# 한국말 하시네요!

## *You Speak Korean!*

## First-year Korean I
## Book I

**Library of Congress Cataloging-in-Publication Data**

한국말 하시네요! / *You Speak Korean!*

First-year College Korean, Volume I
Soohee Kim, Emily Curtis, Haewon Cho.

ISBN 0-9728356-0-1 (paperback)

     1.   Korean language – textbooks.

     2.   Korean language – grammar.


Clip art courtesy of *Microsoft Corporation*.

Additional Clip art courtesy of the *Purdue Japanese Language Project*.

Cover Design by Dianne Gardner.

Printed in Canada.

**PARADIGM***BUSTERS*

*www.ParadigmBusters.com*

# 한국말 하시네요!

## You Speak Korean!

## First-year Korean I
## Book I

**Soohee Kim**
**Emily Curtis**
**Haewon Cho**

## ACKNOWLEDGEMENTS

We would like to acknowledge the Korea Foundation for their sponsorship and support in the form of a publisher's grant. The grant would not have been earned without the much-appreciated letter of review of Dr. Ross King of the University of British Columbia and Concordia Language Villages. Dr. King's review was exceptionally positive, thorough, thoughtful and fair. This edition has benefited enormously from his extensive comments and suggestions as well as his general review and linguistic analyses. We are thrilled to have such a colleague. We also thank Dr. Joe Ree of Florida State University for his letter of review, Nora Tums for editing and managing, and Dianne Gardner for the cover design, Jeehun Kim and Youngji Kim for their valuable feedback and volunteer work. Finally, we thank Microsoft Corporation and the Purdue University Japanese Language program for access to their clip art. Any errors remaining in the current edition are our own.

# TABLE OF CONTENTS

# INTRODUCTION TO THE TEXTBOOK

**NOTE TO STUDENTS**
This textbook was originally intended for a first-year classroom course for students with no background in the Korean language, but can be a fun and useful self-study book as well, especially with the help of a Korean-speaker friend or tutor. There is an accompanying workbook, and some online listening materials are available on the publisher's website. Students are encouraged to read the CONTENT and ORGANIZATION sections below.

**NOTE TO TEACHERS**
This textbook is generally intended for a first-year classroom course for students with no background in the Korean language, although it can be a fun and useful self-study book as well.

The textbook can successfully be used in the classroom under the guidance of an experienced teacher, who will provide some supplementary activities for practice of the grammatical points and vocabulary introduced as well as basic reading, writing, speaking and listening practice.

The textbook exercises are generally intended to be oral, partner or group activities for classroom practice, though many can be used as homework (writing) exercises, even redundantly after classroom use. The accompanying workbook (Workbook to Accompany 한국말 하시네요! You Speak Korean!) provides more homework and listening activities. Audio material is also available on the publisher's website.

**CONTENT**
In determining the grammar and vocabulary to include, we have considered the conventions in many other textbooks – for Korean and other languages, -- and the linguistic structures of Korean and English, and we have tried to keep a balance between expressions and constructions English-speaking college students will want to know at an early learning stage as well as natural, frequently-occurring and useful expressions in Korean. We focus on the -어요 and -으세요 endings, as they are the most commonly used forms in spoken Korean. (-ㅂ니다 and the written -ㄴ다 forms are reserved for the second year course). Once students master the regular consonant- and vowel-ending verbs in the 어요 forms and with other connectors, the irregular verbs and adjectives (ㅂ-, 으-, ㅎ-, ㄹ-irregulars) are more readily learned. All forms and vocabulary are reinforced throughout the textbook, and at various points, summary charts and tables are included to help students to recall and categorize earlier grammar and vocabulary while incorporating new forms.

Vocabulary is introduced thematically and grammar by increasing difficulty or inversely by frequency of use. Both are introduced via natural, spoken dialogues. Grammar explanations are brief and as non-technical as possible, but examples and exercises are ample and carefully chosen to illustrate both usage and semantic nuance. (Explanation of the organization of the textbook is provided below.)

**ORGANIZATION**
The material in this textbook is intended to fill one academic year of a standard, non-intensive college-level introductory course (or a one-quarter, intensive course, where applicable). Earlier chapters are shorter and contain less difficult grammar lessons, so they are covered more quickly.

The **Preliminary** chapter is structured somewhat differently from the others to allow students to learn Han'gul, basic vocabulary and useful phrases before delving into grammar lessons. Having learned the preliminary material, students are prepared for an immersion classroom environment (where only Korean is used). Material in the Preliminary chapter is fundamental and should be taught before beginning Chapter 1. It will also be convenient for students to refer back to the lists and charts therein.

There are then six numbered **chapters** in the year-long course (Volumes 1 and 2). Each numbered chapter presents a unified theme or storyline, such as 'In the Classroom" or "Vacation." Each chapter has four **Lessons** that consist of a main **Vocabulary** lesson, a **Dialogue**[1], **Grammar** points and **Exercises** and finally, a **Checkpoint** that includes short readings including all the grammar points from the lesson. The vocabulary and main grammar point for each section are linked and exemplified in the dialogue. The grammar point is a useful structure, however, and vocabulary is complete along a theme (e.g. classroom items) so that students can go beyond the contents of the dialogue to discuss their own experiences and to understand the experiences of others, especially Koreans.

**Vocabulary** sections introduce basic, useful vocabulary *by theme*. For example, there are vocabulary sections on school subjects, clothing, food and everyday activities (verbs). Vocabulary sections are extensive to allow students to be conversant along a given theme regardless of the dialogue content or their own experiences. Vocabulary sections are thus lessons in their own right and should be covered before moving on to the dialogues. Vocabulary-learning exercises are provided in the textbook and in the workbook to help students to learn the vocabulary, which is essential for communication.

Introducing vocabulary by theme helps students to categorize new words and at times to see linguistic relationships, both of which help students to memorize and recall vocabulary. As much as possible, pictures are used alongside new vocabulary and as models for exercises in order to encourage students to associate Korean words with *concepts*, and not (only) with English words.

**Vocabulary exercises** are included to help students learn tactics for memorizing vocabulary, such as forming semantic categories, and for getting students to use the vocabulary right off the bat.

**Dialogues** make use of the preceding vocabulary from Vocabulary sections and preceding chapters, and they focus on a particular grammatical structure. Dialogues can be read for basic comprehension and as examples of vocabulary usage when the immediately preceding Vocabulary has been learned (passive/recognition stage). Dialogues can be re-examined as *examples* of the grammatical structures presented in the following Grammar section. And finally, the dialogues serve as a review once the Grammar section is completed. They may thus be practiced aloud several times or even memorized for classroom presentation.

**Dialogues** are generally written in the polite (요) form and focus on everyday conversational styles that learners of Korean may encounter and need to be familiar with. Vocabulary and grammar points also focus on spoken Korean and we are careful to point out differences in natural, spoken forms versus more formal, written forms, such as 봐요/보아요 or 그럼/그러면.

Where it arises, additional vocabulary necessary for understanding the dialogue is glossed in the right-hand margin of each dialogue.

**Grammar** sections are divided into one main point or **Focus** and smaller, numbered grammar points. A typical grammar **Focus** is a grammatical structure, such as a verb conjugation (e.g. the past tense, p-irregular verbs, etc.). Many times, the **Vocabulary** section consists of verbs and adjectives that should be conjugated according to the Grammar Focus. The **Dialogue** is intended to thoroughly exemplify the main grammar Focus. **Other Grammar Notes** are smaller lessons, such as new particles. These are also exemplified in the dialogue.

In the **Grammar** sections, care is taken to provide *brief* grammatical explanations that are clear and precise but not overly technical. Where confusion with other forms in Korean is common, a special note is made alongside a warning icon. Examples are provided of correct, and at times incorrect, usage of the grammar structures.

---

[1] The dialogue may be a conversation, a monologue or a written passage, but it is labeled *dialogue* for simplicity.

**Exercises** for all grammar points follow the Grammar section. Early exercises focus on one grammar point, while later exercises may combine grammar points. Each exercise has a title that should help to determine the intended focus. Instructions are provided in English for clarity and simplicity. Most exercises are readily used in the classroom as group or partner activities, and many can additionally be used as homework (written) practice.

At the end of each lesson is a **Checkpoint**; two or more readings that further exemplify and bring together the grammar points learned in the lesson. The idea is that if students can understand the **Checkpoint** materials, they are ready to move on.

**Pronunciation, linguistic and cultural points and songs** are added where relevant between main sections. Instructors may wish to spend class time further exemplifying or discussing these points.

Finer points, reminders and 'asides' about word usage, grammar, pronunciation and culture are presented in call-outs (or. bubbles).

Finally, like some of the materials in the Preliminary Chapter, some topics are best learned as small, individual lessons – for example, telling time. These topics are presented in the **Let's Take a Break** lessons (Chapters 1.5, 2.5, etc.). The Break material is as relevant as the rest, and is integrated into the main text once it has been covered.

### EDITION
This edition has been used in manuscript form by the authors' university Korean language program for both the regular year-long course and the summer intensive course for non-heritage students. Students' and instructors' comments have been integrated and will continue to be integrated in order to make use of the textbook maximally successful. Please feel free to contact the publisher with your comments and suggestions.

## PRELIMINARIES A: GREETINGS

| | |
|---|---|
| **hakseng[2] 1:** | suhnsengnim, annyuhng haseyo? |
| **suhnsengnim:** | ne, annyuhng haseyo? <br> ireum-i mwuh-eyo? |
| **hakseng 1:** | che ireum-eun Seunghi-eyo. <br> chingu ireum-eun Ben-ieyo. |
| **hakseng 2:** | chuh eum bekkessuhyo. |
| **suhnsengnim:** | mannasuh bangawuhyo. |
| **hakseng 2:** | chal butak heyo. |

… … … … … … … … … … … … … … … … … … … … … … … … …

| | |
|---|---|
| **hakseng 1, 2:** | (*Leaving*) annyuhnghi gyeseyo. |
| **suhnsengnim:** | (*Staying*) ne, annyuhnghi gaseyo.   neil bwayo. |

# Vocabulary

| | |
|---|---|
| *suhnsengnim* | teacher, professor |
| *hakseng* | student |
| *annyuhng haseyo* | how do you do, hello |
| *ne / ye* | yes |
| *ireum-i* | name (as subject of the sentence) |
| *che ireum-eun* | as for my name |
| *chingu ireum-eun* | as for my friend's name |
| *mwuh- eyo / ieyo* | what – is / it is |
| *chuh eum beggessuhyo* | first time to see you (=nice to meet you) |
| *mannasuh bangawuhyo* | pleased to meet you |
| *chal butak heyo* | I'll be obliged to you |
| *annyuhnghi gaseyo* | goodbye (to a person who is leaving) |
| *annyuhnghi gyeseyo* | goodbye (to a person who is staying) |
| *neil bwayo* | see you tomorrow |

---

[2] For these first lessons, before you learn to write in Korean, we adopt a transcription system that we think will be easy for American English speakers to use without training—it is not one of the standard transcriptions systems used in Korea and elsewhere for Korean, nor in Linguistics, but we think it will serve the purpose.

**Exercise 1. Greetings**
Greet your friend using the expressions you have just learned. Don't forget to introduce yourself to him/her too.

**Exercise 2. What would you say?**
What would you say in the following situations? Practice with your partner.

1) What would you say if you met a teacher in the street (say hello to her)?

2) What would you say if you were leaving the classroom and wanted to say goodbye to your friend?

3) What would you say if your friend were leaving your room and you wanted to say goodbye to her?

4) What would you say if you met an attractive man/woman at a party and wanted to ask his/her name?

5) What would you say if you also wanted to introduce yourself to that woman/man?

# PRELIMINARIES B: DEFERENCE IN KOREAN CULTURE

## Teachers

> With a Korean teacher, always give and receive papers and objects with two hands, and always show deference to the 선생님. 선생님 is a highly respected title in Korea that stays with the person even when they are no longer your current teacher. Students' parents, past students, and even the teachers' colleagues will always address a teacher as 선생님 and show proper respect. In fact, the 님 in 선생님 is an honorific title reserved for kings, gods, others' parents, and high officials – *and teachers*.
>
> 
> 선생님은 그림자도 밟으면 안 된다.
> **Don't even step on a teacher's shadow.**
> 

## Politeness and respect

With other older people (as well as teachers), Koreans speak and act with deference and respect. Family history, ancestors and parents play a central role in Korean culture. Along with schooling, connections are very important in advancing in one's career and social standing. Therefore, one's parents must be respected and you had better respect other older people too, lest they judge your family according to your behavior. Whatever the origins or basis for the system, Koreans show respect for their elders and superiors in many ways.

**TWO HANDS**: Always give and receive using both hands and full attention.

**BOWING**: Greet elders with a bow. The first time you see them: a full 45° bow, from the waist and with your arms at your sides. Afterwards, you should still bow, but less and less deeply, gradually becoming a nod. Do not make eye contact as this will appear defiant.

Additionally, there is traditional bowing (세배) at the new year, wherein youngsters make a full ceremonial bow, on their knees, to the floor – and then receive a monetary allowance (세뱃돈) from their elders.

**HONORIFICS**: Deference for one's elders and superiors also shows in the language, which has a system of marking politeness and social distance on its verbs and sentences as well as an honorifics system (words and conjugations) of honoring another and humbling oneself.

# PRELIMINARIES C: IN THE CLASSROOM

## Culture Point: Thou Shalt Not...

Remember the saying "Never step on a teacher's shadow"? You should also always use two hands when giving and receiving objects to or from a respected person. You should give full attention to the exchange, making eye contact and then probably bowing (at least your head). In a classroom, you should give a full attention to the teacher and the activities at hand. You should *never* do the following in class or in front of your teacher – How about in the U.S.?

Thou shalt not...

1. call your teacher by their first name – always use 선생님.

2. yawn. Never yawn loudly!

3. chat in class.

4. come to class late (or skip a class).

5. chew gum or eat.

6. do homework or read the newspaper.

7. wear a hat.

8. apply makeup or clip your fingernails.

9. complain about your personal life, making excuses for unfinished work.

10. ask personal questions or make comments about your teacher in class.


Be aware that Koreans in the U.S. bring this culture with them, holding the same expectations of their students (or classmates).

## Classroom Expressions:

(We provide these expressions in the Korean writing system which you will soon learn. This way the list can be used as a reference later.)

1.  질문 있어요?
(chilmun issuhyo)

Do you have any questions?

2.  네, 질문 있어요.
(ne, chilmun issuhyo)

Yes, I have a question.

3.  아니오, 질문 없어요.
(anio, chilmun uhpsuhyo)

No, I don't have a question.

4.  잘 들으세요.
(chal deureu-seyo)

Listen carefully.

5.  따라 하세요.
(ddara haseyo)

Repeat after me.

6.  짝하고 (같이) 하세요.
(jjak hago gachi haseyo)

Please work (together) with a partner.

7.  한국말로 하세요.
(hangung-malo haseyo)

Please speak in Korean.

8.  한 번 더 해 보세요.
(hanbuhn duh he boseyo)

Try it one more time!
(teacher to student)

9.  한 번 더 해 주세요.
(hanbuhn duh he juseyo)

Please do/speak it once more.

10. 천천히 해 주세요.
(chuhn-chuni he juseyo)

Please go/speak slowly.

11. 더 큰 소리로 해 주세요.
(tuh kheun soriro he juseyo)

Please do/speak louder.

**12.** 책 보세요.                                  Please look at your book.
(chek bboseyo)

**13.** 책 보지 마세요.                             Please do not look at your book.
(chek bboji maseyo)

**14.** 여기 보세요.                                Please look here.
(yuhgi boseyo)

**15.** 읽어 보세요.                                Please try reading it.
(ilguh boseyo)

**16.** 써 보세요.                                  Please try writing it.
(ssuh boseyo)

**17.** 숙제 내세요.                                Turn in your homework.
(sukje neseyo)

**18.** 빨리 하세요.                                Do it quickly.
(bbali haseyo)

**19.** 무슨 뜻이에요?                              What does that mean?
(museun ddeushieyo)

**20.** 자기 소개 해 주세요                         Please introduce yourself/yourselves.
(chagi sogee juseyo)

**21.** 외워 오세요.                                Come (to class) with it/them memorized.
(wewuh oseyo)

**22.** 잘 했어요.                                  Good job. (You did well.)
(chal hessuhyo)

# PRELIMINARIES D: THE KOREAN ALPHABET

## What do you know about Korean?
In groups, find the right answer for each question. Guessing is OK! ☺

**True or false?**
1. Korean is spoken as a native language in the Korean peninsula alone.

2. Korean is the same language as Japanese or Chinese; it is called Korean because of where it is spoken.

3. The Korean writing system is pictographic (or ideographic) like Chinese. You can in most cases guess the meaning if you stare at the "characters" for a while.

4. The Korean writing system is truly phonetic. As long as you know the alphabet, you can write what you hear and get the correct spelling of the words.

5. North Koreans speak a variety of Russian and South Koreans speak a variety of Chinese.

**Pick the correct answer:**
1. What is "Hangul"?
    a. Korean alphabet
    b. Korean language
    c. Korean people
    d. Korean food

2. Who created "Hangul"?
    a. King Tan-goon
    b. Kim Dae-joong
    c. Kim Chung-il
    d. King Sejong

3. When was "Hangul" invented?
    a. BC 2333
    b. 15th Century
    c. 18th Century
    d. 1945

4. Korean is spoken as a native language by
    a. 23 million
    b. 44 million
    c. 67 million
    d. 5.6 million

The Korean writing system consists of an alphabet of 21 vowel symbols and 19 consonant symbols. For the most part, each symbol is pronounced individually and in one way (unlike English combinations like 'ch' and 'e' versus 'ee'). The Korean alphabet, **Han'gul**, was created in the 15th century by King *Sejong*. It is based on linguistic considerations of how each sound is made in the mouth! Here is an overview chart of how consonants (on the vertical) combine with vowels (on the horizontal):

## 1. Alphabet chart (simple vowels)

| Vowels / Consonants | ㅏ | ㅑ | ㅓ | ㅕ | ㅗ | ㅛ | ㅜ | ㅠ | ㅡ | ㅣ |
|---|---|---|---|---|---|---|---|---|---|---|
| ㄱ | 가 | 갸 | 거 | 겨 | 고 | 교 | 구 | 규 | 그 | 기 |
| ㄴ | 나 | 냐 | 너 | 녀 | 노 | 뇨 | 누 | 뉴 | 느 | 니 |
| ㄷ | 다 | 댜 | 더 | 뎌 | 도 | 됴 | 두 | 듀 | 드 | 디 |
| ㄹ | 라 | 랴 | 러 | 려 | 로 | 료 | 루 | 류 | 르 | 리 |
| ㅁ | 마 | 먀 | 머 | 며 | 모 | 묘 | 무 | 뮤 | 므 | 미 |
| ㅂ | 바 | 뱌 | 버 | 벼 | 보 | 뵤 | 부 | 뷰 | 브 | 비 |
| ㅅ | 사 | 샤 | 서 | 셔 | 소 | 쇼 | 수 | 슈 | 스 | 시 |
| ㅇ | 아 | 야 | 어 | 여 | 오 | 요 | 우 | 유 | 으 | 이 |
| ㅈ | 자 | 쟈 | 저 | 져 | 조 | 죠 | 주 | 쥬 | 즈 | 지 |
| ㅊ | 차 | 챠 | 처 | 쳐 | 초 | 쵸 | 추 | 츄 | 츠 | 치 |
| ㅋ | 카 | 캬 | 커 | 켜 | 코 | 쿄 | 쿠 | 큐 | 크 | 키 |
| ㅌ | 타 | 탸 | 터 | 텨 | 토 | 툐 | 투 | 튜 | 트 | 티 |
| ㅍ | 파 | 퍄 | 퍼 | 펴 | 포 | 표 | 푸 | 퓨 | 프 | 피 |
| ㅎ | 하 | 햐 | 허 | 혀 | 호 | 효 | 후 | 휴 | 흐 | 히 |

## 2. Alphabet chart (complex-graph vowels)

| Vowels \ Consonants | ㅐ | ㅒ | ㅔ | ㅖ | ㅘ | ㅙ | ㅚ | ㅝ | ㅞ | ㅟ | ㅢ |
|---|---|---|---|---|---|---|---|---|---|---|---|
| ㄱ | 개 | 걔 | 게 | 계 | 과 | 괘 | 괴 | 궈 | 궤 | 귀 | 긔 |
| ㄴ | 내 | 냬 | 네 | 녜 | 놔 | 놰 | 뇌 | 눠 | 눼 | 뉘 | 늬 |
| ㄷ | 대 | 댸 | 데 | 뎨 | 돠 | 돼 | 되 | 둬 | 뒈 | 뒤 | 듸 |
| ㄹ | 래 | 럐 | 레 | 례 | 롸 | 뢔 | 뢰 | 뤄 | 뤠 | 뤼 | 릐 |
| ㅁ | 매 | 먜 | 메 | 몌 | 뫄 | 뫠 | 뫼 | 뭐 | 뭬 | 뮈 | 믜 |
| ㅂ | 배 | 뱨 | 베 | 볘 | 봐 | 봬 | 뵈 | 붜 | 붸 | 뷔 | 븨 |
| ㅅ | 새 | 섀 | 세 | 셰 | 솨 | 쇄 | 쇠 | 숴 | 쉐 | 쉬 | 싀 |
| ㅇ | 애 | 얘 | 에 | 예 | 와 | 왜 | 외 | 워 | 웨 | 위 | 의 |
| ㅈ | 재 | 쟤 | 제 | 졔 | 좌 | 좨 | 죄 | 줘 | 줴 | 쥐 | 즤 |
| ㅊ | 채 | 챼 | 체 | 쳬 | 촤 | 쵀 | 최 | 춰 | 췌 | 취 | 츼 |
| ㅋ | 캐 | 컈 | 케 | 켸 | 콰 | 쾌 | 쾨 | 쿼 | 퀘 | 퀴 | 킈 |
| ㅌ | 태 | 턔 | 테 | 톄 | 톼 | 퇘 | 퇴 | 퉈 | 퉤 | 튀 | 틔 |
| ㅍ | 패 | 퍠 | 페 | 폐 | 퐈 | 퐤 | 푀 | 풔 | 풰 | 퓌 | 픠 |
| ㅎ | 해 | 햬 | 헤 | 혜 | 화 | 홰 | 회 | 훠 | 훼 | 휘 | 희 |

## 3. Vowels　　모음

The following list includes the 21 Korean vowel letters; 10 simple, 11 complex-graph). The name of each vowel letter is the same as its pronunciation. Pronunciation guidelines for each letter are given next to a mnemonic transcription of the sound value of each letter. The vowels are given in the order they would appear in most Korean dictionaries.

1.　ㅏ　　　ah　　　like the *a* sound in *father*

2.　ㅑ　　　yah　　　y + ah

3.　ㅓ　　　uh　　　somewhat like the *uh* sound in *but* or the *au* in *caught*

4.　ㅕ　　　yuh　　　y + uh

5.　ㅗ　　　o　　　like Spanish *o* as in *como*, not as long and gliding as English *low*

6.　ㅛ　　　yo　　　y + o

7.　ㅜ　　　oo　　　*oo* as in *mood* – stick out your lips!

8.　ㅠ　　　yoo　　　y + oo

9.　ㅡ　　　eu　　　like the *oo* in *book* but without rounding your lips

10.　ㅣ　　　ee　　　*ee* as in *teeth*

11.　ㅐ *　　eh　　　*e* as in *bed*

12.　ㅒ +　　yeh　　　y + eh

13.　ㅔ *　　eh　　　*e* as in *bed* or similar to *a* as in *bake*

14.　ㅖ +　　yeh　　　y + eh

15.　ㅘ　　　wah　　　w + *a* as in *father*　　　　　(ㅗ + ㅏ)

16.　ㅙ ˇ　　weh　　　...　　　　　　　　　　　　　(ㅗ + ㅐ)

17.　ㅚ ˇ　　weh　　　　　　　　　　　　　　　　(ㅗ + ㅣ)

18.　ㅝ　　　wuh　　　　　　　　　　　　　　　　(ㅜ + ㅓ)

19.　ㅞ ˇ　　weh　　　　　　　　　　　　　　　　(ㅜ + ㅔ)

20.　ㅟ　　　wee　　　w + *ee* as in *teeth*　　　　　(ㅜ + ㅣ)

21.　ㅢ　　　eu-i　　EU + ee　　　　　　　　　　　(ㅡ + ㅣ)

• The vowels with marks next to them have the same pronunciation in the modern Seoul/Standard dialect. You might encounter native speakers who insist on the difference in the vowel quality, but it is a myth.

• Some people from the older generations (over 50 years old in 2002) might have a VOWEL LENGTH distinction, where the word 말: with a long ㅏ means something different from the word 말 with a short ㅏ, for example.

• It might be helpful to remember that the addition of a stroke adds the pronunciation *y* as in 애 vs. 얘 and that the added [w] sound comes from either an ㅗ or an ㅜ depending on the second vowel.

# 4. Writing out simple vowels

All letters are written from top-to-bottom and left-to-right.

| | | | | |
|---|---|---|---|---|
| ①↓ ├ ②→ | ├ | ├ | ├ | ├ |
| ①↓ ├ ②,③→ | ├ | ├ | ├ | ├ |
| ①→ ┤ ②↓ | ┤ | ┤ | ┤ | ┤ |
| ①,②→ ┤ ③↓ | ┤ | ┤ | ┤ | ┤ |
| ①↓ ┴ ②→ | ┴ | ┴ | ┴ | ┴ |
| ①,②↓ ㅛ ③→ | ㅛ | ㅛ | ㅛ | ㅛ |
| ①→ ┬ ②↓ | ┬ | ┬ | ┬ | ┬ |
| ①→ ㅠ ②,③↓ | ㅠ | ㅠ | ㅠ | ㅠ |
| — → | — | — | — | — |
| │ ↓ | │ | │ | │ | │ |

## 5. Writing out complex-graph vowels

| | | | | |
|---|---|---|---|---|
| ㅐ<br>①↓ ②→ ③↓ | ㅐ | ㅐ | ㅐ | ㅐ |
| ㅒ<br>①↓ ②,③→ ④↓ | ㅒ | ㅒ | ㅒ | ㅒ |
| ㅔ<br>①→ ②,③↓ | ㅔ | ㅔ | ㅔ | ㅔ |
| ㅖ<br>①,②→ ③,④↓ | ㅖ | ㅖ | ㅖ | ㅖ |
| ㅘ<br>①↓ ②→ ③↓ ④→ | ㅘ | ㅘ | ㅘ | ㅘ |
| ㅙ<br>①↓ ②→ ③↓ ④→<br>⑤↓ | ㅙ | ㅙ | ㅙ | ㅙ |
| ㅚ<br>①↓ ②→ ③↓ | ㅚ | ㅚ | ㅚ | ㅚ |
| ㅝ<br>①→ ②↓ ③→ ④↓ | ㅝ | ㅝ | ㅝ | ㅝ |
| ㅞ<br>①→ ②↓ ③→ ④,⑤↓ | ㅞ | ㅞ | ㅞ | ㅞ |
| ㅟ<br>①→ ②↓ ③↓ | ㅟ | ㅟ | ㅟ | ㅟ |
| ㅢ<br>①→ ②↓ | ㅢ | ㅢ | ㅢ | ㅢ |

⚠ The vowel combinations ㅝ, ㅞ, ㅘ, and ㅐ do not occur in Korean.  This has something to do with *vowel harmony* in writing, which you will have a chance to learn more about in later lessons.  For the time being, keep in mind that the vowels ㅗ, ㅘ, ㅐ, ㅏ, ㅐ and ㅒ are considered "bright" vowels whereas vowels ㅜ, ㅝ, ㅞ, ㅓ, ㅔ and ㅖ are "dark" vowels in Korean, and that is why they cannot be mixed.

## 6. Consonants    자음

The following list completes Korean alphabet lesson with the 19 Korean consonant letters (14 simple, 5 "twin"). The name of each consonant is given next to the letter, along with pronunciation guidelines. The consonants are given in the order they would appear in most Korean dictionaries.

| Symbol | Name of the symbol | Pronunciation |
|---|---|---|
| 1. ㄱ (기역) | kee-yuhk | soft k or g |
| 2. ㄴ (니은) | knee-eun | n |
| 3. ㄷ (디귿) | dee-geut | soft t or d |
| 4. ㄹ (리을) | lee-eul | Spanish r or l |
| 5. ㅁ (미음) | me-eum | m |
| 6. ㅂ (비읍) | be-eup | soft p or b |
| 7. ㅅ (시옷) | she-ot | s (sh before 이 or 위) |
| 8. ㅇ (이응)* | ee-eung | ng as in 'si<u>ng</u>' in the final position* |
| 9. ㅈ (지읒) | jee-eut | soft ch or j |
| 10. ㅊ (치읓) | chi-eut | aspirated ch (burst of air) |
| 11. ㅋ (키읔) | khey-euk | aspirated k |
| 12. ㅌ (티읕) | thee-eut | aspirated t |
| 13. ㅍ (피읖) | phee-eup | aspirated p |
| 14. ㅎ (히읗) | he-eut | h |
| 15. ㄲ (쌍기역) | ssang kee-yuhk | hard (tense) kk |
| 16. ㄸ (쌍디귿) | ssang dee-geut | hard (tense) tt |
| 17. ㅃ (쌍비읍) | ssang be-eup | hard (tense) pp |
| 18. ㅆ (쌍시옷) | ssang she-ot | hard (tense) ss (or sh) |
| 19. ㅉ (쌍지읒) | ssang jee-eut | hard (tense) cch |

*ㅇ does not have a sound value when it comes before a vowel (for example, ㅇ + ㅏ). It functions as a place holder, graphically.

 Pay attention to letters containing small strokes. Tiny strokes are sometimes hard to see, especially in print, and once you memorize the incorrect shape of a symbol or syllable, it can come back and haunt you for a long time!!

## 7. Writing out consonants

| | | | | |
|---|---|---|---|---|
| ①→ ↓<br>ㄱ | ㄱ | ㄱ | ㄱ | ㄱ |
| ①↓ →<br>ㄴ | ㄴ | ㄴ | ㄴ | ㄴ |
| ①→ ②↓→<br>ㄷ | ㄷ | ㄷ | ㄷ | ㄷ |
| ①ㄱ ②→ ③ㄴ<br>ㄹ | ㄹ | ㄹ | ㄹ | ㄹ |
| ①↓ ②ㄱ ③→<br>ㅁ | ㅁ | ㅁ | ㅁ | ㅁ |
| ①↓ ②↓ ③→ ④→<br>ㅂ | ㅂ | ㅂ | ㅂ | ㅂ |
| ① ✓ ② ＼<br>ㅅ | ㅅ | ㅅ | ㅅ | ㅅ |
| ① ↻<br>ㅇ | ㅇ | ㅇ | ㅇ | ㅇ |
| ①→ ②✓ ③＼<br>ㅈ | ㅈ | ㅈ | ㅈ | ㅈ |
| ①→ ②→ ③✓ ④＼<br>ㅊ | ㅊ | ㅊ | ㅊ | ㅊ |
| ①ㄱ ②→<br>ㅋ | ㅋ | ㅋ | ㅋ | ㅋ |
| ①→ ②ㄴ ③→<br>ㅌ | ㅌ | ㅌ | ㅌ | ㅌ |
| ①→ ②↓ ③↓④→<br>ㅍ | ㅍ | ㅍ | ㅍ | ㅍ |
| ①→ ②→ ③↻<br>ㅎ | ㅎ | ㅎ | ㅎ | ㅎ |
| ㄲ | ㄲ | ㄲ | ㄲ | ㄲ |

| | | | | |
|---|---|---|---|---|
| ㄸ | ㄸ | ㄸ | ㄸ | ㄸ |
| ㅃ | ㅃ | ㅃ | ㅃ | ㅃ |
| ㅆ | ㅆ | ㅆ | ㅆ | ㅆ |
| ㅉ | ㅉ | ㅉ | ㅉ | ㅉ |

 The letters ㅈ, ㅊ, ㅌ, and ㅎ may look quite different in different fonts and handwriting. Also, the consonant letters ㅎ, ㅂ, ㄷ, ㄹ, ㅁ and the vowel letters ㅏ, ㅓ can look very confusing when cursorily written by hand. Ask your teacher about the alternate ways of writing ㅈ, ㅊ, ㅌ, and ㅎ. Also ask them to write the letters ㅎ, ㅂ, ㄷ, ㄹ, ㅁ and ㅏ, ㅓ *sloppily* on the board!

Here is a little trick to help you memorize the dictionary order of the simple consonants:

C<u>ana</u>da <u>la</u>mps <u>a</u>re <u>J</u>ack <u>Ch</u>urchill,(and) <u>K</u>athy <u>Th</u>ompson's <u>pa</u>rents' <u>h</u>obby.

가 나 다 라 마 바 사 아 자 차 카 타 파 하

15

# 8. Mnemonics for Vowels

| Basic Vowel | Y- series | W- series | Other |
|---|---|---|---|
| ㅏ aah! | 야 | 와 | |
| ㅓ aaw / uh | 여 | 워 | |
| Oh! ☺ | 요 | | |
| boooo! | 유 | | |
| 'eu' | | | *의 [EU-ee] |
| 'ee' | | 위 | *외 [weh] |
| ... F G ㅐ I<br>ㅏ + ㅣ = ㅐ<br>letter "aych" | 애 | 왜 | |
| ㅓ + ㅣ = ㅔ<br>eh? | 예 | 웨 | |

## 9. Mnemonics for Consonants

| | | | | |
|---|---|---|---|---|
| gaga | Kkaw-Kkaw! | c$^h$ough! | ding-do**nnnng** | |
| doe | **Dd**oh! | t$^h$oe | knee | la**dd**er |
| beer | Pbeep-Peep! | p$^h$eeking | mmmwah! | |
| s$^h$aw | Ssassy! | | | hat |
| chew, chew | tchoot-tchoo! | aa-chhhoo! | | |

# 10. Letters into syllables (How to write and read!)

In Korean, each written "character" (called a *keulcha* 글자) is one *syllable* made up of the consonant and vowel symbols you have learned. Some syllables have only a vowel (similar to English *a*), some have a consonant followed by a vowel (similar to English *to*), and some have a vowel followed by a consonant (similar to English *an*). Yet other syllables have a consonant followed by a vowel *and* a consonant (similar to English *pan* or *toll*). Finally, Korean syllables can end in (a limited set of) two consonants (like English *cost* or *bulk*), but they can NEVER begin with more than one consonant (that is, no syllables like English *stop* and *crush*!).

The Korean *keulcha* is written in one of two patterns (where the final consonant is optional):

| beginning consonant | vertical vowel | OR | beginning consonant | |
|---|---|---|---|---|
| final consonant(s) | | | horizontal vowel | |
| | | | final consonant(s) | |

(A 'vertical vowel' is one where the main stroke is vertical.)

The beginning consonant is not optional, however. When there is no consonant sound at the beginning of the syllable, a placeholder, ㅇ, is used. In this case the letter ㅇ ([ng] sound as a final consonant) is not pronounced.

⚠ Also, keep in mind that spellings don't change just because the "syllable" seems to change. That is, there are spelling conventions that you must learn in Korean -- you can't just write Korean words any old way or however you think they sound (*aaz iff thayre wur noh spehleeng roolz*)!

## (1) Vowel-only syllables

Remember you need to have the placeholder ㅇ. Can you read the following syllables?

# 아, 야, 이, 여, 우, 유, 오, 요, 외, 워, 와

If you put some of these syllables together, you have words:

| 아야 | ouch! | 우유 | milk |
|---|---|---|---|
| 오이 | cucumber | 아이 | child |
| 이유 | reason | 요요 | yo-yo |
| 여우 | fox | 이 | teeth |
| 외워요 | Memorize (it/them), please! | 와요 | Come, please! |

 Have you noticed that some vowels come to the right and others underneath the placeholder ㅇ? Do you remember what the principle behind this difference is? (The answer is... the vowels written with a long vertical stroke like "ㅣ" and "ㅔ" come to the right of the consonant (or the place holder), and the vowels written with a long horizontal stroke like "ㅡ" and "ㅜ" are written underneath the consonant.)

## (2) Consonant- vowel syllables

Consonant-vowel syllables look similar to the vowel-only syllables in shape because the vowel-only syllables have the placeholder ○ at the beginning. For consonant-vowel syllables, simply replace the placeholder with the relevant consonant. Try reading the following:

## 가, 뽀, 키, 러, 누, 며, 해, 주, 세, 규, 샤, 그, 배

Here are some words:

| | | | |
|---|---|---|---|
| 꼬마 | kid | 모자 | hat |
| 바나나 | banana | 가짜 | fake |
| 하마 | hippo | 커피 | coffee |
| 포도 | grape | 베개 | pillow |
| 아빠 | daddy | 돼지 | pig |

## (3) (Consonant-) vowel-consonant syllables

Syllables with final consonants are quite common in Korean. The final consonant (called *patchim*, 받침) goes on the bottom regardless of whether the vowel is "vertical" or "horizontal." Here are some examples.

| | | | |
|---|---|---|---|
| 친구 | friend | 맥주 | beer |
| 고양이 | cat | 책상 | desk |
| 똑똑해요 | to be clever | 펜 | pen |
| 빵 | bread | 한글 | Korean alphabet |
| 도서관 | library | 병원 | hospital |

A small number of *keulcha* have two consonants in the *patchim*. Here are some examples.

| | | | |
|---|---|---|---|
| 읽다 | to read | 삶아요 | steam(ing) |
| 값 | price, cost | 없어요 | there is no… |
| 붉어서 | red-so… | 짧고 | short-and… |
| 앉았는데 | sat-but… | 젊은이 | youth (person) |

## Exercises

### Exercise 1.
Practice writing the [consonant + simple vowel] combinations and READ THEM ALOUD!

| Vowels \ Consonants | ㅏ | ㅑ | ㅓ | ㅕ | ㅗ | ㅛ | ㅜ | ㅠ | ㅡ | ㅣ |
|---|---|---|---|---|---|---|---|---|---|---|
| ㄱ | | | | | | | | | | |
| ㄴ | | | | | | | | | | |
| ㄷ | | | | | | | | | | |
| ㄹ | | | | | | | | | | |
| ㅁ | | | | | | | | | | |
| ㅂ | | | | | | | | | | |
| ㅅ | | | | | | | | | | |
| ㅇ | | | | | | | | | | |
| ㅈ | | | | | | | | | | |
| ㅊ | | | | | | | | | | |
| ㅋ | | | | | | | | | | |
| ㅌ | | | | | | | | | | |
| ㅍ | | | | | | | | | | |
| ㅎ | | | | | | | | | | |

- It will be safe to think that the vowel pairs ㅏ-ㅑ, ㅓ-ㅕ, ㅗ-ㅛ, ㅜ-ㅠ, ㅐ-ㅒ, and ㅔ-ㅖ in the ㅈ and ㅊ rows *sound* identical.

**Exercise 2.**

Practice writing the [consonant + complex vowel] combinations and READ THEM ALOUD!

| Vowels / Consonants | ㅐ | ㅒ | ㅔ | ㅖ | ㅘ | ㅙ | ㅚ | ㅝ | ㅞ | ㅟ | ㅢ |
|---|---|---|---|---|---|---|---|---|---|---|---|
| ㄱ | | | | | | | | | | | |
| ㄴ | | | | | | | | | | | |
| ㄷ | | | | | | | | | | | |
| ㄹ | | | | | | | | | | | |
| ㅁ | | | | | | | | | | | |
| ㅂ | | | | | | | | | | | |
| ㅅ | | | | | | | | | | | |
| ㅇ | | | | | | | | | | | |
| ㅈ | | | | | | | | | | | |
| ㅊ | | | | | | | | | | | |
| ㅋ | | | | | | | | | | | |
| ㅌ | | | | | | | | | | | |
| ㅍ | | | | | | | | | | | |
| ㅎ | | | | | | | | | | | |

- Not all of these consonant + complex graph vowel combinations are used with the same frequency in Korean. However, for the sake of learning the pronunciation of each consonant and vowel, read aloud each syllable.

21

## Exercise 3.  Listening I
Circle the vowels that your teacher says. Remember that some vowels have the same pronunciation!

| | | | | |
|---|---|---|---|---|
| 아 | 으 | 왜 | 유 | 외 |
| 웨 | 어 | 여 | 우 | 예 |
| 야 | 에 | 오 | 의 | 애 |
| 워 | 요 | 위 | 와 | 이 |

## Exercise 4.  Listening II
Circle the syllables that your teacher says.

| | | | | |
|---|---|---|---|---|
| 가 | 자 | 까 | 하 | 바 |
| 사 | 빠 | 라 | 따 | 짜 |
| 싸 | 나 | ☺ | 타 | 파 |
| 아 | 다 | 차 | 마 | 카 |

**Exercise 5.  !BINGO!**
Fill out the Bingo table below with possible Korean syllables, using the letters below.
Then, when your teacher calls out a syllable that you have written, you get the square.  Five
squares in a row and you have a Bingo!

ㄱ ㄴ ㄷ ㄹ ㅁ ㅂ ㅅ ㅇ ㅈ ㅊ ㅋ ㅌ

ㅍ ㅎ ㅏ ㅑ ㅓ ㅕ ㅗ ㅛ ㅜ ㅠ ㅡ ㅣ

ㅐ ㅔ

|  |  |  |  |  |
|---|---|---|---|---|
|  |  |  |  |  |
|  |  |  |  |  |
|  |  | ☺ |  |  |
|  |  |  |  |  |
|  |  |  |  |  |

### Exercise 6. !BINGO!

Fill out the Bingo table below with possible Korean syllables, using the *keulcha* below. Then, when your teacher calls out a syllable that you have written, you get the square. Five squares in a row and you have a Bingo!

가 나 다 라 마 바 사 아 자 차 카 타
파 하 아 야 어 여 오 요 우 유 으 이
애 에

|  |  |  |  |  |
|---|---|---|---|---|
|  |  |  |  |  |
|  |  |  |  |  |
|  |  | ☺ |  |  |
|  |  |  |  |  |
|  |  |  |  |  |

## Exercise 7.  Quiz

1) Which of the following consonants (with the vowel ㅏ) are switched?  Put them in the correct dictionary order.

가, 나, 다, 라, 마, 사, 바, 아, 자, 차, 카, 타, 파, 하

2) Which of the following vowels is pronounced differently from the others?

왜, 웨, 외, 위

3) Which of the following vowels is pronounced differently from the others?

내, 네, 늬

4) Which of the following vowels is a true Korean letter combination?

ㅖ, ㅑ, ㅒ, ㅔ

## Exercise 8.

Combine the consonant-vowel combinations with the *patchim* along the vertical axis to create a consonant-vowel-consonant *keulcha*.

| | 가 | 조 | 쓰 | 시 | 후 | 메 | 너 | 대 | 벼 | 웨 | 과 |
|---|---|---|---|---|---|---|---|---|---|---|---|
| ㄱ | | | | | | | | | | | |
| ㄴ | | | | | | | | | 변 | | |
| ㄷ | | | | | | | | | | | |
| ㄹ | | | 싣 | | | | | | | | |
| ㅁ | | | | | | | | | | | |
| ㅂ | | | | | | | 댑 | | | | |
| ㅆ | | | | | | | | | | | |
| ㅇ | 강 | | | | | | | | | | |
| ㅎ | | | | | | | | | | | |

**Exercise 9.**
Write out the following conversation in Han'gul.

| | |
|---|---|
| **hakseng:** | suhnsengnim, annyuhng haseyo? |
| **suhnsengnim**: | ne, annyuhng haseyo? |
| | ireum-i mwuh-eyo? |
| **hakseng:** | che ireum-eun Seunghi-eyo. |

학생:    _____, _____?

선생님:    _____, _____?

_____?

학생:    _____.

# 11. Words borrowed from English (How to write and read!)

- What do you think Korean speakers would do to English words that begin or end with a consonant cluster (like *pro* or *dance*), which is not a possible sequence of sounds in Korean? The answer is -- Koreans use a filler vowel "ㅡ" to compensate for the impossible pronunciation:

| | | | |
|---|---|---|---|
| cost | 코스트 | test | 테스트 |
| milk | 밀크 | strike | 스트라이크 |
| Starbucks | 스타벅스 | chance | 찬스 |
| Budweiser | 버드와이저 | dryer | 드라이어 |
| player | 플레이어 (Have you noticed that the final *r* sound is represented by 어?) | | |
| actor | 액터 | singer | 싱어 |

- Usually, *r* that does not come at the end of the syllable is written (and pronounced) as *one* ㄹ, whereas *l* is written (and pronounced) as *two* ㄹ:

| | | | |
|---|---|---|---|
| radio | 라디오 | curry | 커리 |
| train | 트레인 | romance | 로맨스 |
| ball | 볼 | Bill | 빌 |
| school | 스쿨 | Long Island | 롱 아일랜드 |
| love | 러브 (Have you noticed that *v* is represented by ㅂ?  What about *f*?) | | |

 film 필름,      folk song 포크 송<br>Volvo 볼보,      vanilla 바닐라

- Going back to the <u>filler</u> vowel, the vowel "ㅡ" is also in action when the English word ends in *s* or *z*, sounds that cannot end a word in Korean:

| | | | | | |
|---|---|---|---|---|---|
| coat | 코트 | bus | 버스 | kiss | 키스 |
| DOS | 도스 (For whatever reason, the actual *pronunciation* of the syllable 스 is 쓰!) | | | | |
| jazz | 재즈 | gauze | 거즈 | quiz | 퀴즈 |

- When the word ends in *ch* or *j*, the vowel "ㅣ" is used instead of "ㅡ".

| | | | | | |
|---|---|---|---|---|---|
| touchdown | 터치다운 | lunch | 런치 | punch | 펀치 |
| Grunge | 그런지 | | | | |

• Laypeople use varying spelling conventions for borrowed words. You will find many different spellings for names of English and other origins, for example. This is especially so with vowels and the sounds ㅅ and *f*.

John        잔, 쟌, 존, 죤, and 좐!

Tom         탐, 톰

stop        스탑, 스톱

French fries   프렌치 프라이, 후렌치 후라이

bus         버스, 버쓰, and even 뻐쓰!

Susan       수잔, 수전, 쑤잔, 쑤전

(You got the idea, right?)

Other borrowed words are so common in Korean that their spellings are set in stone – you must memorize the right spelling!

## Exercise 1.
Guess the meaning of the following words.

1) 샌드위치, 햄버거, 핏자, 콜라, 핫도그, 아이스 크림, 커피

2) 비디오, 텔레비전, 카메라, 컴퓨터, 바이오 리듬

3) 포카 혼타스, 피노키오, 미키 마우스, 신데렐라

4) 샴푸, 키, 펜, 크레딧 카드

5) 이메일, 쿠키, 다운로드, 모니터, 스크린

6) 뉴욕 시티, 엘에이, 시카고, 시애틀, 샌프란 시스코, 워싱턴 디씨

7) 방콕, 토쿄, 파리, 마드리드, 하바나

8) 데이트, 스파이, 스키, 버스, 키스, 택시

9) 힙합, 팝송, 로큰롤, 그런지, 하드 록, 헤비 메탈

10) 마돈나, 제임스 딘, 엘리자베스 테일러, 다이애나, 케네디

11) 브렉퍼스트, 런치, 디너, 테이블, 포크, 나이프, 냅킨

## Exercise 2.
1) Write your name in Korean.

2) Write the name of three classmates in Korean.

# PRELIMINARIES E: PRONUNCIATION GUIDE

Korean has many pronunciation rules that may seem overwhelming at first, but they *are* learnable – Korean children can learn them! Start out with these in mind and refer back to this section often, to practice and make the connections between the rules and real words and sentences where they occur, so that you can internalize them like Korean kids do.

These pronunciation rules are changes in the way words and letters are pronounced that take place when you put words together – changes that make the words sound different from how they are written.

> Unlike other languages where the spelling reflects a *historical* pronunciation, and historical sound changes account for the current pronunciation (e.g. *night* in English), Korean pronunciation rules have to do with changes in the pronunciation of words depending on where they occur with respect to other words, syllables and sounds. So these "rules" are applied actively, each time you speak Korean. They are along the lines of the "ch" sound in English "got you."

You will probably best learn how to pronounce words by listening to native speakers and ***mimicking them***. It will all gradually make sense and begin to come naturally the more you speak and listen – just like with Korean-speaking children. The following explanations are offered as guidelines that you can fall back on and to start you off on learning the "rules." We will start out with tips for pronouncing and discerning some of the sounds that are different from English, then list the rules of Korean pronunciation.

 Use this pronunciation guide as a reference throughout this book. Do not try to *memorize* the rules. It will be a lot more effective if you read the examples out and see how spelling interacts and correlates (or doesn't correlate) with the pronunciation.

## Peculiarities of Individual Korean Sounds

### 1. Vowels

- Korean vowels are never glided like they are in English (e.g., *baby)*. Korean vowels are pure vowels; your jaw shouldn't move while pronouncing a vowel. They are much like Spanish or French vowels. Compare *baby* to French *bébé*. Or, consider a bad English pronunciation of Spanish *bueno* [boo-AY-no-u] versus the Spanish pronunciation (bwEH-no). Also, Korean vowels should not be cut short like Japanese vowels often are. Practice reading the following words, paying attention to the vowel quality:

노래        매워요        동생        친구        호호        데이트

Among the Korean vowels, 우, 오, 어, 아 are the most difficult to distinguish. You can only learn to differentiate them by repeated listening and speaking practice! Listen to your teacher or native-speaker friends say the following words *over and over*!

| 거나 | 주조 | 조조 | 주주 | 무모 | 머무니 |
|------|------|------|------|------|--------|
| 소수 | 뭐   | 모   | 무   | 마   | 모국어 |

## 2. Consonants with a questionable identity

Simple stop consonants (ㄱ, ㄷ, ㅂ, ㅈ) have two different sound values in Korean: When they begin a word (especially after a pause or in slow speech) they sound like English *k, t, p,* and *ch.* On the other hand, when they come word-medially (especially in fast speech), they sound like a *weaker* version of English *g, d, b,* and *j.* So, the word 바보 ('fool') in Korean may sound like *pah-bo* in English, although both syllables begin with the letter ㅂ. Practice saying the following phrases and sentences (Better yet, repeat after your instructor or a Korean friend):

| | | |
|---|---|---|
| **다**, **다**림질 | vs. | 아**다다**, 살**다**가 |
| **더**, **더**위 | vs. | 가**더**라, 오**더**라구 |
| **도**레미, **도**자기 | vs. | 인**도**, 기**도** |
| **두**목, **두**부 | vs. | 자**두**, 만**두** |
| **드**세요, **드**니까 | vs. | 뿌**드**득, 고**드**름 |
| **디**젤, **디**지탈 | vs. | **디디**다, 어**디** |
| **바**, **바**위 | vs. | 잠**바**, 누가**바** |
| **보**자기 | vs. | 전**보**, 가**보**자 |
| **기**억, **기**술 | vs. | 아**기**, 도자**기** |
| **반가**워요 | 제 이름은 | 안녕히 **계**세요 |

> No flapping! English speakers, be careful **NOT** to pronounce this word as something like *kiddo*! The 도 should sound harder (like a full D) than *-do* in *kiddo*!

## 3. Tense, aspirated, or plain?

One of the most difficult pronunciations to master in Korean is the distinction between the three members of series such as ㅂ, ㅍ, and ㅃ. The simple or 'plain' consonants ㄱ, ㄷ and ㅂ are pronounced with a slight popping of air but a very low pitch. The tense consonants ㄲ, ㄸ and ㅃ sound very much like *b, d,* and *g* to native English speakers, but they tend to be harsher sounding with a high pitch (or note). Finally the ㅍ, ㅌ, and ㅋ are pronounced pretty much like the English *p, t,* and *k*, but with a much greater puff of air (aspiration) coming out of the mouth. Korean is not a tone language like Chinese or Vietnamese, but it might help to think of the tense and aspirated consonants as having a higher pitch. Have your instructor or a Korean friend say the following triples and test you!

재미 – 채미 – 째미          고 – 코 – 꼬

달 – 탈 – 딸                          모자 – 모차 –모짜                              방 – 팡 – 빵

> These twin letters might sometimes sound "double" between vowels in slow speech. But remember to make them tense.

## 4. ㅅ vs. ㅆ: 시, 쉬

Like the stop-sounds (bursting sounds) in the last section, there are two different Korean *s*'s as well, a plain ㅅ and a tense ㅆ. In this case, though, the tense ㅆ sounds a little more like the English *s* than the plain one. The tense ㅆ in Korean is a just bit more tensed, with a harsher hissing sound that is normal in English, and it has the familiar raised pitch of tense consonants. Try saying 싸 with a good tense ㅆ. (싸 means *cheap, inexpensive*.)

To pronounce a nice 'plain' or soft ㅅ, you might imagine there is an *h* sound before the ㅅ. The pitch should be low and the ㅅ should sound very soft. Try saying 사랑 in a breathy, romantic way, and your ㅅ will probably be about right. (사랑 means *love*.)

| | | | | | |
|---|---|---|---|---|---|
| 사 | 싸 | 소 | 쏘 | 설 | 썰 |
| 삼 | 쌈 | 살 | 쌀 | 생 | 쌩 |
| 상 | 쌍 | 소 | 쏘 | 서 | 써 |

One final note about the Korean *s*'s is that they are pronounced *sh*, plain and tense, before the vowels ㅣ and ㅟ and before vowels with a y- pronunciation (야, 여, 요…). For the *sh* sound before ㅣ and *y-*, you shouldn't round your lips (or stick them out) the way you would in English. You *do* stick them out before ㅟ, as if the ㅜ got stuck on top of the *sh* sound.

Remember to make the difference between plain and tense *sh* sounds, too! Now go and practice!

어서          동생          의사          조수          연설          수시로

사 vs.시          시 vs. 쉬          시 vs. 씨

셔요 vs. 쉬어요 vs. 쉬워요          맛있어요 vs. 맛있었어요 vs. 마시세요 vs. 마시셨어요

## 5. ㄴ and ㅁ

You might occasionally hear Korean speakers say "이름이 버에요?" or "이름이 뷔에요?" when they mean "What is your name?" Word-initial ㄴ's and ㅁ's sometimes sound like ㄷ's and ㅂ's.

Ask your teacher or a native speaker friend to pronounce the following phrases several times for you:

누구세요?　　　　　　　뭐에요?

> Have you noticed something interesting in this row? Most ㄹ-beginning words used in (South) Korea are those recently borrowed from English and other Western languages.

## 6. ㄹ

Be aware that there are two kinds of ㄹ (i.e., two different pronunciations) in Korean. When ㄹ comes between vowels or in the beginning of words, it sounds very much like English *t* or *d* in words like *water, butter, cater, chatty, buddy, daddy,* or *ladder*. Ask your teacher or a native-speaker friend to say the following words for you:

| | | | | | |
|---|---|---|---|---|---|
| 머리 | 다리 | 꼬리 | 노루 | 하루 | 구름 |
| 버리다 | 부르다 | 노란색 | 얼어요 | 살아서 | 돌아도 |
| 라디오 | 라면 | 레몬 | 리본 | 로데오 | 르네 |

When ㄹ comes at the end of a syllable, it sounds like the English *l* when it is pronounced in the beginning of a word (much like *lady, little, low,* or *let*). It does **NOT** sound like the English dark *l* at the end of a word (e.g. in words like *ball, doll, all,* or *cool*). Be careful!!

| | | | | | |
|---|---|---|---|---|---|
| 칼 | 솔 | 돌 | 길 | 달 | 잘 |
| 마을 | 빌다 | 얼다 | 놀다 | 살다 | 갈비 |

## 7. One or two?

Unlike English, where you pronounce only one consonant sound even though there are two in the spelling (e.g., *summer, banner, ladder, shutter*), Korean is very faithful about pronouncing one vs. two consonants in a row. The difference in pronunciation makes important differences in meaning. A double consonant sound is like the two *k* sounds in *book̲c̲ase*, but of course comes in all types of consonant (except ㅎ) in Korean.

Practice making double versus single consonant sounds in the following word sets. A close approximation of the pronunciation of the words is given in square brackets "[　]".

| | | | |
|---|---|---|---|
| 만나 [만나] | 마나 [마나] | 많아 [마나] | 만화 [마나]<br>This in *really* fast speech! |
| 멀리 [멀리] | 머리 [머리] | 멀이 [머리] | |
| 엄마 [엄마] | 엄아 [어마] | 어마 [어마] | |

Be sure to double the ㄹ even before the y-vowels!

빌려요　　　　걸려요

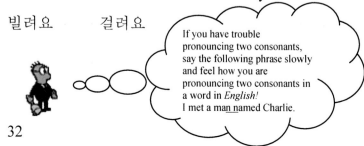

> If you have trouble pronouncing two consonants, say the following phrase slowly and feel how you are pronouncing two consonants in a word in *English!*
> I met a ma̲n̲ named Charlie.

> 머리 and 멀이 have exactly the same pronunciation (due to the liaison rule) although they are two different words. There are *many* such pairs in Korean. This means you will need to memorize their spelling!

## Pronunciation Rules

It is VERY important to learn that words are not pronounced as they are written in Korean. Learn the following "pronunciation rules". They will teach you how to fight SPELLING PRONUNCIATION.

### 1. The seven representatives

Although syllables are spelled as if they end in a variety of consonants - and consonant sequences in some cases - the final consonants that are actually *pronounced* at the end of Korean syllables are very limited. In fact, only seven representative consonants can be pronounced at the end of a syllable or word. They belong to only two categories: **sonorous sounds** ㄴ, ㅁ, ㅇ, ㄹ, and **simple stop sounds** ㄱ, ㄷ, and ㅂ.

```
ㄱ, ㄲ, ㅋ → ㄱ

ㄷ, ㅌ, ㅅ, ㅆ, ㅈ, ㅊ, ㅎ → ㄷ

ㅂ, ㅍ → ㅂ
```

So there are no *s* or *ch* sounds at the end of a syllable in Korean, which is why you cannot pronounce words like *bus* in Korean without the *empty* vowel at the end: 버스). But there is no problem with sonorant sounds at the ends of syllables, so *pen* is 펜.

Q: Can you guess the consonant pronunciations of the following written syllable-final letters?

ㅋ          ㄲ          ㅍ          ㅃ
ㅌ          ㄸ          ㅅ    ·   ㅆ          ㅊ          ㅉ          ㅎ

ANSWER: In pronunciation, [ㄱ] represents ㄱ, ㄲ, ㅋ; [ㅂ] represents ㅂ and ㅍ (syllable-final ㅃ does not occur); and [ㄷ] represents the whole second row above. If you pronounce the pronunciation sounds and the written-letter sounds silently in your mouth – try to feel the movement of your tongue – you can see the reasoning behind this seemingly crazy substitution. ㄲ and ㅋ are sounds made in the back of the mouth, and so is ㄱ – the simplest sound of each sort replaces the more complex, or released sounds! Now, can you guess the other two groups? Pronounce the sounds ㄷ, ㅅ, ㅆ, ㅈ, ㅊ, ㅌ, ㅎ silently and slowly. These are teeth sounds (except for ㅎ) and are represented by the simplest sound ㄷ. How about ㅂ and ㅍ? Obviously, they are lip sounds, and ㅂ is considered simpler than ㅍ.

Practice saying the following syllables:

억 [억]              닭 [닥]              엮 [역]              었 [얻]

숲 [숩]              빵 [빵]              반지 [반지]          문 [문]

**and check out this fun set:**

낫 [낟]              낱 [낟]              낮 [낟]              낯 [낟]

Korean stop final consonants (ㄱ, ㄷ, and ㅂ) are **never** released! Look at your 선생님's mouth carefully when she produces each syllable.

33

## 2. The spill-over rule

One more very important thing to remember about writing and pronouncing Korean syllables is the liaison rule. Although only seven simple consonants are allowed in syllable-*final* position, all that was suppressed comes alive when the next syllable begins with a vowel! In other words, the final consonant of a syllable spills over to the next syllable if the next syllable begins with a vowel (that is, the place holder ㅇ in writing). Compare how the following pairs of sounds are pronounced.

| | | | |
|---|---|---|---|
| 빛 [빋] | vs. | 빛에 [비체] | |
| 낫 [낟] | vs. | 낫이 [나시] | In the second column, the seven representatives rule doesn't apply. |
| 낮 [낟] | vs. | 낮을 [나츨] | |
| 꽃 [꼳] | vs. | 꽃이 [꼬치] | |
| 밖 [박] | vs. | 밖에 [바께] | |
| 앉 [안] | vs. | 앉아 [안자] | |
| 숲 [숩] | vs. | 숲이 [수피] | |
| 있 [읻] and 었 [얻] | vs. | 있었어 [이써써] | |
| 이름 + 은 [이름] + [은] | vs. | 이름은 [이르믄] | |
| 있 + 어요 [읻] + [어요] | vs. | 있어요 [이써요] | |

 Just remember to use the final consonants as the beginning sound of the next syllable if it begins with the place holder ㅇ. Korean LOVES to have consonants and vowels in a row!


## 3. Syllables ending in consonant sequences

Syllables ending in two consonants are far rarer than those ending in single consonants, but they do occur, usually in verbs or adjectives. For example, 앉다, 끊다, 읽다, 젊다, 밟다, 잃다, 없다 are all real words in Korean.

The tricky business about pronouncing words with two final consonants is to figure out which final consonant is actually pronounced. (Remember that Korean can have only ONE representative final consonant.) These pesky complex-consonant words should be tackled as they come along. (The rule of thumb in pronouncing these complex final consonants is that ㄴ and the lip sounds ㅁ,ㅂ will always be pronounced. Also ㄹ tends to be weak (deleted), although ㅎ is the weakest!

*Can't I use the liaison rule for the complex final consonants?* Yes! The second of the final two consonants moves over (*in pronunciation!*) if the following syllable starts with a vowel sound:

앉아    [안자]                        읽어    [일거]

젊은    [절믄]                        밟으니    [발브니]

훑어서    [훌터서]                    읊어요    [을퍼요]

없이    [업씨]  – You will learn why ㅆ is used instead of ㅅ below!

## 4. Tensed out!

Simple consonants ㄱ, ㄷ, ㅂ, ㅅ, and ㅈ become tense-sounding (like ㄲ, ㄸ, ㅃ, ㅆ, and ㅉ, respectively) when they come after other stop sounds. Practice reading the following:

먹고    [먹꼬, 머꼬]

학교    [학꾜, 하꾜]                  Stop sounds are sounds that are pronounced with some stopping of the air in the mouth like k, d, j, p, and ch.

찾지요  [찬찌요, 차찌요]

닫더라  [닫떠라, 다떠라]            작지 [작찌]          없어 [업써]          격분 [격뿐]

Simple stop sounds ㄷ, ㅅ, and ㅈ also become tense when they come after ㄹ:

발달 [발딸]        갈등 [갈뜽]        꿀단지 [꿀딴지]        철사 [철싸]

발전 [발쩐]        돌진 [돌찐]        술잔 [술짠]            밀수 [밀쑤]

 Crazy as it may sound, simple stop sounds ㅂ, and ㄱ do **NOT** become tense after ㄹ:

일본          달걀          솔개          절부          돌김          결과          밀밭

It's actually a bit more complicated that this, but this is all you need to know for now. If you like to take a challenge, see second year textbook.

## 5. ㅎ, you ARE the weakest link!

ㅎ is pronounced like the English *h* in the beginning of the word:

하나          할머니          학교          한글          한국어          화장실

It often disappears in *fast speech* when it comes in the middle of a word or as the final consonant:

많이 [마니]                    넣어요 [너~요]                    실례합니다 [실레암니다]

안녕히 계세요 [안녕이 게세요]              안녕히 가세요 [안녕이 가세요]

## 6. ㅎ-combo

Because it is an "air" sound, ㅎ makes its neighboring sound aspirated:

업혀서 [어펴서]              넣다가 [너타가]              많다면 [만타면]

Practice reading these aloud:

좋지요        넣고        하얗다        박해        족하        밥하는

## 7. Assimilation to the following sound

Sounds made in the back of the mouth (like ㄱ, ㅋ, ㄲ, and ㅇ) tend to win out – neighboring sounds often take on their back-of-the-mouth (velar) pronunciation, especially in fast speech.  Read aloud the following words:

연극 [영극]              친구 [칭구]

못 가 [목까, 모까]        반가워요 [방가워요]

반말 [밤말]      대한민국 [대암밍국]← This in *really* fast speech!

> Pronounce the word *congruent* and the phrase *mean girls* in fast English. Do you say *con-gruent* or *cong-gruent*?  *Mean girl* or *Meang girl*?

## 8. ㄹ-strong

ㄴ and ㄹ are notorious foes in the Korean language.  When they meet, ㄴ usually becomes like ㄹ.

신라 [실라]        전라 [절라]        연락 [열락]        원로 [월로]

원래 [월래]        찰나 [찰라]        실내 [실래]        월남 [월람]

You'll learn exceptions like 신라면 in second-year Korean.

 But don't forget that one ㄹ is more like a *flap* sound and two ㄹ's are like the English *l* sound!

> The *flap* sound is the sound in words like bu**dd**y and cu**t**ie. Compare that with the *l* sound in *pillow* or double *l* in *sale-list*.

## 9. Strong nose!

Final consonants (e.g., ㅂ, ㅍ, ㄷ, ㅌ, ㄱ, ㅋ, ㄲ, ㄳ, ㅅ, ㅆ ㅈ, ㅎ, etc. except ㄹ) become nasal if the next syllable begins with a nasal sound:

| | | | |
|---|---|---|---|
| 닫네 [단네] (ㄷㄴ → ㄴㄴ) | | 학년 [항년] (ㄱㄴ → ㅇㄴ) | |
| 엮는 [영는] (ㄲㄴ → ㅇㄴ) | | 부엌만 [부엉만] (ㅋㅁ → ㅇㅁ) | |
| 갔나 [간나] (ㅆㄴ → ㄴㄴ) | | 잊는 [인는] (ㅈㄴ → ㄴㄴ) | |
| 잇몸 [인몸] (ㅅㅁ → ㄴㅁ) | | 넣네 [넌네] (ㅎㄴ → ㄴㄴ) | |
| 읽나요 [잉나요] (ㄺㄴ → ㅇㄴ) | | 실례합니다 [실레암니다] (ㅂㄴ → ㅁㄴ) | |

Continue pronouncing the following words out loud. Write the pronunciations out if you want!

| | | | | |
|---|---|---|---|---|
| 국내 | 앞날 | 깎니 | 갔네 | 읽는 |
| 잊나 | 입만 | 국민 | 덧문 | 못 만나 |
| 한국말 | 없는데요 | 감사합니다 | 만나서 반갑습니다 | |

## 10. Weird!
When the final consonants ㄷ and ㅌ come before the vowel 이, they turn into ㅈ and ㅊ.

같이 [가치]    낱낱이 [난나치]

맏이 [마지]    미닫이 [미다지]    해돋이 [해도지]

> This rule may not seem so strange after all. Think of how "Got you" is pronounced in fast speech, for example,
> ……………………………………..Gotcha!

## 11. Combined rules!!
Can you pronounce the following words? Can you guess what rules applied?

몇 해                                        → 멷해 → [며태]

갇히                                         → 가티 → [가치]

흘렸는지                                     → 흘럲는지 → [흘련는지]

못 해                                        → 몯 해 → 모태

## 12. Simplicity is the word!
The sounds *w* and *y* occurring in complex vowels in written words are often weakened or dropped, especially in fast speech:

시계 [시게]                     계피 [게피]                     안 돼 [안 대]

줘 [조]                         뭐가 [머가, 모가]

놓아요 [놔요, 나~요]   처음 뵙겠어요 [첨~ 베께써요]

안녕히 계세요 [안녕이 게세요]   실례합니다 [실레함니다; 실레암니다]

## 13. Something about 의!

The syllable 의 is pronounced as [으+이] in one syllable with the emphasis on the [으] when it is at the beginning of a word (e.g. 의자, 의사, 의복, 의도), but is pronounced as 이 otherwise (e.g. 모의). And strangely, 희 is ALWAYS pronounced as [히] regardless of where it comes in the word!

Practice reading out loud the following words. Then write out in square brackets [ ] how they are pronounced.

의문 [        ]        의도 [        ]        편의 [        ]

도의 [        ]        희망 [        ]        희생 [        ]

희다 [        ]        경희 [        ]        의사 [        ]

There is one more; you will learn in a later chapter that the possessive particle 의 is pronounced as 에!

# Peculiarities of Korean Spelling

## 1. Spelling conventions

Like most writing systems, the Korean writing system is a means of representing words, not just sounds. It makes sense to have related words maintain roots with the same spelling. The Korean writing system respects the edges and shapes (spelling) of roots so you can see through all the heavy machinery of endings and particles and identify related words. This will become clear once you start memorizing words, especially verbs.

The following word combinations are pronounced all very distinctly, But they are written with 먹, to show that they are related:

| 먹다 | 먹고 | 먹지 | 먹으니 | 먹니 |
| eat-verb | eat-and | eat-right? | eat-because | eat-? |
| [먹따] | [먹꼬] | [먹찌] | [머그니] | [멍니] |

> This is almost like English words showing word relation by spelling out the K in *knowledge* (~acknowledge), and C in *electric* (~electricity). Well, almost.

 Attention! This spelling convention in turn means that there will be many homonyms that are not spelled the same! The spelling helps to identify the meaning in these cases. Do you know how the following words are pronounced?

도리        돌이        돌리                다리        달이        달리

모가        목아        목가                많아        마나        만나

## 3. Spacing between words

Hand in hand with respecting the spelling and edges of roots is the spacing of Korean words. Like English, independent words are written with spaces between them. Even some small words that require some kind of modifier before them, like the word 데, a dependent noun that indicates a *place* (e.g., *a place to meet* 만날 ˅ 데) is written with a space before it.

엄마 엄마, 이리 와. 요것 보세요. 병아리 떼 뽕뽕뽕 놀고 간 뒤에 미나리 파란 싹이

돈아 났어요. 미나리 파란 싹이 돌아 났어요.

> They are there! Look closely. You'll have to get used to finding the spaces in Korean sentences!

 The one catch to this spacing rule is that suffixes and endings are part of the larger word. And Korean has **many** suffixes and endings!! Also remember that the *be* verb in Korean (이다, 이에요, 이니까, etc.) is not considered a full word and has to be written attached to a preceding noun.

| 먹다 | 먹고 | 먹지 | 먹으니 | 먹니 | 학생이에요. |
|------|------|------|--------|------|------------|
| eat-verb | eat-and | eat-right? | eat-because | eat-? | student-be-polite |

Finally, the demonstrative prefixes (*this, that, that over there*: 이, 그, 저) may or may not have a space after them (before the noun they modify). The space is usually deleted before only short nouns.

이 ˅ 번 = 이번        그 ˅ 것 = 그것        저 ˅ 분 = 저분

## 2. Compounds

When two nouns come together to form a compound, boundaries are marked in Korean. When the first noun ends in a consonant, the first consonant of the second noun is pronounced as a tense consonant.

안 [안] + 방 [방] = 안방 [안빵]
inside        room        inner room 'master bedroom'

When the first noun ends in a vowel, a ㅅ is inserted in the spelling, and the first consonant of the second noun is pronounced as doubly long in slow speech (or tense in fast speech).

고추 [고추] + 가루 [가루] = 고춧가루 [고춘까루, 고추까루]
pepper        powder        ground pepper

바다 [바다] + 가 [가] = 바닷가 (바닫까, 바다까)
sea        side        seaside

코 [코] + 물 [물] = 콧물 [콤물]
nose        water        snot

> How are compounds signaled in English?
>
> a bluebird vs. a blue bird
> The White House vs. a white house

# Exercises

## Exercise 1.
Circle the words that are pronounced the same way.

1) 입만, 임만, 임반            2) 가티, 가치, 같이, 갗이

## Exercise 2.
Fill in the blanks with an appropriate consonant-vowel combination so that the word may have the same pronunciation as the others.

1) 잎이, 입히, 이_____            2) 도리, 돌____

## Exercise 3.
How are the following words pronounced?

1) 젊어, 여덟은, 읽을까            2) 닦아도, 밝아서

3) 입혀, 많아, 같이, 학년, 한국말

## Exercise 4.
How is 몇 해 pronounced?            며채, 며태, 며대

## Exercise 5.
How is 덧문 pronounced? (mark one *fast* and one *slow*)

던문, 덥문, 던문, 덤문

## Exercise 6.
How are the following words pronounced?

1) 학교            2) 수학 (*fast* and *slow*)       3) 많아요

4) 넣고            5) 낙화                    6) 안녕하세요

## Exercise 7.
Mark the words that are pronounced the same way.

1) 만나, 많아, 마나, 만아            2) 달리, 다리, 달이

3) 박이, 밖이, 바끼, 바기            4) 먹기요, 모기요, 막이요, 먹이요, 머기요

## Exercise 8.
Which English word(s) do you think the following Korean word represents?

1) 씽크 (think? sink?)            2) 밴 (van? ban? pan? fan?)

# PRELIMINARIES F: USEFUL EXPRESSIONS

**1.** 실례합니다.                    **Excuse me.**

**2.** 미안합니다. / 죄송합니다.              **Sorry. / I am really sorry.**

**3.** 감사합니다. / 고마워요.              **Thank you. / Thanks.**

**4.** __은/는_____ 한국말로 뭐에요?      **How do you say _____ in Korean?**

(Use 은 after nouns that end in a consonant; use 는 after nouns that end in a vowel.)

**5.** 내일 봐요.                    **See you tomorrow.**

**6.** 그래요?                     **Is that so?**

**7.** 그래요.                     **That is so. / Let's do.**

**8.** 맞아요. / 좋아요.              **That's correct. / That's good.**

**9.** 괜찮아요. / 천만에요.              **That's O.K. / Not at all.**

**10.** 조용히 하세요.                 **Please be quiet.**

**11.** 화장실이 어디에요?              **Where is the restroom?**

**12.** 문제가 뭐에요?                **What is the problem?**

**Exercise 1. Greetings**
Answer the questions below with a partner.

| | |
|---|---|
| How do you greet a friend in the morning? | You forgot to bring your homework. What would you say to your instructor? |
| You forgot your boyfriend's/girlfriend's birthday! What would you say to your boyfriend/girlfriend? | You want to know where the restroom is. What would you ask? |
| Our friend is talking to someone and you need to speak to him/her. How would you interrupt the conversation? | You are studying Korean in the library but the people sitting next to you are talking loudly. What would you say to them? |
| Your friend gave you a nice present on your birthday. What would you say? | You saw an attractive woman/man at a party and want to ask her/his name. What would you say to him/her? |
| What would you say to a friend who is staying? | What would you say to a friend who is leaving? |

**Exercise 2. Asking for Korean words/ English equivalents.**
Ask your partner for Korean words/ English equivalents as shown in the example.

*Example*:       A: fox 한국말로 뭐에요?

                      B: 여우!

# PRELIMINARIES G: NUMBERS 숫자

## 1. Sino-Korean Numbers

The following numbers are Sino-Korean numbers. They were borrowed from Chinese long ago and are now part of the Korean number system. Sino-Korean numbers are used when referring to a *numbered* item, such as a page or a numbered exercise. In this case the numbers are used almost like names.

*Example*        Page One = 일 페이지
                 Bus #1 = 일번 버스

| English | Arabic Numeral | 한글 | |
|---------|----------------|------|---|
| zero | 0 | 영 / 공 | 영 is used in math and 공 is used in reciting phone numbers and addresses. |
| one | 1 | 일 | |
| two | 2 | 이 | |
| three | 3 | 삼 | |
| four | 4 | 사 | Try to say the 's' sound really softly! |
| five | 5 | 오 | |
| six | 6 | 육 | Pronounced [륙] in phone numbers and when in counting [오, 륙, 칠...] |
| seven | 7 | 칠 | |
| eight | 8 | 팔 | |
| nine | 9 | 구 | Make your lips really really round! |
| ten | 10 | 십 | |

| eleven | 11 | 십 일 | |
| twelve | 12 | 십 이 | |
| thirteen | 13 | 십 삼 | |
| … | … | … | |
| sixteen | 16 | 십 육 | [심뉵] |
| … | … | … | |
| twenty | 20 | 이 십 | |
| twenty-one | 21 | 이 십 일 | |
| … | … | … | |
| thirty | 30 | 삼 십 | |
| forty | 40 | 사 십 | |
| (one) hundred | 100 | 백 | |
| (one) thousand | 1000 | 천 | |
| ten thousand | 10,000 | 만 | |
| hundred thousand | 100,000 | 십 만 | [심만] |
| million | 1,000,000 | 백 만 | [뱅만] |
| ten million | 10,000,000 | 천 만 | |
| hundred million | 100,000,000 | (일)억 | |

## Notes: 만

Note that the Korean word for *ten thousand* is 만, and that the larger numbers are based on 만, not on *thousand* and *million* as in English. This is a source of some confusion in translating. Be sure to practice using *man* and *uhk* and not to look for a direct translation for the words 만 and **million**.

## Exercise

Practice reading the following years. (Ask your teacher what 기원전 and 서기 mean!)

1) 2005 년     2) 1984년     3) 1776 년     4) 2000년     5) 1492년     6) B.C. 14 년

## 2. Native Korean Numbers

The following numbers are native Korean numbers. They are used to express the *quantity* of items that are counted individually, but they must be used with a proper *counter*. This grammar point will be discussed in a later chapter. When ordering food at a restaurant, however, you may use the number without a *counter*.

e.g.,     one page = 한 페이지          cf.) Page 1 = 일 페이지

one book = 책 한 권  (권 is the counter for books)

One order of *bibimbap*, please. = 비빔밥 하나 주세요.

| English | Arabic Numeral | 한글 |
|---------|:--------------:|:----:|
| one | 1 | 하나, 한 |
| two | 2 | 둘, 두 |
| three | 3 | 셋, 세 |
| four | 4 | 넷, 네 |
| five | 5 | 다섯 |
| six | 6 | 여섯 |
| seven | 7 | 일곱 |
| eight | 8 | 여덟 |
| nine | 9 | 아홉 |
| ten | 10 | 열 |

silent ㅂ!

| | | | |
|---|---|---|---|
| eleven | 11 | 열 하나 | |
| twelve | 12 | 열 둘 | |
| thirteen | 13 | 열 셋 | |
| fourteen | 14 | 열 넷 | [열렌] |
| … | … | … | |
| twenty | 20 | 스물, 스무 | |
| twenty-one | 21 | 스물 하나 | |
| thirty | 30 | 서른 | |
| forty | 40 | 마흔 | |
| fifty | 50 | 쉰 | |
| sixty | 60 | 예순 | |
| seventy | 70 | 일흔 | |
| eighty | 80 | 여든 | |
| ninety | 90 | 아흔 | |
| (one) hundred | 100 | 백 | |
| (one) thousand | 1000 | 천 | |
| ten thousand | 10,000 | 만 | |
| hundred thousand | 100,000 | 십만 | [심만] |
| million | 1,000,000 | 백만 | [뱅만] |
| ten million | 10,000,000 | 천만 | |
| hundred million | 100,000,000 | (일)억 | |

## Notes: HANA, HAN

Some native Korean numbers have alternate pronunciations such as 하나 and 한. The shortened forms (e.g., 한) are adjective forms of the full forms (e.g., 하나). They are used when followed by a counter or a noun.

one = 하나     vs.     one person = 한 사람

Starting from 100, Sino-Korean number vocabulary is used, mixed with native Korean number vocabulary. For example, 121 people = 백 스물 한 사람.

# Exercises

**Exercise 1.**
Quiz yourself using only the Arabic digits (1-10) and the Hangul column. Cover the other columns and try not to rely on the English translation. Also, make flash cards with Arabic numerals on one side and 한글 numbers on the other. Make a set for Sino-Korean and another for native-Korean numbers.

**Exercise 2.**
From now on refer to pages and exercises *in Korean*, using the Sino-Korean numbers: 십 페이지, 일 번... .

**Exercise 3.**
From now on, count out items, such as handouts, homework, snacks, your steps and so on *in Korean*, using the Native Korean numbers: 하나, 둘, 셋, 넷, ... .

**Exercise 3. !BINGO!**
Fill in the following Bingo chart with Arabic numerals. When your teacher calls out numbers, find the right square, if you have it and you get the square.

| | | | | |
|---|---|---|---|---|
| | | | | |
| | | | | |
| | | ☺ | | |
| | | | | |
| | | | | |

**Exercise 4. Slap it!**
Using your flashcards, arrange them so that the Arabic number side is facing up. In a group of 3-4, try to be the first to slap the right card when your teacher calls out the number in Korean. If you are first, you get the card, but if you slap the wrong card, you have to put one back.

## Ordinal Numbers

**First    second    third**       **...**

첫째    둘째    셋째    넷째, 다섯째        일곱째  여덟째  아홉째 열째

여섯째

last
마지막

Also, 첫번째 = the first time
*How would you say the fifth time?*

### Exercise

Tell your partner something about each of the runners in the picture above. Or, assign names to the runners in the picture with your partner.

# PRELIMINARIES H: DAYS AND MONTHS

## 오늘이 몇월 며칠이에요?
### What's the date today?

## Vocabulary

### 1. Months

| Months | Meaning |
|---|---|
| 일월 [이뤌] | January |
| … | … |
| 유월 | June |
| … | … |
| 시월 | October |
| 십 일월 [시비뤌] | November |

### Days of the month

| Days | Meaning |
|---|---|
| 일일 [이릴] | the 1st (day) |
| 이일 [이:리] | 2nd day |
| 삼일 | 3rd day |
| … | … |
| 삼십일 | 30th day |
| 삼십 일일 [삼시비릴] | 31st day |

| 지금 | now |
| 오늘 | today |

| 몇월 [며뤌] | what month |
| 며칠 | what date |

| 생일 | birthday |

> When you say the name of the months, **June** and **October**, the final consonants ㄱ and ㅂ disappear!

## Grammar Notes

**1. What month is it now?**
A: 지금 **몇 월**이에요?
B: 6 월이에요.

**2. What's the date today?**
A: 오늘이 **며칠**이에요?
B: 오늘은 1 일이에요.

**3. What's the month and the date today?**
A: 오늘이 **몇월 며칠**이에요?
B: 오늘은 10 월 10 일이에요.

# Exercises

### Exercise 1.  What date?
Ask your partner what today's date is according to the pictures.

가)           나)           다)           라)

### Exercise 2.  Date & month practice
Read the following months and dates aloud.

1)  12 월 8 일

2)  1 월 1 일

3)  4 월 5 일 – 식목일[싱모길] (Arbor Day)

4)  3 월 1 일 – 삼일절[사밀쩔] (Korean Independence Movement Day)

5)  10 월 9 일 – 한글날[항글랄] (Korean Language Day)


### Exercise 3.  When is…?
Do you know when the following days are?  Ask your partner for the dates of each.

1) 크리스마스

2) 미국 독립 기념일 (U.S. Independence Day)

3) New Year's Day

4) 발렌타인 데이

5) 할로윈

6) 제일 친한 친구 생일 (best friend's birthday)

7) 엄마/아빠/친구 생신 (생신 = honorific form of 생일)

8) 할머니/할아버지 생신


### Exercise 4. When is your birthday?  생일이 언제에요?
Ask 5 of your classmates when their birthdays are. Report to the rest of the class!

# PRELIMINARIES I:   NATIONALITIES

## 어디 사람이에요? 어느 나라 사람이에요?
### Where are you from?

## Vocabulary

**1. Country names and languages**

| 나라 이름<br>Country Names | 언어<br>Languages | 국적<br>Nationality | |
|---|---|---|---|
| 한국 | 한국어 | 한국 사람 | Korean |
| 중국 | 중국어 | 중국 사람 | Chinese |
| 일본 | 일본어 | 일본 사람 | Japanese |
| 베트남 | 베트남어 | 베트남 사람 | Vietnamese |
| 미국 | 영어 | 미국 사람 | English/American |
| 영국 | 영어 | 영국 사람 | English/British |
| 프랑스 | 프랑스어 | 프랑스 사람 | French |
| 독일 | 독일어 | 독일 사람 | German |
| 이탈리아 | 이탈리아어 | 이탈리아 사람 | Italian |
| 스페인 | 스페인어 | 스페인사람 | Spanish/Spaniard |
| 러시아 | 러시아어 | 러시아사람 | Russian |
| 캐나다 | 영어 | 캐나다 사람 | English/Canadian |
| 호주/오스트레일리아 | 영어 | 호주 사람 | English/Austrailian |
| 대만 | 중국어/대만어 | 중국사람/대만사람 | Taiwan/Taiwanese |

In language names, −어 can be replaced by 말. 말 is a native Korean word that means *speech* or *word*. −어 means the same, but it is of Chinese origin.

All 사람 words can be replaced by 인 to sound a little more sophisticated: 한국인, 중국인, 일본인, 미국인, 영국인, etc.,

51

## 2. Other words you should know

| | |
|---|---|
| 저는 | I (topic) |
| 이 분은 | this person (honorific) -(topic) |
| _____ 씨는 | Ms. _____;  Mr. _____; <br> Ms. / Mr. _____, you |
| 사람 | person |
| 어디 | where |
| 어느 | which |
| 나라 | country |
| 국적 | nationality |

## Asking about nationalities

A: **한스** 씨는 어디 사람이에요?

B: (**한스** 씨는) 독일 사람이에요.

A: **알랙세이** 씨는 어느 나라 사람이에요?

B : 저는 러시아 사람이에요.

A: **지니** 씨는 어디 사람이에요?

B : 저는 대만 사람이에요.

> You will see over and over that the second person pronoun "YOU" is hardly ever used in Korean. In formal and polite speech styles, you can address the person you are talking *to* or talking *about* by using their name *plus* 씨:
>
> **한스** 씨… Hans, he…
>
> **알랙세이** 씨… Alexei, you

## Language Point          It's in the names!

As you know, Korea is divided by the Demilitarized Zone, and there are two Koreas in the Korean Peninsula.  South Korea is called 남한 (literally South-Korea), and North Korea is called 북한 (literally North-Korea).  You might also hear some other terms such as 북조선 and 남조선. These are the names of North and South Korea that are used by North Koreans and older generation Japanese.

Although the complete name of 한국(South Korea) is 대한민국 (Republic of Korea), it is only used in official or governmental documents (like on one's passport), very much like the use of the 'United States of America.'

## Language Point        It's all in the history!

Korea is a country of a long literary history, and much of that history is owed to the Chinese language. Much like the English language having two words that mean similar things (e.g., "ascend" which has a *Latinate* root and "go up" which is *Germanic*), Korean has many synomym sets with one word from Chinese (Sino-Korean) and one that is native Korean. Just as "ascend" and "go up" are used in different contexts, so are Sino-Korean and native Korean pairs.

Sino-Korean words tend to be decomposable, where you can usually detect the meaning of each syllable. You will learn more about this as you go along.

One other exciting (well, *crazy*) thing about Korean is that you will find many words that mean the *same* thing! 스페인어 and 프랑스어, for example, are also as widely called 서반아어 and 불어, respectively. The latter is the Korean pronunciation of the names of these countries written in Chinese. The picture became more complicated when Korean started using recent Western borrowings. Can you guess what the following words mean?

프랑스      불란서
월남       이태리        멕시코

| 중 | 국 | 어 |
|---|---|---|
| center | country | language |
| 중 | 국 | 인 |
| center | country | person |

## Exercises

**Exercise 1. Where are you from?**
Ask your classmates their names and where they are from. Then introduce each classmate to another.

A: 이름이 뭐에요?

B: 제 이름은 _____ 이에요.

A: 어느 나라 사람이에요?

B: 저는 _____ 사람이에요.

A: ___(C)___ 씨, 이분은 _____A_____씨에요. __(나라)__ 사람이에요.

C: 반갑습니다.

> You may hear 만나서 반갑습니다 [방갑씀니다] instead of 만나서 반가워요 [방가워요], and 잘 부탁합니다 [잘 부타캄니다] for 잘 부탁해요 [잘 부타캐요]. The -ㅂ니다 ending is quite formal and used for formal broadcasting (e.g. by newscasters), in the military (e.g. to address senior officers). On a daily basis, men tend to use the —ㅂ니다 ending to their seniors at work, or to those they are just introduced to. Normally, -ㅂ니다 will soon ease into —어요 ending. It will be useful to memorize both pairs of expressions!

53

A: 어느 나라 사람이에요?

B: 저는 미국 사람이에요.

A: 재미동포에요?

B: 네.

> If you want to express that you are Korean-American or Japanese-American, you can add 계 and say:
> 한국계 미국사람이에요.
> 일본계 미국사람이에요.
> You might also hear the expressions 재미동포 and 재일동포. They mean Korean ex-patriots (Korean people living in the U.S. or in Japan).

## Exercise 2. Where are they from?
Ask your partner where the following people are from.

| | | | |
|---|---|---|---|
| 마오 쩌뚱 | 알래니스 모리셋 | 제임스 본드 | 김대중 |
| 마이클 잭슨 | 루드윅 베토벤 | 레오 톨스토이 | 호지민 |
| 요코 오노 | 레오나르도 다빈치 | 마리 퀴리 | 훌리오 이글레시아스 |
| 나폴레옹 | 티 에스 엘리옷 | 에밀졸라 | 펄벅 |

# 노래 하고 갑시다!

## 사랑해 -- I love you

사랑해 당신을... 정말로 사랑해... 당신이 내 곁을... 떠나간 뒤에... 얼마나
눈물을... 흘렸는지 모른다오...

| 사랑해 | 당신을 | 정말로 | 사랑해 |
|---|---|---|---|
| (I) love | you-poetic (object) | really | love |

| 당신이 | 내 곁을 | 떠나간 | 뒤에 |
|---|---|---|---|
| you (subject) | my side | left | after |

| 얼마나 | 눈물을 | 흘렸는지 | 모른다오 |
|---|---|---|---|
| how much | tears | shed | (I) don't know-(poetic) |

예예예 예예예 예예예 예예예 예예예 예예예 예예예
예예예 예예예 예예예 예예예 예예예 예예예 예예예
예 ~

| 사랑해 | 당신을 | 정말로 | 사랑해 |
|---|---|---|---|

# CHAPTER 1 그게 뭐에요?

**What's that?**

## Preliminary Dialogue

| | |
|---|---|
| 학생: | 선생님, 안녕하세요? |
| 선생님: | 네, 안녕하세요? |
| | 이름이 뭐에요? |
| 학생: | **타미**에요. 잘 부탁해요. |
| 선생님: | 네. **타미** 씨, 만나서 반가워요. |

이름이
뭐에요?

Between people of similar age or to a younger person, 이름이 뭐에요 is used to ask for one's name. To older people, it is considered impolite to ask their name, but if you must, use 성함이 어떻게 되세요? [성아미 어떠케 되세요]

You may see "What is …?" spelled 뭐|에요 in other Korean language texts instead of 뭐에요 adopted in this book. 뭐 에요 is considered *standard*, but 뭐에요 reflects more widely accepted pronunciation and spelling.

The pronunciation of 뭐에요 is usually either [머에요] or [모에요].

**Dialogue practice.**

Practice the preliminary dialogue with a classmate.

# LESSON 1
# 내일 시험이 있어요.

## Lesson 1 vocabulary          Classroom Nouns

| | | |
|---|---|---|
| 1. 뭐 = 무엇 | **what** | |
| 2. 내일 | **tomorrow** | |
| 3. 숙제 [숙쩨] | **homework** | |
| 4. 시험 [시험, 시엄] | **test** | |
| 5. 질문 | **question** | |

For all words that begin with 시, don't forget to make the s sound like the *sh* sound in English only with no lip rounding!

| | |
|---|---|
| 6. 선생님 | **teacher** |
| 7. (남) 학생 [학쌩] | **(male) student** |
| 8. (여) 학생 | **(female) student** |
| 9. 짝 | **partner** |

| | |
|---|---|
| 10. 교실 | **classroom** |
| 11. 사무실 | **office** |
| 12. 문 | **door** |
| 13. 창문 | **window** |
| 14. 벽 | **wall** |

| | |
|---|---|
| 15. 책상 [책쌍] | **desk** |
| 16. 탁자 [탁짜] | **table** |
| 17. 의자 | **chair** |
| 18. 칠판 | **chalkboard** |
| 19. 시계 [시게] | **clock, watch** |
| 20. 전화 [저놔, 저나] | **telephone** |
| 21. 컴퓨터 | **computer** |
| 22. 프린터 | **printer** |
| 23. 텔레비전 = 텔레비젼 | **T.V.** |
| 24. 비디오 | **VCR** |

Though some Korean words such as **컴퓨터** and **텔레비전** were borrowed from English (and other languages), they were adapted into the Korean language. They are similar to the English words, but should be pronounced according to Korean pronunciation rules and written according to Korean spelling conventions.

| | |
|---|---|
| 25. 있어요 [이써요] | **there is/exists/one has (polite form)** |
| 26. 없어요 [업써요] | **there is no/is lacking/one does not have (polite form)** |
| 27. 예 = 네 | **yes** |
| 28. 아니오 | **no** |
| 29. -이 | **subject marker (after a noun ending in a consonant)** |
| 30. -가 | **subject marker (after a noun ending in a vowel)** |
| 31. -에 | **in, at, on** |

Many Korean speakers still use 테레비, which is a form borrowed through the Japanese language.

**Vocabulary Exercise 1.  Word Search!**

| 숙 | 제 | 슈 | 교 | 테 | 요 | 멸 | 의 |
|---|---|---|---|---|---|---|---|
| 선 | 내 | 님 | 실 | 공 | 이 | 추 | 자 |
| 구 | 일 | 굿 | 비 | 주 | 장 | 블 | 사 |
| 가 | 공 | 남 | 디 | 생 | 교 | 무 | 벽 |
| 녀 | 방 | 책 | 오 | 과 | 실 | 문 | 툐 |
| 벽 | 전 | 시 | 공 | 펜 | 장 | 쳐 | 낮 |
| 술 | 험 | 계 | 험 | 상 | 류 | 바 | 닥 |
| 칠 | 필 | 카 | 줌 | 리 | 테 | 종 | 이 |
| 장 | 판 | 간 | 메 | 몸 | 죠 | 이 | 창 |
| 텔 | 레 | 비 | 전 | 라 | 질 | 문 | 블 |

1)  homework        _____        2) tomorrow        _____

3)  test            _____        4) desk            _____

5)  table           _____        6) chair           _____

7)  chalkboard      _____        8) video           _____

9)  notebook        _____        10) paper          _____

11) clock           _____        12) classroom      _____

13) television      _____        14) office         _____

15) question        _____        16) book           _____

17) window          _____        18) door           _____

19) wall            _____

**Vocabulary Exercise 2.  Categories**
Organize the vocabulary according to natural sets or categories of 3-4 items.  Draw pictures
of the items or of where you find them together, if you like.

1) 문, _____, _____

2) _____실, _____

3) 시계, _____, _____, _____

4) 전화, _____, _____, _____

5)  *Start with your own word!*

*Additional office supplies*

| Words | Meaning |
|-------|---------|
| 가위 | scissors |
| 칼 | knife |
| 자 | ruler |
| 복사기 | copier |
| 마커 | highlighter |
| 화이트 | white-out |
| 필통 | pencil case, holder |

## Lesson 1 dialogue    내일 시험이 있어요?

학생:   선생님! 질문 있어요.

선생님: 네, 질문이 뭐에요[1]?

학생:   내일 시험이 있어요?

선생님: 아니오, 시험이 없어요.

학생:   그럼[2], 숙제가 있어요?

선생님: 네, 숙제가 있어요.

[1] What is…

[2] if so, then

네 is often used as an acknowledgment that you have heard someone or are allowing turn-taking in a conversation. In this case, it doesn't mean *yes*. It means, *Yes, go ahead.*

In this dialogue, 학생 and 선생님 are talking about whether or not there is a test or homework. They are not discussing a main topic and referring back to "it." This is why 숙제 and 시험 are marked with the subject marker 이/가 even in 선생님's answers.

## Lesson 1 grammar

### 1. Focus                    *there is / there is no*

| | |
|---|---|
| A 이/가 있어요 | there is A |
| A 이/가 없어요 | there is no A |

In this first lesson, you should learn two important points about basic sentence structure in Korean. The first is that the **verb** always comes **last** in a Korean sentence.
The second is that other parts of the sentence, like the *subject* and the *object* of the *verb*, as well as location words, have a special **suffix-like marker** whose function is to indicate the grammatical role (*Subject*, etc.) of the noun it attaches to.

Languages tend to have a special way of expressing the concept of simple existence, such as the English expression *there is/there are*. In Korean, the verb 있어요 expresses existence (it means *exists* or *there is*) and the verb 없어요 expresses a lack (*there is no*), or, the opposite of 있어요. Both verbs can be used regardless of the number of items in existence (or lacking). Since they are verbs, they come at the end of the sentence.

> Talking about grammar and grammatical *Subject* of the verb, the *Subject* is the noun that *does* the action communicated by the verb.

 Since 있어요 and 없어요 are *verbs*, the items in existence or lacking are their (grammatical) *subjects*:

"시험이 있어요" is literally *A test exists*, which is parallel to *A boy cried.*, *My dog eats.* – all have a **subject** + **verb** structure (in English and Korean).

*Subjects* in Korean are marked with -이, when they end in a consonant, like 시험, and with -가 when they end in a vowel, like 의자. So we say the subject marker is -이/가.

62

Put it all together and you get a good sense of Korean sentence structure:

| Subject | Subject Marker | Verb | (natural) English translation |
|---------|----------------|------|-------------------------------|
| 시험<br><br>test | 이<br><br>-- | 있어요.<br><br>exists | There is an exam/there are exams. |
| 의자<br><br>chair | 가<br><br>-- | 없어요.<br><br>not-exist | There is no chair/there are no chairs |
| 창문<br><br>window | 이<br><br>-- | 있어요.<br><br>exists | There is a window/there are no windows. |
| 숙제<br><br>homework | 가<br><br>-- | 없어요.<br><br>lacks/<br>not-exist | There is no homework. |

In spoken Korean, the subject marker is frequently omitted.

내일 시험이 있어요?                     Is there a test tomorrow?

내일 숙제가 없어요.                      There is no homework tomorrow.

It might sometimes be awkward to *have* the subject marker -이 or -가 in spoken Korean, but we insist that you practice with it in the sentence. According to our teaching experience, students find it easier to naturally drop the subject marker once they have firmly learned how it works. So keep reminding yourself to put the subject marker after all subjects!

## 1. Other Grammar Notes

### 1. 뭐/무엇          *what*

There are two forms of *what* in Korean. One is 무엇, the full form, and the other is 뭐, the shortened form. 뭐 is used in **conversational** Korean, and 무엇 usually in **written** Korean. There are some points to remember about the use of 뭐 in Korean.

 When you make questions, the question word is *not* placed at the front of the sentence. Simply change the noun in question to 뭐, which stays where the original noun would be:

내일 뭐가 있어요?   What is there tomorrow?          and **NOT** 뭐가 있어요 내일?

When you are asked for the subject of the sentence with the *subject* marker (뭐가 있어요? or 무엇이 있어요?), you *must* answer with the subject of the sentence marked with the *subject* marker.

A: 내일 뭐가 있어요?        What's there tomorrow?
B: 내일 시험이 있어요.        There is a test tomorrow.

A: 내일 무엇이 있어요?      What's there tomorrow?
B: 내일 숙제가 있어요.        There is homework tomorrow.

 This point may sound too obvious to make now, but there will be more noun markers to learn, and it is a good idea to get into the habit of answering with the subject marker -이/가 when you are asked the question "뭐가/무엇이 있어요?"

> In grammatical terms, it is called a *locative phrase* and the *locative marker.*

## 2. -에        Location marker *in, at, on*

You have learned that nouns are marked for their grammatical function in Korean; for example, nouns that are **subjects** are marked with -이/가.  Another useful marker is -에 which marks a *location* and means *in/at/on.*  In *there is* sentences, the location phrase comes first, then the subject, and finally the verb:

| Location noun | Location marker | Subject noun | Subject Marker | Verb |
|---|---|---|---|---|
| 교실 | 에 | 창문 | 이 | 있어요. |
| classroom | -- | window | -- | exists |

*There is a window in the classroom.*

| 사무실 | 에 | 의자 | 가 | 없어요. |
|---|---|---|---|---|
| office | -- | chair | -- | not-exist |

*There is no chair/there are no chairs in the office.*

 Unlike the subject marker, -에 is never dropped after a noun.

## Lesson 1 exercises

> As you will learn later in this chapter, 에 can be dropped after place *adverbs* like 어디 (where), 여기, 거기, and 저기 (here, there, over there)

### Exercise 1.    Dialogue practice
Practice the dialogue with a classmate.

**Exercise 2.　-이 or -가?**
Which subject marker would you use in each case?

1) 의자_______ 있어요.

2) 공책_______ 없어요.

3) 종이_______ 있어요.

4) 펜_______ 있어요.

5) 연필_______ 없어요.

6) 지우개_______ 없어요.

7) 가방_______ 있어요.

8) 숙제_______ 있어요.

9) 오빠_______ 있어요. (오빠: brother)

10) 돈_______ 없어요. (돈: money)

**Exercise 3.　Is there a …?**
Talk to your partner about another classroom, teacher's office or his/her desk at home. Ask what items are in the room. For example, is there a window? Write down the list of the items you have come up with.

1) What is in the classroom? (교실에 뭐가 있어요?)
There is/are … in the classroom. (교실에 …….이/가 있어요.)

2) What is not there in the classroom? (교실에 뭐가 없어요?)
There is/are no … in the classroom.

3) What is there in the teacher's office?
There is/are … in the teacher's office.

4) What is not there in the teacher's office?
There is/are no … in the teacher's office.

5) What is there in the house? (house: 집)
There is/are … in the house.

6) What is not there in the house?
There is/are no … in the house.

Be careful with the order of the final consonants when you write the verb 없어요. There is no final consonant in Korean with a ㅅㅂ combination!

## Lesson 1       Checkpoint

### 대화 1       오늘 시간 있어요?

철수: **영희** 씨 오늘 시간[1] 있어요?

영희: 아니오, 오늘 시간 없어요. 숙제가 있어요.

철수: 내일도[2] 숙제 있어요?

영희: 아니오, 내일 숙제 없어요.

철수: 그럼[3] 내일 시간 있어요?

영희: 네, 내일 시간 있어요.

### 대화 2       뭐가 있어요?

케이: **마이크** 씨, 선생님 사무실에[4] 뭐가 있어요?

마이크: 책상이 있어요.

케이: 책상에 전화가 있어요?

마이크: 네, 전화가 있어요.

케이: 그럼, 한국어 교실에 뭐가 있어요?

마이크: 의자가 있어요.

케이: 네? 뭐가 있어요?

마이크: 의자가 있어요. 그리고[5], 책상이 있어요.

---

[1] time
[2] also (marker)
[3] well then
[4] in, on, at
[5] and

# LESSON 2
# 그게 뭐에요?

## Lesson 2 vocabulary          *Other Basic Nouns*

| | | |
|---|---|---|
| 1. | 누구 | who |
| 2. | 친구 [칭구] | friend(s) |
| 3. | 엄마/어머니 | mom/mother |
| 4. | 아빠/아버지 | dad/father |
| 5. | 이름 | name |
| 6. | 펜 | pen |
| 7. | 카메라 | camera |
| 8. | 이메일 | email (address) |
| | | |
| 9. | 가방 | bag |
| 10. | 책 | book |
| 11. | 교과서 | textbook |
| 12. | 워크북 | workbook |
| 13. | 공책 | notebook (blank book that you will fill in!) |
| 14. | 종이 | paper |
| 15. | 연필 | pencil |
| 16. | 지우개 | eraser |
| 17. | 지도 | map |
| 18. | 전화번호 [저나버노] | phone number |
| | | |
| 19. | 이, 그, 저 | this, that/it, that over there (adj.) |
| 20. | 거/것 | thing (cf. written form 것) |
| 21. | 이거, 그거, 저거 | this, that/it, that thing over there (N.) |
| 22. | 이게, 그게, 저게 | this, that/it, that thing over there (subject) |
| 23. | 이건, 그건, 저건 | this, that/it, that thing over there (topic) |
| 24. | 누구 거 [누구꺼] | whose (thing) |
| 25. | 저(는) | I - humble (shown with the topic marker) |
| 26. | 제 | my (humble) |
| 27. | 저희 | our (humble) |
| 28. | 네/예 | yes |
| 29. | 아니오 | no |
| 30. | 씨 | Mr., Ms. |
| 31. | 분 | honorifically, person (after 이, 그, 저 and numbers ) |

Unlike Mr. and Ms. in English, the Korean name suffix 씨 is added to *first names* in polite relationships with people of roughly the same age, such as with colleagues, acquaintances that are not bosom buddies or college classmates -- unless 선생님 or another title applies.

## Vocabulary Exercise 1. 뭐에요?    What is it?
Write the name of each item in Korean.

*Examples:* 책!

1)

2)

3)

4)

5)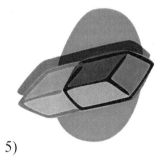

6)

7)

8)  Tel: 987-654-3210

9)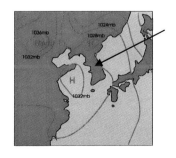

10)  koreanlg@u.washington.edu

**Vocabulary Exercise 2.  Odd one out**
Which vocabulary item does not fit with the others?

1) 사람, 학생, 선생님, 전화번호

2) 책, 카메라, 공책, 종이

3) 지우개, 연필, 가방, 펜

4) 한국, 한국사람, 이름

5) 엄마, 이름, 전화번호, 이메일

6) 어머니, 아버지, 선생님, 가방

7) *Make up your own sets and pairs!*

## Lesson 2 dialogue   그게 뭐에요?

선생님:  그게 뭐에요?

학생:     펜이에요.

선생님:  스파이 카메라가 아니에요?

학생:     아니에요, 이건 그냥 [1] 펜이에요.

선생님:  저건 뭐에요?

학생:     그건 제 한국어 책이에요.

[1]. just

Pay special attention to the use of the word 그건 in the last sentence by 학생. He could have used 저건 to mean **_That_** (*is my Korean book*). By using 그건, he actually said **_It_** (*is my Korean book*).

⚠️ 그 refers to things that are physically close to the hearer, but it also talks about what is common knowledge between the speaker and the listener, namely *it*!

In English, it is O.K. to use the same demonstrative pronoun *that* for both people and things and ask *What is that?* and *Who is that?* In Korean, it is terribly rude to call a person 그거. To properly honor a third person (*he, she*), you should say 그 분: 그 분 누구에요? (*Who is that person?*) If it is someone of similar age or younger than you, you can say 그 사람 누구에요? (*Who is that person?*) Of course, it is impolite in any culture to ask 이 사람 누구에요? *Who is this guy?* (in their presence). You will learn more about the word *who* and honorific expressions in later chapters!

## Lesson 2 grammar

### 1A. Focus                    *A is B*

| A 은/는   B 이에요/에요 | A   am, are, is   B |
|---|---|

이에요/에요 is the *BE* verb (*it is, they are, you are, I am, etc.*).  It comes at the end of the sentence, of course, and like all Korean verbs, does not "conjugate" for Person and Number (*I, we, you, he, she, it* or *they.*).  BUT!  -에요 is used after a word that ends in a **vowel** and -이에요 is used after a word that ends in a **consonant**.  These two forms are (already) conjugated with a polite ending and are ready to be used in conversations with colleagues and acquaintances.

이에요/에요 is used in sentences identifying an item or person: *This **is** a _____* or *She **is** the teacher.*  Don't forget to use 있어요 for locating items – see Lesson 1 if you need to review these sentences.

The **subject** in a sentence with 이에요/에요 is usually marked with -은/는, which is grammatically a *topic* marker. When a noun that begins a sentence is flagged with the marker -은 or –는, you can assume that the sentence is **about** that noun, that is, the noun is the **topic** of the sentence. Sometimes it might be easier to grasp the concept if you translate the sentence with a noun marked with –은/는 with *as for...* or *in regards to...* :

> 저희 선생님**은** 한국 사람**이에요**.     *My teacher* is a Korean. (*As for the teacher, he is...*)

> 이 분**은** 저희 어머니**에요**.        *This* person is my mother. (*In regards to this person, she is...*)

 Use **-은** when the noun being marked ends in consonant, and use **-는** when it ends in vowel.

> As you have already observed, it is *very* important for you to pay attention to whether a noun ends in a vowel or a consonant when it comes to selecting noun markers (-이 vs. -가, and -은 vs. -는).  The same holds true when you start "conjugating" verbs.

### *Wait a minute!!*

When you are asked "X 가 뭐에요? (What is X?)" with the subject marker, be sure to answer with the topic marker "X 는 Y 에요/이에요. (X is Y.)"  By asking the question "X 가

72

뭐에요?", you are already making X the **topic** of the sentence, thus you must use the topic marker when you answer the question. The same holds for the question "X 가 누구에요?"

> Here you used the subject marker '가' because it is the subject of the sentence, and it is NOT a topic yet. You are *making* it a topic. When the listener hears your question, the X becomes the topic. Hang in there. You'll get the hang of it soon!

Now, observe the interplay between the subject marker -이/가 and the topic marker -은/는:

A: 이름이 뭐에요?　　　　　　What's (your) name?

B: 제 이름은 모린이에요.　　　*(My) name* is Maureen. (*As for my name, it's…*)

A: 저분이 누구에요?　　　　　Who is that person (honored)?

B: 저분은 저희 어머니에요.　*That person* is my mother. (*As for that person, she is…*)

A: 저 학생이 누구에요?　　　Who is that student (that is, *person*)?

B: 저 사람은 제 친구에요.　*That person* is my friend (*As for that person, he/she is…*)

 Finally, do not forget that the verb has to come at the very end of the sentence, and that you must *always* have a verb in each sentence!

이름이 뭐에요? What's your name?　　　　And **NOT**　이름이 뭐?

> The verb *BE* is often considered sub-minimal or parasitic, since it is so short. It also sometimes totally disappears after a noun ending in a vowel (hence the form '에요'). For this reason, this verb is said in one breath along with the preceding noun and is written attached to it. All other verbs in Korean act far more independently, and you need to put a space between other verbs and their preceding words.

## 1A. Other Grammar Notes

### 1. *this, that, that over there*　이, 그, 저

While in English we have only *this* and *that*, Korean establishes three referent locations. 이 is a demonstrative adjective (like *this*) that indicates that the item is *near the speaker*. 그 denotes a location *near the listener*. And 저 denotes a location *far from both the speaker and the listener*.

이 책                                    this book (close to ME)

그 연필                    that pencil (close to YOU)

저 공책                                  that notebook over there

 You already know that Korean does not have articles *the* and *a*. Then how do Koreans express definiteness or specificity (not any book but "the book we both know")? They do so by using the demonstrative adjective 그. This seems the most logical choice among the three demonstrative adjectives 이, 그, and 저 in Korean, as 그 assumes the proximity to the listener (that is, the listener should know about what is talked about).

A: 어제 그 사람 누구에요?        Who is the person (from) yesterday?
B: 그 사람은 제 친구에요.         He is my friend.

A: 그 책 읽었어요?               Did you read the book?
B: 네, 그 책 읽었어요.            Yes, I read it.

> Although it is possible to use the words *this* and *that* as nouns in English, the same is not true for Korean. Always explicitly say the noun you are discussing!
> 이가 뭐에요?  **WRONG WAY**  What is *this*?

## 2. 거/ 것    *thing*

Just like 뭐 and 무엇, there are two forms that mean *thing* in Korean. One is the full form 것, which is used more often in written texts, and the other is 거, the shortened form of 것, which is used more often in conversational Korean.

**이것**이 무엇이에요?                    What is this? – written

**이거**가 뭐에요?                        What is this? - conversational

In conversational speech, because the word 거 is so frequently used with the demonstrative markers 이, 그, 저 and the subject/topic marker, they have merged to yield a set of very compact expressions. Learn the following useful forms by heart!

| | Written (full) forms | Intermediate contracted forms | Conversation forms |
|---|---|---|---|
| | 것 | 거 | 거 |
| 이, 그, 저 + 것/거 + 이/가 | 이것이, 그것이, 저것이 | 이거가, 그거가, 저거가 | 이게, 그게, 저게 |
| 이, 그, 저 + 것/거 + 은/는 | 이것은, 그것은, 저것은 | 이거는, 그거는, 저거는 | 이건, 그건, 저건 |

A: **이게** 뭐에요?              What is this?
B: **이건** 제 공책이에요.        This is my notebook.

> Forms in the third row are the most widely used in spoken Korean.

A: **저게** 뭐에요?                          What is that?
B: **그건** 제 한국어 교과서에요..              It is my Korean textbook.

거 or 것 is so called a dependent noun, and it may not be used by itself – instead, it always has to be modified by something (e.g. an adjective or a demonstrative adjective)

~~것이 있어요.~~       There is a thing.

You should also not directly translate English expressions involving the word *thing* into Korean. Most of the time, they don't work. The following expressions do not make any sense in Korean!

~~것은... 것아~~     (to mean "The thing is...")
~~카메라 거~~      (to mean "The camera thing..." when you forgot the exact name for the item you are talking about)

## 1B. Focus        *A is not B*

| A 은/는  B 이/가  아니에요 | A  am not, are not, is not  B |
|---|---|

아니에요 is a negative *BE* verb. It negates the identity of two items (e.g., *X is not Y*).

책상은 탁자가 아니에요.                       A desk is not a table.

Note in the previous sentence that the first noun is flagged with the topic marker -은 and the second noun is flagged with the subject marker -가. This is because you can only negate something that is already defined (that is, which is a topic). Here are some more examples:

저 선생님은 한국어 선생님이 아니에요.    That teacher is not a Korean teacher.

저 선생님은 그 한국어 선생님이 아니에요.  That teacher is not the Korean teacher
                                        (that I talked about).

이 책은 제 책이 아니에요.                    This book is not my book.

그 가방은 제 친구 가방이 아니에요.          That bag is not my friend's bag.

A: 이게 선생님 가방이에요?              Is this the teacher's bag?
B: 아니오, 그건 선생님 가방**이 아니에요.**   No, it is not the teacher's bag.

> It is O.K. and quite natural to repeat nouns in Korean. You can also avoid saying the nouns repeatedly by using 거, right? 이건 제 책이 아니에요. (This is not my book).

 Again, in spoken Korean, the subject marker is frequently omitted.

그건 선생님 가방이 아니에요.              No, it is not the teacher's bag.

그 가방은 제 친구 가방이 아니에요.          That bag is not my friend's bag.

저 사람은 제 친구가 아니에요.            That person is not my friend.

*Wait a minute!!*

Recall that the verb 이에요 does not act independently but attaches to the preceding noun. Remember not to put the subject marker before this verb!

이건 펜<u>이</u>에요.        This is a pen.    ~~이건 펜이 이에요.~~

이건 펜이 아니에요.        This is not a pen.

> This is part of the verb 이에요, right?

## 2B. Other Grammar Notes

### 1. *my, our, your*    제, 저희, ...씨

Some expressions in Korean are used to heighten the status of the listener (e.g. -님 in 선생님) and others to humble oneself, such as 저, 제, and 저희 in Korean. 저 is a humble first person pronoun ("I"), and 제 is its possessive form that means *my*, and 저희 means *our*. To talk about one's family members and what might be considered family/communal property, get used to using 저희, instead of 제.

| 저희 어머니 | our mother |
| 저희 집 | our home/house |
| | |
| 제 가방 | my (-humble) bag |
| 제 이름 | my name |
| 제 친구 | my friend |

If you want to talk about something belonging to someone other than yourself, (e.g. *your* or *his/her*), you can simply use the person's name + 씨, followed by the object possessed.

| **제임스** 씨 어머니 | James, your mother | OR | James's mother |
| **다니엘** 씨 펜 | Daniel, your pen | OR | Daniel's pen |

 The expression "*name* 씨" can only be used when you are talking to or about your equals such as colleagues and friends. **Do not refer to yourself using the word 씨!** You will also learn other ways to address people respectfully in later lessons.

## 2. Noun compounds

When two nouns are put together, the first noun either *describes* the second noun, or it acts as a *possessor* of the second noun.

Description
| 전화번호 | telephone number |
| 한국 사람 | Korean (person) |
| 스페인어 교과서 | Spanish textbook |

Possession
| 선생님 가방 | teacher's bag |
| 친구 어머니 | friend's mother |
| 아버지 카메라 | father's camera |

> Much like the confused use of English compounds that are sometimes considered one words and sometimes hyphenated (e.g., blackboard, baby-sitter, math teacher), Korean compound nouns also allow various spacing between nouns:
> 한국 대학 학생회
> 한국대학 학생회
> 한국 대학학생회
> 한국대학학생회
> "Hankuk University Student Union"

## 3. Yes and No in Korean

*Yes* is 네/예 and *No* is 아니오 in Korean  The usage of 네/예 versus 아니오 in Korean is a little bit different from English. 네/예 implies "you are right" while 아니오 implies "you are not right:"

A: **찰스**는 미국 사람이에요?
B: **아니오**, 미국 사람이 아니에요. 영국 사람이에요.
A: **찰스**는 미국 사람이 아니에요?
B: 네. 영국 사람이에요.

> Of course, questions and answers all depend on the intention of the speaker. As you are saying "찰스는 미국 사람이 아니에요?", if you mean "That's what I've always thought", the answer can be 네. 미국사람이에요. (or, 아니오, 미국사람이 아니에요.)

77

Be aware that 아니오 means *no*, which is a simple answer, and 아니에요 is a sentence, which means (*No, it*) *isn't.*

| | |
|---|---|
| 이게 가방이에요? | Is this a bag? |
| 아니오. | No (*somewhat blunt!*) |
| 아니에요. | No, it's not (the case). |

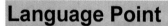

## Language Point          *Topic markers -은 and -는*

People usually talk *about* things already known to both the speaker and the listener. That being the case, in what situations do you think -은/는 is predominantly used?

When a noun is followed by the demonstrative adjectives 이, 그, 저 (that is, to talk about something or some one in one's presence), you are likely to use the topic marker -은/는, because you are talking about something apparent, obvious, and plain to see:

| | |
|---|---|
| 이 분은 한국어 선생님이에요. | This person (you see) is a Korean teacher. |
| 그 가방은 제 가방이에요. | That bag (right there) is my bag. |

Another case is when both the speaker and the listener already know about the person or thing in question. In such a case, pronouns are typically used in English:

| | |
|---|---|
| 그 사람은 제 친구가 아니에요. | *He* is not my friend. |
| 그건 제 펜이에요. | *It* is my pen. |

## Lesson 2 exercises

**Exercise 1.     Dialogue practice**
Practice the dialogue with a classmate.

**Exercise 2.     What's your phone number?**
Exchange phone numbers and email addresses with three of your classmates.  Don't forget to introduce yourself politely and ask their names!

**Exercise 3.     Where are your parents from?**
Ask five of your classmates whether they are from Korea (or other countries).  Ask about their parents.  Try to use as many nationality terms as you remember, and don't forget to use the humble possessive forms when you answer!

*Example:*
제시:     **제임스** 씨는 미국 사람이에요?

제임스: 네, 저는 미국 사람이에요.

제시:     **제임스** 씨 어머니는 미국 사람이에요?

제임스: 아니오, 저희 어머니는 영국 사람이에요.

**Exercise 4.     What is this?**
Point to or pick up various objects and ask your partner what they are.  Remember to use the correct distance term in your response!

*Example:*
A: "이게 _____ (이)에요?"
B: "네 **(yes)**, 그건 _____ (이)에요." or "**아니오 (no)**. 그건 "_____ (이)에요."

**Exercise 5.     은/는**
Fill in the blanks with 은 or 는.

1) 한국어 선생님____ 한국 사람이에요.

2) 저 분____ **샌디** 씨 아버지에요.

3) 이 카메라____ 제 카메라에요.

4) 저희 엄마____ 일본 사람이에요.

5) 저____ 고등 학생이 아니에요. (고등학생: high school student)

**Exercise 6.    Negative Sentences**
Negate the question your partner proposes.

*Example:*
제시:    저 사람은 학생이에요?
제임스: 아니오. 학생이 아니에요. 선생님이에요.

1) 저 선생님은 미국 사람이에요?

2) 저 분은 **리사** 씨 아버지에요?    (**리차드** 씨)

3) 이 카메라는 제 카메라에요?

4) ____ 씨 아빠는 독일 사람이에요?

**Exercise 7.    제 or 저희**
Fill in the blanks with 제 or 저희.

1) 이 분은 _____어머니에요.

2) 이건 _____ 가방이 아니에요.

3) _____ 이름은 **파멜라 앤더슨**이에요

4) 이건_____ 집이에요. (집: house, home)

**Exercise 8.    Contracted forms**
Practice changing the full (written) forms 이것이/이것은, 그것이/그것은, and
저것이/저것은 to the contracted, more conversational forms 이게/이건, 그게/그건, and
저게/저건.

> 이것은 제 책이에요.  저것은 제 공책이 아니에요.  그것은 제 친구 공책이에요.
> 이것이 제 공책이에요.
>
> This is my book.  That is not my notebook.  That is my friend's notebook.
> *This* is my notebook.

## Lesson 2     Checkpoint

**대화 1**      이게 **타미** 씨 연필이에요?

지미: 이게 **타미** 씨 연필이에요?

타미: 아니오, 그건 **수미** 씨 연필이에요.

지미: 이건 **수미** 씨 핸드폰[8]이에요?

타미: 아니오, 그건 제 핸드폰이에요.

지미: 이건 뭐에요?

타미: 제 한국어 책이에요.

**대화 2**      이메일 있어요?

케이:     **마이크** 씨, 이메일 있어요?

마이크: 아니오, 이메일 없어요.

케이:     그럼, 전화 있어요?

마이크: 네, 전화 있어요.

케이:     전화번호가 뭐에요?

마이크: 네, 3456-6543 이에요.

케이:     3456-654 가 아니에요?

마이크: 아니오. 3456-6543 이에요.

---

[8] Transliteration of *handphone* (cell phone).

대화 3        이게 선생님 책상이에요?

수미:     이게 선생님 책상이에요?

선생님: 네, 그 책상이 제 거에요.

수미:     이건 뭐에요?

선생님: 학생들[9] 한국어 공책이에요.

수미:     학생들이 미국사람이에요?

선생님: 네, 학생들이 미국사람이에요.

읽기 1        친구 수미

    제 친구 이름은 **김수미**에요. **수미**는 한국 사람이에요. 이건 **수미** 전화번호에요. 9876-6789 에요. 이건 **수미** 이메일이 아니에요. 이건 제 이메일이에요. 저게 **수미** 이메일이에요. **수미** 이메일은 soomee@abc.edu 에요.

읽기 2        **지미의 컴퓨터**

    이것은 제 컴퓨터에요. **지미** 컴퓨터가 아니에요. **지미** 컴퓨터는 노트북[10]이 아니에요. 제 컴퓨터가 노트북이에요.

---

[9] plural marker (usually after an animate being)
[10] laptop

## Culture Point       "학생!"

학생 is used to refer to both male and female students of all ages; of course at a university, one assumes you are referring to college students. 여- can be prefixed to 학생 to specify female students and 남- to specify male students. In addition, 학생 may be used, especially by older people, as a term of address for someone of school age (including college) whose name is not known. Be ready to respond when someone calls "학생!"

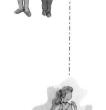

Just as it would be rude to say "Hey, you!" to the wrong person in English, it is also important to learn correct vocatives in Korean.

## Language Point    *Korean nouns: plurality and indefiniteness*

Determiners such as *a* and *the* are not used with Korean nouns; the number (plural or singular) and definiteness (*a* or *the*) of nouns is not expressed, unless reporting a specific number (*one, five, fifty-seven*) of items or using a demonstrative (*this, that*).

Similarly, nouns are not often marked as plural (such as by adding –*s* as in English). At times, to clarify that a noun is indeed plural, the suffix –들 is added to the noun. This plural marking is largely limited to animate nouns (generally people).

| | |
|---|---|
| 교실에 학생이 있어요? | *Are there any/is there a* student in the classroom? |
| 네, 교실에 학생이 있어요. | Yes, there is a/are student(s) in the classroom. *OR* |
| 네, 교실에 학생들이 있어요. | Yes, there are students in the classroom. *OR* |
| 네, 교실에 학생이 많아요. | Yes, there are many students in the classroom. |

In the last sentence, the adjective 많아요 (to be many) makes it clear that there is more than one student in the classroom, and therefore, the use of -들 would be redundant. -들 is not commonly used in such cases.

# LESSON 3
# 사탕도 있어요?

## Lesson 3 vocabulary     More Nouns & Markers

| | | |
|---|---|---|
| 1. 잡지 [잡찌] | magazine | |
| 2. 신문 | newspaper | |
| 3. 지갑 | wallet | |
| 4. 돈 | money | |
| 5. 학생증 [학쌩쯩] | student ID card | |
| 6. 운전면허증 [면허쯩] | driver's license | |
| 7. 열쇠 [열쐬, 열쎄] | key | |
| 8. 칼 | knife | |
| 9. 자전거 | bicycle | |

Don't be misled by the ㅇ in 학생증. The word is NOT 학생증 and be careful with this minute graphic difference!

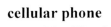

| | |
|---|---|
| 10. 핸드폰 | cellular phone |
| 11. 워크맨 | portable CD player |
| 12. 시디, 씨디 [씨디] | CD (compact disc) |
| 13. 레터 오프너 | letter opener |
| 14. 신용카드 | credit card |
| 15. 기타 | guitar |

Aside from 신용카드, 크레딧 카드, 크레디트 카드, or just 카드 can also be used.

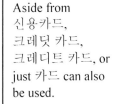

| | |
|---|---|
| 16. 오토바이 | motorcycle ("auto-bike") |
| 17. 버스 | bus |
| 18. 택시 | taxi |

| | |
|---|---|
| 19. 사탕 | candy |
| 20. 과자 | snack crackers, chips |
| 21. 껌 | chewing gum |
| 22. 초컬릿, 초콜렛, 초코렛 | chocolate |
| 23. 아이스크림 | ice cream |
| 24. 주스 or 쥬스 | juice |
| 25. 샌드위치 [쌘드위치] | sandwich |

| | |
|---|---|
| 26. -도 | also (noun particle) |
| 27. -하고 | and (noun particle) |
| 28. 또 | again, what else (adverb) |
| 29. 여기 | here |
| 30. 거기 | there |
| 31. 저기 | over there |
| 32. 누가 | who (subject) |
| 33. 제(가) | I - *humble* (shown with the subject marker) |

**Vocabulary Exercise 1.  Tell me what you have!**
Work with at least three classmates and find out what is in their bag. Report your findings to the rest of the class.  Use –도 and 하고 as many times as possible!

*Example:*            _____씨 가방에는 _____이/가 있어요?

                    _____이/가 있어요/ 없어요?

                    _____도 있어요/없어요?

**Vocabulary Exercise 2.   What might you find there?**
Fill in the blanks with items you might find in each location.

1)  for lunch:  _____, _____, _____

2)  in my snack bag:  _____, _____

3)  locations: 여기, _____, _____

4)  in my wallet:  _____, _____

5)  in my (jeans) pocket:  _____, _____, _____

**Vocabulary Exercise 3.   In prose...**
Modifying the exercise above, ask questions and answer.

*Example:*
Q: 카페테리아에 뭐가 있어요?

A: 카페테리아에 샌드위치가 있어요. 주스하고 껌도 있어요.

1) 교실
2) 가방
3) 여기
4) 지갑
5) 주머니

## Lesson 3 dialogue    사탕도 있어요?

### At the airport security checkpoint

(Looking inside a bag, talking to the student)

경찰 [1]:   여기 뭐가 있어요?

학생:   워크맨이 있어요. 시디도 있어요.

경찰:   또, 뭐가 있어요?

학생:   지갑하고 열쇠가 있어요.

경찰:   칼은 없어요? [2]

학생:   네, 칼은 없어요.

경찰:   이거 칼이 아니에요?

학생:   아니오, 그건 칼이 아니에요. 레터 오프너에요.

경찰:   여기 과자도 있어요?

학생:   네, 있어요.

경찰:   사탕도 있어요?

학생:   네, 있어요.

경찰:   그럼, 사탕하고 과자 좀 주세요 [3].

[1.] police officer

[2.] How about a knife? Do you have a knife?

[3.] Give (me) a little

Koreans don't really use letter openers to open letters. Instead, they use scissors and razor blades. You can hear Koreans use the word 오프너 to refer to a bottle opener. As for the word *letter opener*, the closest translation would be 편지 따개, literally, a letter opener.

## Lesson 3 grammar

### 1. Focus          *have / don't have*

| A 는 B 가 있어요 | A has B |
|---|---|
| A 는 B 가 없어요 | A does not have B |

You might have already discovered that 있어요/없어요 expresses ownership or possession of an item. 여기 뭐가 있어요? in the dialogue above can mean either "What do you have here?" or "What's here?"

The item in existence or possessed is marked with -이/가 , and the possessor is often left out, especially when it is *I* or *You*.

| 마이클: | (제니 씨는) 워크맨이 있어요? | Jenny, do you have a Walkman? |
|---|---|---|
| 제니: | 네, (저는 워크맨이) 있어요. | Yes, I have a Walkman. |

 It's important to remember that the item **possessed** is marked by the subject marker -이/가. The literal English translation for "…이/가 있어요" is perhaps "a … exists (unto me)", such that the item possessed is clearly the *subject* of the sentence (e.g. *A boy* goes, *A boy* takes…, *A boy* exists).

> Can you translate the following sentences? Which corresponds to which?
> Jack has a roommate.          Jack's roommate is here.
> ➔     잭 씨 룸메이트는 여기 있어요.     잭 씨는 룸메이트가 있어요.

### 2. Other Grammar Notes

#### 1. -도          *also*

-도 is a noun particle that means "also." In English *also* can occur in several places in the sentence. In Korean, however, -도 immediately marks the *new* or *added* noun, which is italicized in the following examples:

| 스티브는 연필이 있어요. | | 스티브는 펜도 있어요. |
|---|---|---|
| Steve has a pencil. | ➔ | Steve also has a *pen*./Steve has a *pen*, too. |

| 스티브는 연필이 있어요. | | 조엔도 연필이 있어요. |
|---|---|---|
| Steve has a pencil. | ➔ | *Joan* also has a pencil. |

88

## 2. Noun-하고 Noun-하고 Noun          Noun …, *and* Noun

하고 is a marker that means *and,* which connects two **nouns**:

| | |
|---|---|
| 펜**하고** 연필 | a pen and a pencil |
| 책**하고** 공책**하고** 가방 | a book, a notebook, and a bag |
| 선생님**하고** 학생 | teacher and the student |
| 탁자**하고** 책상**하고** 의자 | a table, a desk, and a chair |

⚠ **It is ungrammatical to say:** 이건 책이에요. ~~하고~~ ~~저건 공책이에요.~~
In future lessons, you will learn other ways of connecting sentences and adjectives.

## 3. 여기, 거기, 저기          *here, there, over there*

You already know that 이, 그, and 저 are adjectives that mean *this, that,* and *that over there.* 여기, 거기, 저기 are related words that mean *here; this place* (close to me, the speaker), *there; that place* (close to you, the listener; also the place "we" both know), and *that place over there* (yonder, place far from me and you).

> To say "Come here" or "Go over there", you need to say 이리 (*here*), 그리 (*there*), and 저리 (*over there*).

## Lesson 3 exercises

**Exercise 1.     Dialogue practice**
Practice the dialogue with a classmate.

**Exercise 2.     -은/는 or -이/가 or NO MARKER?**
Fill in the blanks with most natural sounding markers.

1) 선생님_____ 가방_____ 있어요.          The teacher has a bag. (statement, not an answer to a question)

2) **동현이**_____ 과자_____ 있어요.     **동현이** has snacks.(talking *about* **동현**)

3) **바바라**_____ 워크맨_____ 없어요.     Barbara does not have a Walkman. (talking *about* Barbara)

4) A: **스테이시**는 씨디가 있어요? A: 네. **스테이시**_____ 씨디_____ 있어요. (Yes, she does.)

4)  Q: 누가 씨디가 있어요?  A: **스테이시**_____ 씨디_____ 있어요.  (*Stacy* does.)

5) 제 이름은 **이 소영**_____이에요.          My name is **이 소영**.

6) 제 이름은 **이 은비**_____ 아니에요.          My name is not **이 은비**.

7) 저____ 한국 친구 ____ 있어요.

8) 누가 **제임스** 씨 친구에요? A: _____가 **제임스** 씨 친구에요. (*I* am James's friend.)

**Exercise 3.    What do you have?**
Tell your partner what you have in ONE sentence using -하고 between the nouns.
*Example*: 여기 책이 있어요. 가방**도** 있어요.        →        여기 책**하고** 가방이 있어요.

1) 가방에 CD 가 있어요.  워크맨도 있어요. →

2) 주머니에 사탕이 있어요. 과자도 있어요. → (주머니 pocket)

3) 저기 책이 있어요. 공책도 있어요.  →

4) 가방에 칼이 있어요. 열쇠도 있어요. →

**Exercise 4.    What else?  -도**
In response to the sentences, say what else is in the location given.

1) 가방에 책이 있어요.

2) 교실에 학생이 있어요.

3) 맥도날드에 햄버거가 있어요.

4) 스타벅스에 커피가 있어요.

**Exercise 5.    Who else?  -도**
In response to the sentences, say who else has the item mentioned.

1) 제이레노는 멋있는 넥타이가 있어요. (멋있는 stylish)

2) 선생님은 한국어 교과서가 있어요. (교과서 textbook)

3) 제 친구는 사탕이 있어요.

4) 핑크는 남자친구가 있어요. (남자친구 boyfriend)

**Exercise 6.    -도 and  -하고**
Translate the following sentences into Korean. (For sentences that begin with '*you*', you can simply omit the subject.)

1) Chris has a bag and a wallet.

2) There is a teacher and a student.

3) Do you have chips? Do you have candy too?

4) Do you have a credit card?  Do you have a student ID too?

5) Doug has a chocolate bar and gum.

**Exercise 6.    What else you got in there?**
Work with at least three classmates and find out what they have in their bag or pocket (주머니) and report your findings to the rest of the class.  Practice using -도 and -하고 as many times as possible!

**Exercise 7.    Conversation**
Substitute the person listed below for the police officer role and change parts of the following dialogue according to what they might be suspicious of or looking for.

경찰: 가방에 뭐가 있어요?

학생: <u>워크맨</u>이 있어요. <u>씨디</u>도 있어요.

경찰: 또, 뭐가 있어요? <u>칼</u> 있어요?

학생: 아니오, <u>칼</u>은 없어요.

경찰: 이거 <u>칼</u>이 아니에요?

학생: 아니에요. 그건 <u>펜</u>이에요.

1) a guard at a nightclub entrance

2) a guard/ranger at a zoo entrance

3) a bouncer at a concert entrance

4) a clerk at a shop exit

# Lesson 3    Checkpoint

대화 1        지갑이 없어요!

영희:  앗,[11] 지갑이 없어요.

철수:  지갑에 뭐가 있어요?

영희:  크레디트 카드하고 학생증이 있어요.

철수:  지갑에 돈도 있어요?

영희:  아니오, 지갑에 돈은 없어요.

---

[11] interjection to express surprise

## 대화 2      먹을 거[12] 있어요?

지미: **타미** 씨, 먹을 거 있어요?

타미: 네, 샌드위치하고 아이스크림이 있어요.

지미: 초컬렛도 있어요?

타미: 아니오, 초컬렛은 없어요.

지미: 그럼, 아이스크림 좀 주세요.

## Culture Point      *Once upon a time in Korea…*

You couldn't call this a 가방 but it is sort of a backpack, used in the olden days in Korea. Farmers used to carry wood on their backs using this ingenious instrument 지게. You can still see this instrument in the remote rural areas of Korea.

Although modern 경찰 dress like western policemen, here is what they looked like in the days of 지게, and they were called 포졸. Ask your teacher or Korean friends about proverbs involving 포도청, the old police station.

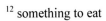

---

[12] something to eat

# LESSON 4
# 선생님의 사무실

## Lesson 4 vocabulary  *Location Nouns*

1. 건물 = 빌딩 [빌딩, 삘딩]　　　building

2. Noun 앞(에)　　　　　　front (in front of Noun)
3. Noun 뒤(에)　　　　　　back (behind Noun)
4. Noun 오른쪽(에)　　　right side (to the right of Noun)
5. Noun 왼쪽(에)　　　　left side (to the left of Noun)
6. Noun 위(에)　　　　　　top (on top of, above Noun)
7. Noun 아래(에)　　　　below (below Noun)
8. Noun 밑(에)　　　　　　underside (underneath Noun)
9. Noun 옆(에)　　　　　　side (next to, beside Noun)

10. Noun 안(에)　　　　　inside (inside of Noun)
11. Noun 속(에)　　　　　within (deep inside of Noun)
12. Noun 밖(에)　　　　　outside (out side of Noun)
13. N₁ 하고 N₂ 사이(에)　between (between $N_1$ and $N_2$)
14. Noun 가운데(에)　　　center (in the center of Noun)
15. N₁ 하고 N₂ 중간(에)　middle (in the middle of $N_1$ and $N_2$)
16. Noun 맞은 편(에) = 건너편 (에) across (across Noun)
17. Noun 주위(에)　　　　around (around Noun)
18. Noun 근처(에)　　　　(in the) vicinity (of Noun)

19. 어디(에)　　　　　　　where
20. –의 [에]　　　　　　　possessive (Noun's)
21. 여기, 거기, 저기　　　here, there, over there

> 윗사람 (위 + 사람) means people who are older than you (and thus should be respected), 아랫사람 (아래 + 사람) means people who are younger than you.

> If you listen to Korean folk songs or rock songs, you will hear the word 곁 a lot, which also means *next to* or *beside*. 곁 is usually used to *poetically* describe a person being next to another person.

**Vocabulary Exercise 1. 뭐가 있어요?**
Tell your partner what you see in/on/at the following place.

1) 지갑 안

2) 교실 안

3) 오른쪽

4) 책상 뒤

5) 선생님 오른쪽

6) 가방 안

**Vocabulary Exercise 2.  It's on the table**
Your instructor will tell you about the location of some items. Mark the location of each item in the picture below.

**Vocabulary Exercise 3.  Where is Kane Hall?**
Ask your partner where a specific building on campus is.  Use location words in your response.

A: __B___ 씨, (building x) 이/가 어디에 있어요?

B: _____ 앞/뒤/옆/위/아래에 있어요.

> 어디에 있어요 is usually pronounced as 어뎄어요 (after 에 is dropped out).

## Lesson 4 monologue    선생님의 사무실

여기는 선생님의 사무실이에요.   책상하고 의자가 있어요. 책상 위에 전화가 있어요.   전화 옆에 컴퓨터가 있어요. 프린터는 없어요. 책상 위에는 또, 책하고 공책도 있어요. 책상 안에는 과자가 있어요. 사탕도 있어요. 선생님의 한국어 책은 어디에 있어요?

**Comprehension Exercise 1.**
Based on the reading passage above, answer the following questions.

1) 선생님의 사무실에는 책상이 있어요?

2) 선생님의 책상 위에 전화가 있어요?

3) 전화 옆에는 뭐가 있어요?

4) 선생님의 사무실에는 프린터도 있어요?

5) 책상 안에는 뭐가 있어요?

> Don't forget to use the 은/는 once the topic you are discussing is distablished, understatood, or expected.

**Comprehension Exercise 2.**
Based on the reading passage above, draw the objects on the teacher's desk.

## Lesson 4 grammar

### 1. Focus          Location Expressions

| A  앞, 옆, 뒤...에 | in front of, next to, behind... A |
|---|---|

To be precise about location (*inside*, *next to*, and so on), Korean uses the location words 안, 옆, and 위, etc. These words are similar to English prepositions, but are grammatically *nouns* in Korean.  In a sense they are possessed by the preceding noun indicating the reference point:

은행 옆                                          the bank's side
선생님 책                                        the teacher's book

The location words (*side, top, front*, etc.) *must follow* the reference point (which may seem the reverse of English).  Then the phrase is marked with the location marker-에:

| reference point | location word | location marker | |
|---|---|---|---|
| 은행 bank | 옆 side | 에 at | at the bank's side = *beside the bank* |
| 가방 bag | 위 top | 에 at | on the bag's top = *on top of the bag* |
| 제 my | 오른쪽 right side | 에 at | at my right side = *on my right* |
| 책하고 공책 book and notebook | 사이 between (noun) | 에 at | on the book and the notebook's between = *between the book and the notebook* |

Can you translate these sentences?
타일러 씨는 누구 앞에 있어요?                                    Who is Tyler in front of?

타일러 씨는 누구하고 누구 사이에 있어요?                          What two people is Tyler between?

### 2. Other Grammar Notes

#### 1. Possessive marker          -의
You have learned that when two nouns are put together, the first noun expresses possession of the second noun:

선생님 가방                                      teacher's bag

There is a more explicit way to express possession in Korean, using the possessive marker 의:

선생님의 가방                          teacher's bag

아버지의 카메라                         father's camera

Remember how to say "I" humbly? (e.g., 저는 미국인이에요, 제 친구는 프랑스 사람이에요.) The humble form of "I" you know is in fact a contracted form of 저 + 의, which is used mainly in written Korean:

저의 친구도 미국 사람이에요.  My friend is also American.

제 친구도 미국 사람이에요.    My friend is also American.

> The possessive marker 의 is used more often in *written* texts than in everyday conversations.

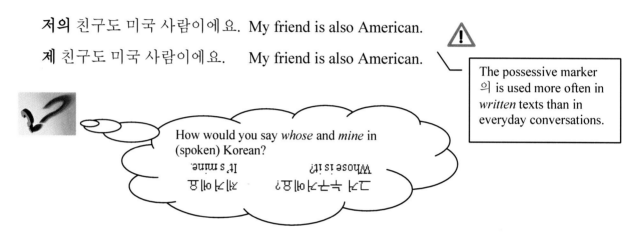

How would you say *whose* and *mine* in (spoken) Korean?

Whose is it?    It's mine.
누구 거에요?      제 거에요.

## 2. Use of the word 어디

The location particle -에 can be left out after such words as 어디 and 여기, which can be considered either nouns or adverbs.

선생님 한국어 책이 **어디**에 있어요?   Where is the teacher's Korean book?

                                    or Where is your Korean book, teacher?

제 한국어 책은 **여기**에 있어요.      Here is my Korean book.

As in the case of the question word 뭐, **어디** simply replaces the noun in question (instead of moving to the beginning of the sentence as in English):

제 한국어 책이 **어디**에 있어요?      Where is my Korean book?

~~**어디** 제 한국어 책이 있어요?~~      ~~(Where is my Korean book?)~~

## 3. -은/는                    contrast

You already know -은 and -는 as a *topic* marker. They can also mark **contrast** to a preceding referent.

전화 옆에 컴퓨터**가** 있어요. 프린터**는** 없어요.
There is a computer next to the phone. As for a *printer*, there is none.
(i.e., There is no *printer*, however.)

When -은/는 is used to flag *contrast*, the noun can be a newly introduced topic. Study the interplay of markers in the conversation below. The use of the markers is explained on the right:

경찰:    그**게** 뭐에요?                    (subject M: introducing a new noun 그것)

학생:    이**건** 지갑이에요.        (topic M: talking about the noun just introduced)

경찰:    그 안에 뭐**가** 있어요? (subject M: unidentified subject of the sentence 뭐)

학생:    지갑하고 열쇠**가** 있어요.      (subject M: introducing a new noun 열쇠)

경찰:    칼**은** 없어요?                      (contrast M, introducing a new topic, giving contrast)

학생:    네, 칼**은** 없어요.        (topic M, talking about the noun just introduced)


## 4. Contracted forms (review)

The following table summarizes the full and contracted forms of 이것, 그것, and 저것. You should be familiar with the first several lines. You will learn about the others later.

| | **Written (full) forms** | **Conversation forms** |
|---|---|---|
| what | 무엇 | 뭐 |
| thing | 것 | 거 |
| 이것, 그것, 저것 + 이 | 이것이, 그것이, 저것이 | 이게, 그게, 저게 |
| 이것, 그것, 저것 + 은 | 이것은, 그것은, 저것은 | 이건, 그건, 저건 |
| 저 + 는 | 저는 | 전 |
| 저 + 의 | 저의 | 제 |
| 저 + 도 | 저도 | 저도 (No change!) |
| 저 희 + 는 | 저희는 | 저흰 |
| 저 희 + 의 | 저희의 | 저희 |
| 저 희 + 도 | 저희도 | 저희도 (No change!) |

The forms 전 and 저흰 are probably new to you, but you can guess how they have come about, can't you? Say 저는 over and over really fast! In conversations, this sort of *blending* takes place quite often even between a regular noun and the topic marker 는...even after people's names!
**스티븐** 어디 있어요?      Where is Steve?
**메린** 제 친구에요.      Mary is my friend.

## Lesson 4 exercises

### Exercise 1.    Dialogue practice
Practice reading the reading passage aloud, heeding the pronunciation of each word.

### Exercise 2.    어디에 있어요?
Complete the sentences with the correct location expressions or subject marker.

가)    테이블 _____ 의자_____ 있어요.
There is a chair under the table.

나)    칠판_____ 선생님_____ 있어요.
The teacher is in front of the chalkboard.

다)    책상_____ 펜_____ 있어요?
Is there a pen in the desk?

라)    책_____ 지우개_____ 있어요.
There is an eraser next to the book.

마)    책_____ 연필_____ 있어요.
There is also a pencil next to the book.

바)    공책_____ 종이_____ 있어요.
There is paper under the notebook.

**Exercise 3.** _____는 어디에 있어요?
Ask your partner where a certain object is in the classroom. Try to internalize the use of the marker -은/는!

*Example*
A: 시계가 어디에 있어요?
B: 시계는 칠판 위에 있어요.
A: 의자는 어디에 있어요?
B: 의자는 칠판 위에 있어요.

A: B 씨 가방은 어디에 있어요?
B: 제 가방은 책상 오른쪽에 있어요. A 씨 가방은 어디에 있어요?
A: 제 가방은 의자 뒤에 있어요.

**Exercise 4.** -은/는
Draw a picture of your belongings, carefully positioning the items with respect to each other. Hide the picture from your partner and describe it to him/her so he/she can draw a picture. Compare your drawing with your partner's when he/she is done. See what is different. Don't forget to use -은/는 when you pick an object to talk about its location!

**Exercise 5.** -에 or -이/가
Fill in the blanks with -이 or -가 marking the subject and -에 marking the location.

*Example:* 교실에 책상이 있어요.          There is a desk in the classroom
                                          /there are desks in the classroom.

1) 가방_____ 칼_____ 있어요.            There is a knife in the bag.

2) 테이블_____ 사탕_____ 없어요.        There is no candy on the table.

3) 지갑_____ 열쇠_____ 있어요.          There is a key in the wallet.

4) 가방_____ 과자_____ 있어요.          There are crackers in the bag.

5) 테이블_____ 스파게티*_____ 있어요.   There is spaghetti* on the table.

6) 의자_____ 교실_____ 없어요.          There is no chair in the classroom
                                          /there are no chairs in the classroom.

7) 씨디_____ 워크맨_____ 있어요.        There is a CD in the Walkman.

8) 지우개_____ 칠판_____ 있어요.        There is an eraser in front of the chalkboard.

**Exercise 6.    Practicing -에, -이/가, -하고, -도**
Translate the following sentences into Korean.

1) I have a wallet and a bag.

2) I have a wallet in a bag.

3) I have a bag.  I have a wallet, too.

4) There is a teacher and a student.

5) Is there a table in the classroom?  Is there also a desk?

6) There is a key and a book and a CD and a notebook on the table.

7) Do you have chips? Do you have candy too?

## Lesson 4      Checkpoint

**대화 1        어디 있어요?**

케이:    여보,[13] 제 책이 어디 있어요?

마이크: 책상 위에 있어요.

케이:    여보, 씨디는 어디 있어요?

마이크: 컴퓨터 앞에 있어요.

케이:    여보, 기타는 어디 있어요?

마이크: 기타는 텔레비전 아래 있어요.

**대화 2        학교가 어디에 있어요?**

철수: **영회** 씨 어디 있어요?

영희: 학교에 있어요.

철수: **영회** 씨 학교가 어디에 있어요?

영희: 저희 학교는 은행 옆에 있어요.

철수: 은행이 어디 있어요?

영희: 은행은 경찰서[14] 오른쪽에 있어요.

---

[13]A way to call one's spouse.

## 읽기 1          로미오의 방

여기는 **로미오**의 방이에요. **로미오**의 방에는 책상과 탁자가 있어요. 탁자는 책상의 왼쪽에 있어요. 책상 앞에는 의자가 있어요. 책상 위에는 한국어 책하고 가방이 있어요. 가방에는 공책하고 연필하고 워크맨이 있어요.

## 읽기 2          케이의 가족 사진

**케이**의 탁자 위에 가족 사진[15]이 있어요. **케이**의 어머니는 영국사람이에요. **케이**의 아버지는 미국사람이에요. 사진에 **케이**의 아버지는 어머니의 오른쪽에 있어요. **케이**는 어머니의 왼쪽에 있어요. **케이**의 어머니는 아버지하고 **케이**의 가운데에 있어요.

## 노래하고 갑시다!

**엄지 어디 있어?**

엄지 어디 있어?

엄지 어디 있어?

엄지 여기 있어!

엄지 여기 있어!

안녕하세요, 오늘?

재미있어요, 오늘?

딩동댕 딩동댕

[14] Police station
[15] family photo

3. 중지 (셋째 손가락)

4. 약지 (넷째 손가락)        2. 검지(둘째 손가락)

5.애지

(새끼 손가락)          1. 엄지

(첫째 손가락)

## Language Point *Right under your nose!*

Some vowels (e.g. ㅏ, ㅑ, and ㅗ, ㅛ) are considered 'small' in Korean, giving the impression that what you are describing is light or small. So saying 요거, 고거, 조거 instead of 이거, 그거, 저거 implies that the object you are pointing to is *small*. What do you think 요기, 고기, 조기 mean?

# 쉬어갑시다!
# LET'S TAKE A BREAK!

What time is it?
What day is it today?

# CHAPTER 1.5 A 오늘이 무슨 요일이에요?

**What day is it today?**

## Vocabulary

| | |
|---|---|
| 무슨 요일 | what day (of the week) |
| 오늘 | today |
| 지난 주 | last week |
| 이번 주 [이번 쭈] | this week |
| 다음 주 [다음 쭈] | next week |

| | |
|---|---|
| 월요일 | **Monday** |
| 화요일 | *Tuesday* |
| 수요일 | *Wednesday* |
| 목요일 | *Thursday* |
| 금요일 | *Friday* |
| 토요일 | *Saturday* |
| 일요일 | *Sunday* |

월-화-수-목-금    M-F  (Monday through Friday)

# Exercises

## Exercise 1.  What day is it? 무슨 요일이에요?

Report to your partner what Xiao Li is doing today.  You partner will tell you what day of the week it is, based on Xiao Li's schedule below.

A:

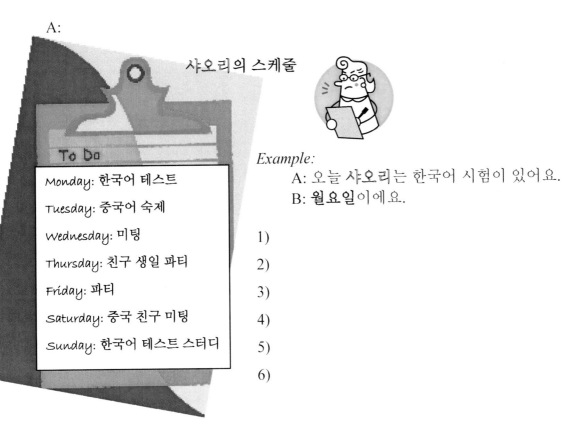

샤오리의 스케줄

To Do

Monday: 한국어 테스트

Tuesday: 중국어 숙제

Wednesday: 미팅

Thursday: 친구 생일 파티

Friday: 파티

Saturday: 중국 친구 미팅

Sunday: 한국어 테스트 스터디

*Example:*

A: 오늘 샤오리는 한국어 시험이 있어요.

B: 월요일이에요.

1)
2)
3)
4)
5)
6)

## Exercise 2.  What day is it? 무슨 요일이에요?

Based on Xiao Li's schedule above, make up sentences to report what she does on each day of the week.  For each thing on Xiao Li's schedule that *you* do, tell what day you do the activity.

*Example*

Q: 샤오리는 무슨 요일에 한국어 테스트가 있어요?

A: 샤오리는 월요일에 한국어 테스트가 있어요.

저는 금요일에 한국어 테스트가 있어요.

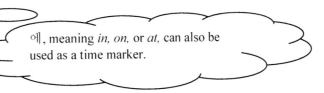

에, meaning *in*, *on*, or *at*, can also be used as a time marker.

107

# CHAPTER 1.5 B 몇 시 몇 분이에요?

**What time is it?**

## Vocabulary

| | | |
|---|---|---|
| 1. | 몇 | how many |
| 2. | 시 | hour |
| 3. | 분 | minute |
| 4. | 반 | half past (30 minutes after the hour) |
| 5. | 정각 | on the nose, on the dot (e.g. 정각 3 시) |
| 6. | 지금 | now |
| 7. | 오전 | A.M. (around 7 A.M. ~ 11 A.M.) |
| 8. | 오후 | P.M. (around 1 P.M. ~ 5 or 6 P.M.) |
| 9. | 오늘 | today |
| 10. | 새벽 | dawn, early morning (around 3, 4 A.M. ~ 6 A.M.) |
| 11. | 아침 | morning (around 7 A.M. ~ 11 A.M.) |
| 12. | 점심 | day time (around 11:30 A.M. ~ 2:30 P.M.) |
| 13. | 저녁 | evening (around 5, 6 P.M. ~ 8 P.M.) |
| 14. | 밤 | night (around 10, 11 P.M. ~ 2, 3 A.M.) |

> To say "this morning" or "tonight" in Korean, you need to say "today" first:
>
> 오늘 아침  this morning
> 오늘 밤   tonight

> 아침, 점심, 저녁 also refer to meals (breakfast, lunch, and dinner)

## Grammar Notes 1

**1. What time is it now?    지금 몇 시에요?**

Use the Native Korean numbers (한, 두, 세...) for telling hours, and the Chinese numbers (일, 이, 삼...) for telling minutes!

> '몇 시에요', in reality, is often pronounced as '메씨' or '며씨'

A: 지금 몇 시에요?
B: (오후) 여섯 시 오 분이에요.

# Exercises 1

### Exercise 1.  What time is it?
Write the time in Korean.  Take turns reading the clocks.  Remember to use the correct numbers for the hour and the minutes!

가) 오전

나) 새벽

다) 오후

라) 오후

마) 아침

바) 밤

(다) 1 시 30 분 can also be said as 1 시 반.
(라) 1 시 53 분 can also be said as 2 시 7 분 전 (7 till).
(마) 10 straight up is said 10 시 정각.

How would you say 2 시 45 분 in another way?

**Exercise 2.    What time is it?**
Say what time it is in Korean. Your partner will find the clock which shows the time you say.
Take turns.

_____

_____

_____

**Exercise 3.    When do you do this?**

What time do you usually do the following activities on weekdays? How about on weekends?  Write the time in Korean

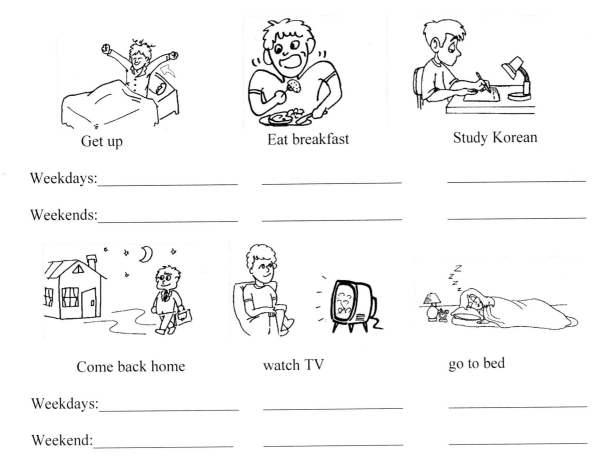

| Get up | Eat breakfast | Study Korean |

Weekdays:_____    _____    _____

Weekends:_____    _____    _____

| Come back home | watch TV | go to bed |

Weekdays:_____    _____    _____

Weekend:_____    _____    _____

# Grammar Notes 2

Remember the marker -에? It means *in, on,* or *at* after place nouns, right?

책상 위에 책하고 공책이 있어요.

-에 still means *in, on,* or *at* when it comes after nouns that express time:

저는 월요일 오후 세 시에 학교*에 있어요.          *학교: school

토요일 밤에 집*에 있어요.          *집: house, home

> While the English order is usually from most specific (smaller) to least specific (larger), the Korean order is the opposite.

111

# Exercises 2

**Exercise 4. Where are you then?  그 때 어디에 있어요?**

Using the expressions 학교 (school) and 집 (home), ask your partner where they are during the times given below:

Example: 아침 7 시

A: ___ 씨는 아침 7 시에 어디에 있어요?
B: 네, 저는 아침 7 시에 집에 있어요.

        or

A: ___ 씨는 아침 7 시에 집에 있어요?
B: 아니오, 저는 아침 7 시에 집에 없어요. 학교에 있어요.

1) 토요일 오후 4 시

2) 일요일 새벽 3 시

3) 월요일 오전 9 시 30 분

4) 수요일 밤 11 시

5) 금요일 저녁 5 시

# CHAPTER 2　뭐 해요?

## What are you doing?

## Preliminary Dialogue

데이빗: 테리 씨, 선생님 사무실이 어디에 있어요?

테리:　　선생님 사무실은 저 쪽, 도서관 [1] 뒤에 있어요.　　library

데이빗: 그럼, 도서관은 어디에요?

테리:　　도서관은 선생님 사무실 앞에 있어요!

You can use 어디에요 in place of 어디에 있어요 *if* you are asking about the location of a PLACE or a building.
선생님 사무실이 어디에요?
과자가 어디에 있어요?
~~과자가 어디에요?~~

**Dialogue practice**

Practice the preliminary dialogue with a classmate.

# LESSON 5

# 어디 가요?

## Lesson 5 vocabulary        *Place Nouns*

| | | |
|---|---|---|
| 1. | 학교 | school |
| 2. | 대학교 | university, college |
| 3. | 백화점 [배콰점] | department store |
| 4. | 서점 | bookstore |
| 5. | 병원 | hospital |
| 6. | 대학원 | graduate school |
| 7. | 체육관 | sports complex/gym |
| 8. | 도서관 | library |
| 9. | 학생회관 | student center |
| 10. | 주차장 | parking lot |
| 11. | 운동장 | ball field |
| 12. | 우체국 | post office |
| 13. | 약국 | drug store |
| 14. | 은행 | bank |
| 15. | 기숙사 | dormitory |
| 16. | 집 | house, home |
| 17. | 방 | room |
| 18. | 공원 | park |
| 19. | 식당 | diner, cafeteria |
| 20. | 노래방 | karaoke room |
| 21. | 영화관 = 극장 | movie theater |
| 22. | 컴퓨터실 | computer lab |
| 23. | 커피숍 | coffee shop |
| 24. | PC 방 / 게임방 | internet cafe |
| 25. | 비디오방 / DVD 방 | rental video viewing rooms |
| 26. | 노래방 | karaoke in private rooms |
| 27. | 호프집 | pub |
| 28. | 꽃집 | flower shop |
| 29. | 슈퍼(마켓) | grocery store |
| 30. | 아파트 | apartment |
| 31. | 누가 | who (used only as the subject of the sentence) |
| 32. | 누구 | who, whom |
| 33. | -하고 | (together) with |
| 34. | 저 | I, me (humble) |
| 35. | 혼자 | by oneself |
| 36. | 어느 | which |

> Did you guess that "서" in 도서관 and 서점 has something to do with "books"?

> Hey kids, I know this is a LOT of words to memorize. But keep working on them. What you memorize today will serve as a building block. It'll get easier and easier. I promise!

115

## Culture Point     SCHOOL

Student-age kids are often called to simply with "학생!" as you know.  In addition, more often than talking about a kid's *age*, Koreans ask their year in school, 몇 학년이에요?. Here's the system and some vocabulary to help:

유치원 preschool and kindergarten (optional)        어린이 little kid, toddler

초등학교 elementary school 6 years        초등학생 elementary school student
중학교 middle school three years      중학생 middle school student
고등학교 high school three years      고등학생 high school student

In Korea, school years are not counted sequentially from elementary school through high school; counting starts in each school-level. So a senior in American high school is equivalent to a high school third-year student, 고등학교 삼 학년, abbreviated 고삼.

고등학교 일 학년      고일    high school first year
고등학교 이학년      고이    high school second year
고등학교 삼 학년      고삼    high school third year

The same works for 중학교 (중일, 중이, 중삼), but for elementary school students you have to say the full mouthful: 초등학교 일 학년, etc.

Also, be forewarned that 삼학년 students have a special status in Korean society (-- support, pity, stress, honor …), because they must spend long hours cramming for college or high school entrance exams.

### Vocabulary Exercise 1.  Association Game
Give a vocabulary item that is associated with each of the following items.  More than one answer may be possible.

보기 (example): 돈 (money): 은행

1) 책: _____

2) 프린터: _____

3) 커피: _____

4) 풋볼 (football): _____

5) 편지 (letter): _____

6) 침대 (bed): _____

7) 숙제: _____

**Vocabulary Exercise 2.    What kind of place?**
Label the following places in Korean.

1) Nordstrom / Saks

2) Gold's Gym

3) University of Washington

4) US Bank

5) Denny's

6) Safeway / IGA / Top Foods

7) Barnes and Noble / Walden Books

8) Bartell's /Walgreen's/ Rite-Aid

9) Safeco Field/ Yankee Stadium

10) Central Park

11) Starbucks

12) (your local library)

# Language point    *Part of the word: building suffixes*

You might have noticed the grouping of the vocabulary above by suffix. Each suffix has a different meaning or nuance, as follows:

-실      **a single room**

-점      **a store**

-원      **an institution**

-관      **a large hall**

-장      **ground, field**

-국      **office, official or government department**

These fragments of a word cannot stand alone as an independent word in a sentence:

실이 있어요. ~~There is a room.~~

Instead, they have to combine with other words or part of a word to form a full noun:

교실    classroom (literally, "teaching room")

Being aware of the parts of these quasi-compounds will help you increase your vocabulary power fast.  What do the following words have in common?  Can you guess the meaning?

학교, 학생, 학생회관        사무실, 연구실, 교실

방, on the other hand, is an independent noun, which means *room* and when used on its own, it refers to a bedroom.

## Lesson 5 dialogue   어디 가요?

**On the street**

시은: 어, **현진** 씨, 어디 가요?

현진: 커피숍에 가요.

시은: 어느 커피숍에 가요?

현진: 학교 앞 카페 **알레그로**요.

시은: 누구하고 가요?

현진: 저 혼자 가요. **시은** 씨는 어디에 가요?

시은: 저는 친구하고 도서관에 가요.

현진: 누구하고 가요?

시은: 제 친구 **피터**하고 가요.

# Lesson 5 grammar

## 1. Focus          The verb *GO*

| 가요 | go/goes, is/are going |
| --- | --- |

The word 가요 used in the dialogue means *go*. It is conjugated for the *polite present tense*. To break it down, 가 is the verb stem, –요, is a politeness marker that indicates that the speaker has some social distance and respect for the listener, and the lack of other suffixes indicates a simple present tense.

The present tense in Korean is equivalent to either the English simple present (*goes*), or present progressive or proximate future (*is going).*

도서관에 가요.          I go to the library (regularly, or everyday).   *or*
                             I am going to the library (now or soon).

Korean verbs are not marked or conjugated differently based on the Person or Number of the Subject; that is, the same verb form is used whether the subject is *I, we, he* or *they*, etc. In fact, the subject can be left out if it is *I, you, it* or the same as in the preceding sentence. Inferring the subject depends on the context.

도서관에 가요.       literally means, "go(es) to the library".

## 2. Other Grammar Notes

### 1. -에      *to (a place)*

-에 was used in Chapter 1 to mark the stationary *location* of an object, and was translated roughly as *in, at, on.*

친구가 은행에 있어요.      A friend of mine *is **at** the bank.*

-에 can also be used to mark a *destination* when used with verbs like 'go':

저는 내일 은행에 가요.      I am going ***to the bank*** tomorrow.

## 2. -요          Politeness marker

-요 can be added to any part of speech (or after any sentence fragment) to show the speaker's politeness or social distance between the speaker and the listener:

까페 **알레그로**요.     (I am going to) Café Allegro (and I am saying it politely).

빨리요.          Quickly, please.

## 3. -은/는        Change of topic

You learned in the previous chapter that the discourse marker 은/는 can be used to talk about an item that has already been introduced or to mark the contrast to a preceding noun. Similarly, it can be used to switch the topic. In the dialogue, **현진** asks **동호**:

**동호** 씨는 어디에 가요?

And the best translation for the sentence is something like "How about you Dongho? Where are *you* going?" or "As for *you*, Dongho, where are *you* going?"

## 4. *(together) with*      -하고

In the previous chapter, you learned that -하고 is a marker that connects two nouns:

학교하고 기숙사              school *and* the dormitory

When -하고 is attached to a *person* noun and there is no second noun following it, -하고 means "(together) with someone"

친구하고 도서관에 가요.        I am going to the library *with* a friend.

## 5. *who/whom, who*        누구, 누가

The word 누구 means *who* or *whom*, but when used as a **subject**, it is 누가.

A: 선생님 사무실에 가요.        (Someone) is going to the teacher's office.

B: **누가요?** *or* **누가 가요?**   Who? – subject *or* Who is going?

A: 저 사람 누구에요?           Who is that person?

B: 누구요?                  Who (are you talking about)?

 Remember that WH-words such as *why* and *who* do not come at the beginning of the question but stay where they would be in a statement.

체육관에 **누구하고** 가요?      Who are you going to the gym with tomorrow?

체육관에 친구하고 가요.        (I) am going to the gym with a friend.

121

## Lesson 5 exercises

**Exercise 1.　　Dialogue practice**
Practice the following dialogues with a classmate.

*Practice Dialogue A*

A: 어, 안녕하세요, ___B__ 씨? 지금 어디 가요?

B: _____ 에 가요.  __A___ 씨는 어디에 가요?

A: 네, 저는 친구하고 _____에 가요.

B: 그래요? 그럼, 안녕히 가세요. (그래요 Is that right?)


*Practice Dialogue B*

A: 어, 안녕하세요, ___B_____ 씨? 지금 어디 가요?

B: _____ 에 가요.

A: 어느 _____이요?

B: _____요. ____A____ 씨는 어디에 가요?

A: 네, 저는 친구하고 _____에 가요.

B: 어느 친구하고 가요?

A: ____하고 가요.

B: 네, 그럼, 안녕히 가세요.

**Exercise 2.　　누구 or 누가?**
Fill in the blanks with 누구 or 누가 appropriately.

1) _____ **제이슨**하고 도서관에 가요?　　Who is going to the library with Jason?

2) _____도 도서관에 가요?　　　　　　　Who is also going to the library?

3) **토비**가_____하고 우체국에 가요?　　Who is Toby going to the post office with?

4) _____ 집에 가요?　　　　　　　　　　Who is going home?

**Exercise 3.**    어디에 가요?

Ask at least three classmates where they are going after class today.  Then report the results of your survey to the class.

*Example*        Q: _____씨는 오늘 어디에 가요? 누구하고 가요?

                  A: 저는 오늘 체육관에 가요. 혼자 (alone) 가요.


Classmate 1:

Classmate 2:

Classmate 3:


**Exercise 4.**    -은/는

Take turns asking your partner where the following people are going.  Follow the pattern given in the example.

*Example*: **제이콥** - 은행, **케이디** - 집

   A: **제이콥** 씨가 어디에 가요?

   B: 은행에 가요.

   A: **케이디** 씨는 어디에 가요?

   B: 집에 가요.

1) **롤디**-식당, **카메론**-공원

2) **로라**-선생님 사무실, **모린**-도서관

3) **제인**-기숙사, **사라**-은행

4) **데이빗**-체육관, **리차드**-우체국

5) **브루스**- 성당, **리치**- 엄마 집 (성당 catholic church)

6) **아만다**-약국, **로저**-서점


**Exercise 5.  누가 누구하고 어디에 가요?**

Fill in the blanks (with the right particles and 누구 or 누가) to ask your partner who is going where with whom.  Your partner will answer the questions according to the pictures.

1) _____ 은행___ 가요?         **데이빗** 씨

2) **티나** 씨___ _____하고 커피숍___ 있어요?    **티나**        **제임스**

3) _____ 우체국___ 가요?      **테일러**

4) **지미**하고____ 서점___ 가요?        **지미**  **피터**

5) _____ 도서관___ 가요?

6) 또, _____도 도서관에 가요?      **다니엘**
**리카**

## Lesson 5      Checkpoint

**대화 1**      금요일에 어디에 가요?

---

몽룡 : **춘향** 씨, 금요일에 어디에 가요?

춘향: 도서관에 가요.

몽룡: 도서관이 어디에 있어요?

춘향: 도서관은 학생회관 앞에 있어요.

몽룡: 도서관에 누구하고 같이 가요?  (같이 together)

춘향: 저 혼자 가요.

몽룡: 그럼 저하고 같이 가요.

---

## 대화 2      공원에 식당이 있어요?

손오공: **저팔계** 씨, 지금 어디에 가요?

저팔계: 지금 식당에 가요.

손오공: 어느 식당에 가요?

저팔계: 한국 식당에 가요. **손오공** 씨는 어디에 가요?

손오공: 저는 공원에 가요.

저팔계: 누구하고 같이 가요?

손오공: 저 혼자 가요.

저팔계: 그럼, 저하고 같이 가요. 그런데,[16] 질문이 있어요.

손오공: 질문이 뭐에요?

저팔계: 공원에 식당이 있어요?

## Culture talk     *Where are you going?*

Asking "어디 가요?" is not usually considered intrusive in Korean. It is a friendly gesture, showing that one cares. Also, if the word 가요 follows a pause, the question simply means "Hello." (literally, 'going somewhere?') In that case, you can respond with "네, 어디 가요." (Yes, I am going somewhere.) Find out how to say "어디 가요?" in two different ways!

## Language point     *Borrowed words*

Many words borrowed from Western languages seem long in Korean, especially compared to Sino-Korean or Native Korean nouns, which are often only two syllables long. These borrowed words are sometimes shortened, such as 아파트 (*apartment*), 에어콘 (*air-conditioner*), and 오토바이 (*motorcycle/auto-bike*).

---

[16] By the way

# LESSON 6

# 뭐 해요?

# Lesson 6 vocabulary  해요 Verbs

> Have you noticed that the -구 words introduced in this lesson involve a ball?

| Verbs | Meaning | Verbs | Meaning |
|-------|---------|-------|---------|
| 숙제해요 | do homework | 배구해요 | play volleyball |
| 공부해요 | study | 야구해요 | play baseball |
| 아르바이트해요 | do part-time work | 축구해요 | play soccer |
| 일해요 | work | 농구해요 | play basketball |
| | | | |
| 애기해요 | talk | 운동해요 | exercise (sports) |
| 전화해요 | phone | 죠깅해요 | jog |
| 노래해요 | sing | 산책해요 | take a walk |
| 쇼핑해요 | do shopping | 등산해요 | hike |
| 외식해요 | eat out | 수영해요 | swim |
| | | | |
| 설거지해요 | do dishes | 목욕/샤워해요 | take a bath/shower |
| 청소해요 | clean (house, rooms) | 세수해요 | wash one's face |
| 빨래해요 | do laundry | 화장해요 | put on make-up |
| 요리해요 | cook | 사랑해요 | love |
| 해요 | do | 같이 [가치] | together |

> In fast speech, ㅎ may drop out. On the other hand, if you are not talking quickly and you drop the ㅎ sound, it will sound like (이)에요, and the listener may be confused.

## Vocabulary Exercise 1.  Odd one out
Which of the following activities does not fit with the others?

1)  설거지해요        노래해요        빨래해요        청소해요

2)  요리해요          외식해요        축구해요        설거지해요

3)  노래해요          애기해요        외식해요        전화해요

4)  죠깅해요          숙제해요        공부해요

5)  아르바이트해요    일해요          사랑해요

6)  운동해요          산책해요        죠깅해요        화장해요        등산해요

7)  세수해요          요가해요        목욕해요        화장해요

8)  축구해요          공부해요        농구해요        배구해요

## Vocabulary Exercise 2.  뭐 해요?
Write the verb that is associated with each person.

1)  대학생은 _____.

2)  **이치로**는 _____.

3)  **오프라**는_____.

4)  학생은_____.

5)  **브리트니 스피어스** 는_____.

6)  선생님은_____.

7)  **마이클 조던**은_____.

8)  틴에이저는_____.

9)  Housewife/househusband 는_____.

**Vocabulary Exercise 3.  What are they doing?**
Complete the sentence describing each picture.

 1)  민우는_____

 2)  정아는_____

 3)  동철이는_____

4)  경수는_____

 5)  현지하고 민수는_____

6)  동현이는_____

## Lesson 6 dialogue     뭐 해요?

**After class**

정민: **수진** 씨, 오늘 뭐 해요?

수진: 산[1] 에 가요.

정민: 등산해요?

수진: 네. 등산해요. **동호** 씨는 오늘 뭐 해요?

동호: 학교 운동장에 가요. 거기에서[2] 친구하고 같이 야구해요. **정민** 씨는요?

정민: 저는 한국어 공부해요. 내일 시험이 있어요.

[1] mountain

[2] there

Notice the use of the marker -은/는 in response to the change of topic.

**동호** 씨는 오늘 뭐 해요?
How about *you*, **동호**, what are *you* doing?

**정민** 씨는요?
How about *you*, **정민**?

저는 한국어 공부하고...
(*Me?*) *I* am studying Korean, and...

130

## Lesson 6 grammar

### 1. Focus                    The verb *DO*

| 해요 | do/does, is/are doing |
|------|----------------------|

해요 means *do, does,* or *is/are doing* and is conjugated for the polite present tense. It is a very useful word to know as it is used with many nouns to form *verb compounds:*

| Noun | Meaning | Verb compound | Meaning |
|------|---------|---------------|---------|
| 숙제 | homework | 숙제해요. | to do homework |
| 전화 | telephone | 전화해요. | to phone |
| 공부 | study | 공부해요. | to study |
| 죠깅 | jogging | 죠깅해요 | to jog |

In fact, 해요 can be used very actively after borrowed nouns to make new verbs: 키스해요, 에어로빅해요, etc. It's a very useful verb!

**NOTE**: 한국말 (을) 해요 means *to speak Korean* – similarly for other languages.

> The direct object of a verb is the noun that undergoes the action denoted by the verb: *I drink coffee.*

### 2. Other Grammar Notes

#### 1. -을/를    Object marker

You have already learned three important noun markers: the subject marker, the topic marker and the location marker. Here is the last of the main markers, the *Object marker*.

The marker -을/를 marks the (*direct*) *object* of the verb. Use -을 when the object ends in a consonant and -를 when the object ends in a vowel.

In the vocabulary section, you learned a series of NOUN+해요 verb compounds. These compounds can also be broken down into noun + object marker + 해요 phrases. That is, the noun may be separated from 해요 and then be marked with -을/를 as the object of the verb 해요 (*do*). (Note that the basic order of words is subject-object-verb in Korean, unlike English which is subject-verb-object.)

|   | Subject | Subject marker | Object | Object marker | Verb | |
|---|---------|----------------|--------|---------------|------|---|
| 1 | 수지 | 가 | 숙제 | 를 | 해요. | Susie does homework. |
| 2 | 정미 | 가 | 운동 | 을 | 해요. | Chungmi does exercise. |
| 3 | 에밀리 | 가 | 농구 | 를 | 해요. | Emily plays basketball. |

**NOUN + -을/를 + 해요** treats the noun as an independent word, so there should be a space after the noun + -을/를. But NOUN + 해요 is a compound verb (single word) with no object marker and no space:

> Like the subject marker, -을/를 also often drops out, and then the words are written as a compound (with no space).

등산을 ˇ 해요 → 등산 ˇ 해요 → 등산해요    does/is hiking

사랑을 ˇ 해요 → 사랑 ˇ 해요 → 사랑해요    love/is loving

There is no apparent meaning difference between 등산해요 and 등산을 해요, although some native speakers of Korean may feel that 등산을 해요 seems to emphasize what they are doing a little more than 등산해요.

 The *object* marker -을/를 is not for literally physical "objects" like *desk* or *phone*. It is a marker to be used after a noun that is the grammatical **direct object** in a sentence.

~~책상에 전화를 있어요.~~             (There is no **direct object** in this sentence!)

책상 위에 전화가 있어요.          There is a phone on the desk.

~~영미가 운동이 해요.~~

영미가 운동을 해요.          Youngmee is doing exercise/ does exercise.

## 2. 같이     *together*

You already know that -하고 is a marker that means *with (someone)*. 같이 means *together* and is often used with the marker -하고 to redundantly emphasize the companionship.

친구하고 학교에 가요.          I go to school with a friend.

친구하고 같이 학교에 가요.       I go to school (together) with a friend.

 -하고 is required whether the adverb 같이 is used or not.

친구하고 학교에 가요.          I go to school with a friend.

친구하고 같이 학교에 가요.       I go to school with a friend.

친구 같이 학교에 가요.                    I go to school with a friend.

 And, don't forget the pronunciation and the spelling of the word 같이 [가치]!

### 3. -에서      Location particle for activities

-에서 is a particle that marks the *location of an activity that has some duration*.  That is, while 학교에 있어요 is fine, because there is no *activity*, 학교에 공부해요 is **ungrammatical** in Korean.  When the meaning of the verb involves an activity such as *do, play, write, run,* or *study,* -에서 must be used:

이번 학기에 체육관**에서** 에어로빅해요.       I do aerobics *at* the gym this quarter.

이번 학기에 체육관**에** 에어로빅해요.

## Lesson 6 exercises

### Exercise 1.    Dialogue practice
Practice the dialogue with a classmate.

### Exercise 2.    What are you doing today?
Interview two classmates about what they are doing today.  Fill in the following chart with the information you get. Then, report the results of your survey to the class.

|       | Classmate 1 | Classmate 2 |
|-------|-------------|-------------|
| 아침  |             |             |
| 오후  |             |             |
| 저녁  |             |             |
| 밤    |             |             |

**Exercise 3.   -을/ -를 해요**
Give out the word so that your partner can complete the sentence with appropriate object marker + 해요. Take turns.

*Example*: 아르바이트 (→ 아르바이트를 해요)

|  |  |
|---|---|
| 1) 노래 | 2) 얘기 |
| 3) 세수 | 4) 목욕 |
| 5) 운동 | 6) 전화 |
| 7) 화장 | 8) 외식 |
| 9) 빨래 | 10) 쇼핑 |
| 11) 청소 | 12) 설거지 |

**Exercise 4.   -은/는 and -을/를**
Find the subject and object in the following sentences and fill in the appropriate markers. Assume that you are talking *about* the subjects and mark the subjects with the topic marker 은 or 는.

1) **제이슨**＿＿＿＿ 세수＿＿＿＿ 해요

2) **메리**＿＿＿＿ 운동＿＿＿＿ 해요

3) **승미**＿＿＿＿ 얘기＿＿＿＿ 해요

4) **정희**＿＿＿＿ 숙제＿＿＿＿ 해요

5) **정호**＿＿＿＿ 청소＿＿＿＿ 해요

6) **철희**＿＿＿＿ 외식＿＿＿＿ 해요

**Exercise 5.   Happy together**
Make a sentence explaining who you do each activity with.  Then ask a classmate who they work with (on each activity).

*Example*: do laundry: 저는 룸메이트하고 같이 빨래해요.

1)  study: ＿＿＿＿＿＿＿＿＿＿＿＿＿＿＿＿＿＿＿＿＿＿＿＿＿＿＿

2) clean house: _____

3) eat out: _____

4) take a walk: _____

5) talk on the phone: _____

6) sing: _____

7) (make your own): _____


**Exercise 6.    What do you do there?**
Work with a partner.  Your partner will pick a place/building, and you need to say what you usually do there.  Pick at least five places/buildings.

*Example*        A: 레스토랑!        B: 외식을 해요.


**Exercise 7.    -에 or -에서?**
Fill in the blanks with markers of destination, stationary location, or location for activity according to the context.

1) 저는 도서관_____ 공부 안 해요. 기숙사_____ 친구하고 공부해요.

2) **로저** 씨는 학교 앞 레스토랑____ 오늘도 외식해요.

3) 제 친구 **리차드** 씨는 집_____ 있어요.

4) **스콧** 씨는 어디_____ 아르바이트를 해요?

# Lesson 6        Checkpoint

### 대화 1        오늘 시간 있어요?

몽룡:    춘향 씨, 지금 뭐 해요?

춘향:    한국어 공부해요. 내일 오전에 시험이 있어요.

몽룡:    내일 오후에 뭐 해요?

춘향:    내일 오후에 엄마하고 요리해요.

몽룡:    그럼, 춘향 씨, 수요일에 저하고 같이 쇼핑해요.

춘향:    쇼핑요? 돈이 없어요.

몽룡:    그럼, 같이 요가해요.

### 대화 2        아르바이트를 해요?

손오공:    저는 오늘 친구하고 같이 아르바이트해요.

사오정:    아르바이트를 해요?

손오공:    네, 사무실을 청소해요. 사오정 씨는요?

사오정:    저는 춘향 씨하고 한국어 공부해요.

손오공:    내일은 뭐 해요?

사오정:    내일은 저도 아르바이트해요.

### 읽기  1      누가 월요일에 뭐 해요?

저는 월요일에 운동해요. 농구를 해요. 또, 축구도 해요.

지미 씨는 월요일에 아르바이트를 해요. 선생님의 사무실에서 일해요.

춘향씨 는 월요일에 쇼핑해요.

몽룡씨 는 월요일에 조깅을 해요. 또, 요가도 해요.

사오정 씨는 월요일에 외식을 해요. 또, 노래방에 가요.

손오공 씨는 월요일에 빨래를 해요.

읽기  2      오늘 뭐 해요?

> 저는 아침에 친구하고 도서관에 가요. 친구하고 같이 한국어를 공부해요. 내일
> 시험이 있어요. 오후에 혼자 체육관에 가요. 거기에서 요가를 해요. 저녁에
> 몽룡씨하고 외식을 해요. 또, 영화관에 가요. 밤에 집에 가요. 친구하고 전화해요.
> 친구하고 얘기해요.

## Pronunciation Point  ㅌ and ㄷ before ㅣ

You won't see it very often, but if you do, remember that ㄷ and ㅌ are pronounced as ㅈ and ㅊ before the vowel ㅣ. One word you have already learned is 같이. Another rather common word you might see is 맏이, which means the *oldest child*.

# LESSON 7

# 평일에 별로 공부 안 해요.

# Lesson 7 vocabulary      *Time Adverbs*

| | | |
|---|---|---|
| 1. | 나 | I (familiar |
| 2. | 내 | my (familiar) |
| 3. | 우리 | we, our (familiar) |
| 4. | 시간 | time |
| 5. | 언제 | when |
| 6. | 오늘 | today |
| 7. | 내일 | tomorrow |
| 8. | 모레 | the day after tomorrow |
| 9. | 평일에 | on week days |
| 10. | 평소에 | usually, on regular days |
| 11. | 매일 | everyday |
| 12. | 이번 주에 | this week |
| 13. | 다음 주에 | next week |
| 14. | 주말에 | on weekend(s) |
| 15. | 이번 주말에 | this weekend |
| 16. | 다음 주말에 | next weekend |
| 17. | 이번 달에 | this month |
| 18. | 다음 달에 | next month |
| 19. | 금년에 = 올해에 | this year |
| 20. | 내년에 | next year |
| 21. | 시험 때(에) | when there is a test |
| 22. | 방학 때(에) | during vacation |

> Remember! To say "this morning" or "tonight" in Korean, you need to say "today" first:
>
> 오늘 아침    this morning
> 오늘 밤      tonight

## 23-29. Frequency adverbs

| 항상 | 자주 (잘) | 보통 | 가끔 | 별로 | 거의 | 전혀 |
|---|---|---|---|---|---|---|
| always | often/ frequently | usually, "*normally*" | occasionally/ sometimes | rarely | hardly ever "*almost*" | never "*not at all*" |

(used with 안 in negative sentences)

**Remember the days of the week?**

| | |
|---|---|
| 월요일 | Monday |
| 화요일 | Tuesday |
| 수요일 | Wednesday |
| 목요일 | Thursday |
| 금요일 | Friday |
| 토요일 | Saturday |
| 일요일 | Sunday |

 Note:  *this Wednesday* is not 의 수요일 but  이번 주 수요일 [이번 쭈 수요일].


**Vocabulary Exercise 1.  누구에요?**
Talk to your classmates to find someone who does each of the following activities at the times or frequencies specified. Write their name down next to each question.
*Example*:        누가 매일 기숙사 청소를 해요?
        →        : _____ 씨는 매일 기숙사 청소를 해요?


1) 누가 가끔 저녁에 목욕해요?

2) 누가 주말에 자주 외식해요?

3) 누가 매일 요리해요?

4) 누가 평소에 전혀 운동을 안 해요?

5) 누가 매일 밤 친구하고 전화해요?

6) 누가 수요일에 아르바이트해요?

7) 누가 주말에 항상 빨래해요?

8) 누가 쇼핑을 별로 안 해요?

9) 누가 주말에 도서관에 전혀 안 가요?

10) 누가 <u>이번 주 토요일에</u> 데이트 (date)가 있어요?

11) 누가 <u>오늘</u> 도서관에 가요?

12) 누가 <u>평소에</u> 화장을 <u>거의 안</u> 해요?

13) 누가 <u>내일</u> 체육관에 가요?

## Vocabulary Exercise 2.  Birds of a feather flock together
Fill in the blanks with the appropriate familiar counterpart to the humble pronouns given.

    1) 저    _____

    2) 우리   _____

    3) 제    _____

## Vocabulary Exercise 3.  Fill in the blanks
Fill in the blanks with a logical vocabulary item.  More than one may be possible.

1) _____ 은/는 3 월 13 일이에요. _____ 은/는 3 월 14 일이에요. _____은/는 3 월 15 일이에요.

2) 내일 _____ 있어요?

3) 아버지는 _____ 일해요.

4) 나는 _____ 숙제 해요.

5) _____ 숙제해요? -- 아니오!

6) 승희씨, _____ 집에 가요?

---

방학 때(에), 시간, 언제, 오늘, 내일, 모레, 평일에, 매일

---

## Lesson 7 dialogue  평일에 별로 공부 안 해요.

정민: **경희** 씨, 오늘 시간 있어요?

경희: 아니오, 오늘은 시간 없어요. 나는 평일 6 시에
아르바이트에 가요. **정민** 씨는요? **정민** 씨는
평일에 보통 뭐 해요?

정민: 나는 아르바이트를 안 해요. 나는 내 친구
**집**하고 배구해요. 가끔 우리는 축구도 해요.

경희: **정민** 씨는 공부는 안 해요?

정민: 나는 평소에 거의 공부 안 해요.

경희: 그럼 언제 해요?

정민: 시험 때 해요!

## Lesson 7 grammar

### 1. Focus                          *not*

| 안 | not |
|----|-----|

안 is added directly before the verb to make a statement negative:

| 베키 씨는 평일에 학교에 가요. | Becky goes to school on weekdays. |
| 베키 씨는 오늘 학교에 안 가요. | Becky doesn't go to school today. |

For Noun + 해요 verb compounds, you *always* have to split them into Noun (-을/를) + 해요 in order to insert 안 **Noun (-을/를) + 안 해요.** The object marker -을/를 may be dropped.

| 아타샤 씨는 주말에 공부해요. | Atasha studies on weekends. |
| ~~아타샤 씨는 주말에 안공부해요.~~ | ~~Atasha doesn't study on weekends.~~ |
| 아타샤 씨는 주말에 공부 안 해요. | Atasha doesn't study on weekends. |
| 아타샤 씨는 주말에 공부를 안 해요. | Atasha doesn't study on weekends. |

### 2. Other Grammar Notes

#### 1. Pronouns        나, 내, 우리; 저, 제, 저희

The pronoun system of Korean is quite complex, with changes depending on markers and honorifics. Since pronouns refer to things or persons already established in the context, they are commonly left out or used with -은/는, the topic marker, to give the sense of "as for…" or "how about…?"

Two useful pronouns are 우리, which means *we*, and 나, which is a familiar form of *I*.

| 나는 축구해요. | *I* play soccer. |
| 우리는 배구해요. | *We* play volleyball. |

Second person pronouns (*you*) are hardly ever used in Korean. To talk about *you*, use NAME + 씨:

| 정민 씨하고 철희 씨는 뭐 해요? | What are you doing, 정민 and 철희? |

Do you recall the humble first person pronoun forms 저 (*I*) and 제 (*my*)? Do you also recall the possessive marker 의? 제 is from 저+의.

저는                     vs.                   제 공책 = 저의 공책;  제 가방 = 저의 가방

The familiar forms of the first person work in a parallel way. (But *note the spelling* of the possessive, based on 나 +의 → 나 ㅣ → 내 *versus* 저 + ㅣ →제).

나는                     vs.                   내 친구 = 나의 친구;  내 펜 = 나의 펜

The first person plural possessive (*our*) is usually expressed without the possessive marker:

우리 집              or                   저희 어머니

 Try not to use 나 and 우리 until you have established that you and the person you are talking to are equals (e.g. friends or colleagues), as in the dialogue above. If you are not sure which form to use, stick to 저 and 저희!

NOTE:  Recall from Chapter 1 (Lesson 1) grammar that Koreans use the *plural* first person possessive to refer to family members and household belongings. It sounds very odd to use the singular, so that even 'singles' may use the plural possessive to refer to their own houses, etc.

~~내 어머니~~     →     우리 어머니          my/our mother
~~제 집~~              →     저희 집 [저이집]      my/our house

## 2. Use of markers
You might have already noticed that you cannot "memorize" a particular marker to always show up in a certain context. The topic marker (-은/는) may show up where you would expect the subject marker (-이/가), and the addition marker (-도) may appear where you would expect the subject marker *or* the object marker (-을/를).

우리는 축구를 해요.                   (We) play soccer.

우리는 축구도 해요.                   We play *soccer* also.

우리도 축구를 해요.                   *We,* too, play soccer.

우리가 축구를 해요.                   We (not anyone else) play soccer.

Sometimes, if need be, one marker can show up more than once in the sentence. What nuance do you get out of the following sentence?

144

정민 씨는 공부는 안 해요?                        You, 정민, don't you ever *study*?

The first -는 after 정민 씨 is used because we are addressing the person **you,** 정민. The second -는 plays a role to switch the topic: *What about* **studying**? *Don't you*

Which marker to use in a sentence largely depends on what *you* want to say.  Be flexible!

## 3.  Frequency adverbs

Frequency adverbs such as 가끔 and 자주 normally come directly before the verb phrase (i.e., object), but might be placed elsewhere in the sentence, with *very* slight emphasis differences.

| | |
|---|---|
| 우리는 가끔 축구를 해요. | We occasionally play soccer. |
| 우리는 축구를 가끔 해요. | We occasionally play *soccer*. |
| 가끔 우리는 축구를 해요. | We *occasionally* play soccer. |
| 우리는 공부를 별로 안 해요. | We don't really study much. |
| 우리는 별로 공부를 안 해요. | We don't really *study* much. |

## 4.  Position of time adverbs

While place and time adverbs tend to come after the verb in English, they come *before* the verb in Korean.  The typical order of the adverbs is **time-place** in Korean. The subject (or the topic you are talking about) can come either before or after these adverbs:

| | |
|---|---|
| 주말에 저는 아르바이트에 가요 | I go to work on weekends. |
| 쟈니 씨는 평소에 청소를 해요. | Johnny cleans (his house) on regular days. |

## 5.  -에          *at (time)*

You learned two different uses of the marker -에.  One was for stationary location, and the other was for destination, both after a *location* noun:

| | |
|---|---|
| 덕이는 집에 있어요. | Doug is *at* home. |
| 캐씨가 산에 가요. | Kathy goes *to* the mountains. |

-에 can also come after a *time* noun to mean *in, on,* or *at.*

| | |
|---|---|
| 몇 시에 집에 가요? | (At) what time are you going home? |
| 세 시에 집에 가요. | I am going home at 3 o'clock. |

이번 주에 같이 산에 가요.        We are going to the mountains together this week.

다음 주말에 산에 가요.        We are going to the mountains next weekend.

⚠ -에 marks a time noun, such as *Monday,* or __ *o'clock.*  Do not use 에 with *adverbs* of time, such as 오늘에 *(on today)* or 매일에 *(on everyday)*

## Lesson 7 exercises

**Exercise 1.    Dialogue practice**
Practice the dialogue with a classmate.

**Exercise 2.    내? 제? 우리? 저희?**
Which *first person* pronoun should you use for each case?  Work with a partner.

1) _____ 엄마 (talking to a close friend of the same age)

2) _____ 연필 (talking to the teacher)

3) _____ 집 (talking to your friend's grandfather)

4) _____ 아버지 (talking to an elderly neighbor)

5) _____ 한국어 책 (talking to a younger sibling)

**Exercise 3.    No, she doesn't. -- Yes, she does!**
Someone is making erroneous statements about what people do.  Tell him/her that the following people *don't* do what he/she says they do or that they *do* do what he/she says they don't.

*Example*: 영준씨는 경희씨 집에 가요. → 아니에요.  영준씨는 경희씨 집에 **안** 가요.

1) **경준** 씨는 공부를 해요.

2) **창길** 씨는 축구해요.

3) **제인** 씨는 세수를 안 해요.

4) **파커** 씨는 쇼핑해요.

5) **상희** 씨는 청소를 안 해요.

6) **덕균** 씨는 도서관에 있어요.

7) **샤넌** 씨는 친구하고 전화해요.

146

## Exercise 4.    Frequency adverb practice
Change the following sentences according to the words in parentheses.

1)  동호 씨는 항상 공부를 해요. (never)

2)  한나 씨는 가끔 축구해요. (often)

3)  소영 씨는 거의 세수를 안 해요. (often does)

4)  은비 씨는 평소에 쇼핑해요. (doesn't)

5)  지나 씨는 청소를 전혀 안 해요. (on any regular day)

6)  시은 씨는 보통 도서관에 있어요. (occasionally)

## Exercise 5.    Time marker –에/ reading time in Korean
Choose chart A or B from below, and have your partner use the other chart.  Then cover up
the chart that you did not choose. Ask questions to find out what your partner does today
(according to the covered chart) and write it down in the table. Also answer your partner's
questions so that your partner can figure out what you do today (according to your chart).

*Example*: _____ 씨는 _____ 시 _____ 분에 뭐 해요?

**A**

| 나 | | 파트너 | |
|---|---|---|---|
| 8:30 | Korean class | 8:30 | |
| 12:30 | Part-time job | 12:30 | |
| 2:00 | Korean homework | 2:00 | |
| 5:00 | | 5:00 | |
| 8:00 | | 8:00 | |
| 10:00 | | 10:00 | |

## B

| 파트너 | | 나 | |
|---|---|---|---|
| 8:30 | | 8:30 | |
| 2:30 | | 12:30 | |
| 2:00 | | 2:00 | |
| 5:00 | | 5:00 | |
| 8:00 | | 8:00 | |
| 10:00 | | 10:00 | |

## Exercise 6.    나 or 저?

Read the following conversations and fill in the blanks with appropriate first person pronouns and possessives.

### Conversation 1

선생님: 그거 _____ 펜이에요?
Is that **my** pen?

학생 1: 아니오, 선생님. 이건 _____ 펜이에요.
No, teacher. This is **my** pen.

학생 2: _____ 펜 여기 있어요. _____ 펜은 _____ 짝 책상 위에 있어요.
Your  pen is here. **My** pen is on **my** partner's desk.

*Conversation 2*

학생:　　선생님, 저기가 _____ 집이에요. _____ 엄마가 문 앞에 있어요.
Teacher, there is **my** house.  **My** mother is in front of the door.

선생님: 네.

학생:　　_____ 남동생도 _____ 엄마 옆에 있어요.
**The** baby (sister/brother) is there, too.

*Conversation 3*

학생 1:　_____ 책이 어디 있어요?
Where is **my** textbook?

학생 2:　_____ 씨 가방 안에 없어요?
Isn't it in **your** bag?

학생 1: 아니오, 거기 없어요.
No, it's not there.

학생 2: 아, _____ 책상 위에 있어요.
A-ha. It's on **my** desk.

> For *you* and *your*, use the person's name and 씨 – we are assuming that you are speaking with a colleague.

**Exercise 7.    오늘, 내일, 모레**
Complete the following conversation three times in three different ways, using different time references and verbs (오늘, 내일, 모레, 이번 주에…; 빨래, 쇼핑, 청소, 외식…).

A: _____씨, _____ 시간 있어요?

B: 아니오. 시간이 없어요.

A: 왜요? 뭐 해요?

B: _____.

A: 그럼 _____ 시간 있어요?

B: 아니오. 시간이 없어요.

A: 또요? _____ 뭐 해요?

B: _____.

A: 그러면, _____ 시간 있어요?

B: 네, _____ 시간 있어요. 왜요?

A: 나/저하고 같이 _____ 해요! (*or* _____ 에 가요!)

B: 싫어요. (No, I don't want to.)

### Exercise 8. Interviews
Ask five classmates what things they do on weekdays or weekends and how often they do them. Make up sentences to report your findings.

## Lesson 7 Checkpoint

**대화 1        오늘 시간 있어요?**

---

춘향: **몽룡** 씨, **몽룡** 씨는 언제 운동해요?

몽룡: 저는 보통 주말에 운동해요. **춘향** 씨는요?

춘향: 저는 거의 운동을 안 해요.

몽룡: **춘향** 씨 평소에 거의 운동을 안 해요?

춘향: 네, 평소에 시간이 없어요.

몽룡: 이번 주말에 우리 같이 운동해요.

춘향: 어느 운동이요?

몽룡: 우리 같이 조깅해요.

---

**대화 2        우리 같이 한국어 공부해요.**

---

춘향: **몽룡** 씨, **몽룡** 씨는 언제 한국어 공부해요?

몽룡: 저는 보통 매일 한국어를 공부해요. **춘향** 씨는요?

춘향: 저는 거의 한국어 공부를 안 해요.

몽룡: **춘향** 씨 평소에 거의 공부를 안 해요?

춘향: 네, 평소에 시간이 없어요.

몽룡: 이번 주말에 시간 없어요?

춘향: 아니오, 이번 주말에 시간이 있어요.

몽룡: 그럼, 우리 같이 한국어 공부해요.

---

## Cultural Talk   *Hey you!*

We introduce the name suffix 씨 because you will likely use it most often. In American university classrooms and in dealings with Korean business associates, where you interact as acquaintances, colleagues, or associates, *first name* + 씨 is appropriate.

If you meet someone significantly older than you, for example, an older clerk at a Korean grocery store, you should **NOT** use *Name* + 씨. Instead, use 아주머니 (*aunt*) for an older woman, and 아저씨 (*uncle*) for an older man.

In Korea, one enters and graduates schools, including college, with the same classmates, forming a tight-knit group. Therefore, Korean students do not use 씨 amongst themselves.

You might hear them address each other using the familiar vocative marker -아/야 and refer to each other using the familiar marker -이, after the name.

# LESSON 8

# 동호의 하루

**UNIVERSITY**

# Lesson 8 vocabulary          *Connectors & Time Words*

1. 그리고                          **and**
2. 그렇지만 [그러치만]              **but**
3. 그래서                          **so**

> Another very frequently used word that means *but* is 하지만. Learn this word too, and it will come in handy!

4. 얼마나                          **how**
5. 얼마나 자주                     **how often**
6. 몇                             **how many**
7. 몇 번 [뻔]                      **how many times**

8. 무슨 NOUN                      **what (NOUN)**
9. 수업                           **class (course)**

10. 요일                          **day(s) of the week**
11. 무슨 요일                      **what day(s) of the week**

12. 매주                          **every week, each week**
13. 매일                          **every day, each day; always, all the time**
14. 하루에                        **per day**
15. 일 주일에 [일쭈이레]           **per week**

16. 전공 [전공, 정공]             **major**
17. 학년 [항년]                   **year (in school)**
18. 학기                          **quarter/semester**
19. 대학생                        **college student**
20. 대학원생                      **graduate student**

21. -쯤                           **about, approximately**
22. 여러분                        **you all (respect)**

23. 들어요                        **take (a class); hear, listen**

> 얼마나 is a *degree* adverb, and 몇 is a *numeral* adverb. You can ask "to what degree" only with the question word 얼마나 (e.g. *how pretty* and *how fast*). To ask "how many" of something, you have to use the question word 몇 (e.g, 몇 학년이에요? 몇 살이에요? 몇 번... etc.?).

> Remember the word 무엇? It is a written form of the word 뭐 (*what*), right? To modify a noun, an adjective form of this word 무슨 has to be used in Korean: 무슨 학교, 무슨 요일, 무슨 전공, 무슨 운동, etc., etc. English doesn't have an adjective form of *what* (what day, what major, etc.), so be sure to to use 무슨 when you need to!

> The nasal sound ㄴ ([n]) becomes ㅇ ([ng]) before the consonants ㄱ, ㅋ, and ㄲ. Practice saying the following words.
> 한국어 [항구거]    전공 [정공]
> 안 가요 [앙가요]    안경 [앙경]
> 연구실 [영구실]    인간 [잉간]

## Supplementary Vocabulary     *Majors*

| 전공/수업 | Major/class | |
|---|---|---|
| 미술 | Art/Painting | |
| 생물학 | Biology | |
| 경영학 | Business and Administration | |
| 경제학 | Economics | |
| 화학 | Chemistry | |
| 컴퓨터 공학 | Computer Science | |
| 기계 공학 | Mechanical Engineering | |
| 전자 공학 | Electrical Engineering | |
| 역사학 | History | |
| 한국학 | Korea Studies | |
| 언어학 | Linguistics | |
| 문학 | Literature | |
| 수학 | Math | |
| 음악 | Music | |
| 물리학 | Physics | |
| 정치학 | Political Science | |
| 심리학 [심니악] | Psychology | |
| 사회학 | Sociology | |
| 여성학 | Women Studies | |
| 신문방송학 | Media and Communications | |

**Vocabulary Exercise 1.   About you.**
Ask the following questions of your partner.

1)  전공이 뭐에요?

_____

2)  몇 학년이에요?

_____

3)  대학생이에요?

_____

4)  대학원생 친구가 있어요?

_____

5)  이번 학기에 무슨 수업을 들어요?

_____

6)  그 수업은 무슨 요일에 있어요?

_____

7)  한국어 공부를 하루에 몇 시간 해요?

_____

8)  매일 학교에 가요?

_____

9)  하루에 몇 번 샤워해요?

_____

10) 일주일에 몇 시간쯤 운동을 해요?

_____

## Language Point    학

학 means *to learn* or *study* as you have seen in words like 학생, 학교 and 학원. Based on the parts you know, can you guess the meaning of the following words?

학년 (년 means *year*)                    학기 (기 means *term* or *period*)
대학생 (대 means *big*)                    방학 (방 means *release*)
학번 (번 means *number*)                   전학 (전 means *transfer*)
독학 (독 means *self*)                      유학 (유 means *to cross*)
휴학 (휴 means *rest*)

When 학 is used as a suffix (i.e., comes *after* the noun), it means something similar to English '-ology', *the study of* some field. Can you guess what these words mean?

문학 (문 means *written text*)
미학 (미 means *beauty*)

## Lesson 8 monologue   동호의 하루   *(Dongho's day)*

제 이름은 **김동호**예요. 저는 대학생이에요. 그리고 저는 2학년이에요. 제 전공은 화학이에요. 그렇지만 저는 이번 학기에 한국어를 들어요. 그래서 매일 한국어를 공부해요. 하루에 3시간쯤 공부해요.

평일에 저는 도서관에서 아르바이트를 해요. 주말에는 학교에 안 가요. 친구하고 항상 체육관에서 배구를 해요. 주말에는 또, 기숙사 청소도 해요. 저는 돈이 별로 없어요. 그래서 외식은 자주 안 해요. 일 주일에 한 번쯤 해요. 여러분은 얼마나 자주 외식해요? 무슨 음식을 좋아해요? 이번 학기에 무슨 수업을 들어요?

**Comprehension Exercise 1.  True or False**
Based on the passage above, mark whether the following questions are true (T) or false (F).

1) **동호**는 대학교 삼학년이에요. 그리고 **동호**의 전공은 수학이에요. (   )

2) **동호**는 이번 학기에 한국어를 들어요. 그래서 매일 공부해요. (   )

3) **동호**는 하루에 1시간쯤 한국어 공부를 해요. (   )

4) 평일에 **동호**는 아르바이트를 해요. 주말에는 친구하고 체육관에서 운동해요. (   )

5) **동호**는 돈이 별로 없어요. 그렇지만 매주 외식해요. (   )

## Lesson 8 grammar

### 1. Focus            Stacking of markers

| | |
|---|---|
| -에도 | Also at this place / Also at that time |
| -에는 | At that place / at that time - contrast |
| -에서도 | Also at that place (some activity takes place) |
| -에서는 | At that place (some activity takes place) – contrast |

You might have noticed that sometimes more than one marker comes after a noun.  Typically, the addition marker -도 and -은/는 as a contrast marker may come after time and location words:

> **알렉세이**는 평일에 일해요.  그리고 주말**에도** 일해요.
> Alexei works on weekdays, and he also works on weekends.

> 집**에서는** 설거지를 안 해요.  그렇지만 기숙사**에서는** 해요.
> At home, I don't do dishes, but in the dorm, I do.

> 이번 주말에는 레스토랑에 가요. 그리고 백화점**에도** 가요.
> This weekend I am going to a restaurant.  I am also going to a department store.

The subject marker -이/가 and the object marker -을/를 may **NOT** be used with other markers.  Other markers **REPLACE** them:

제이콥은 ~~수학을도 잘 해요.~~
제이콥은 수학도 잘 해요.        Jakob is also good at math (Jakob does math well, too).

### 2. Other Grammar Notes

#### 1. 그리고, 그렇지만, 그래서, 그럼        *and, but, so, well then*

When you learned the noun connector -하고, you were promised *sentence connectors.*
그리고 *and*, 그래서 *so*, and 그렇지만 *but* are such connectors, and they usually follow a period "." or a comma ",".

> 기숙사에서 설거지는 제가 해요.  그리고 청소는 제 친구가 해요.
> I do the dishes and my friend cleans in the dormitory.

저는 외식을 자주 해요. 그래서 항상 돈이 없어요!
I frequently eat out, so I never have money!

저는 이번 학기에 한국어를 공부해요. 그렇지만 제 전공은 수학이에요.
I study Korean this quarter, but my major is Math.

## 2. -에　　　　　per

You have learned that -에 marks a the time word, such as *Monday,* or __ *o'clock.* -에 can also be used to mean *per,* as in *per day* or *per week.*

하루에 네 번 세수해요.　　　　　　　I wash my face four times a day.

일 주일에 두 번 방 청소해요.　　　　I clean my room twice a week.

## 3. 몇...　　　　　*how many*

Korean has a single word, 몇, that means *how many.* It cannot be used on its own (like the question fragment "how many?" in English), but must directly precede the counter in Korean – the word that is needed to count particular items, such as 번 *times* or, you may have heard, 개 *things (that can be held in the hand).*

일주일에 <u>몇 번</u> 운동을 해요?　　<u>How many times</u> per week do you exercise?

연필이 <u>몇 개</u> 있어요?　　　　　<u>How many</u> pencils do you have?

## 4. *how often*　　　　얼마나 자주..., 몇 번...

There are two ways to ask about how frequently someone does something. One way is to use 얼마나, an adverb which means *how much* with the word 자주 – altogether *how often.* Another way is to directly ask *how many times* in a given time period by using the words 몇 (*how many*) and 번 (*times*) and a time period phrase. (하루에 *per day* or 일주일에 *per week*).

A: 얼마나 자주 세수해요?　　　How often do you wash your face?
B: 하루에 두 번 해요.　　　　　I do (wash my face) twice a day.

A: 일 주일에 몇 번 엄마하고 전화해요?
How many times per week do you phone your mother? (OR talk to your mother on the phone?)

B: 일 주일에 두 번쯤 해요.　　　I call about twice a week.

Of course, you know how to continue the conversation using 무슨 요일에...
A: 일 주일에 몇 번 엄마하고 전화해요?
B: 일 주일에 두 번쯤 해요.　　　I call about twice a week.

159

A: 무슨 요일에 해요?          On what days (do you phone her)?
B: 수요일하고 토요일에 해요.  I call about on Wednesday and Saturday.

## Lesson 8 exercises

### Exercise 1.    Dialogue practice
Practice the dialogue with a classmate.

### Exercise 2.    Word meaning
What do you think 대 might mean, based on the following words?

| 대학생 college student; 대학교   college, university; 대문 (main) gate |
| --- |

### Exercise 3.    Interview Bingo!
*Ask your classmates!* If they say what's in the box, you get that box! You should walk around asking one question of each person until you have five boxes in a row, a column, or a diagonal line.  Don't forget to write your classmates' names in the boxes!

*Example*:        질문: _____ 씨는 *얼마나 자주* 기숙사 청소를 해요?
             대답: 저는 매일 기숙사 청소를 해요.

| 매일 | 자주, 종종 | 가끔 | 별로_안 | 전혀_안 |
| --- | --- | --- | --- | --- |
| 친구하고 전화해요 | 아르바이트해요 | 목욕해요 | 청소해요 | 한국어 공부해요 |
| 세수해요 | 엄마하고 얘기해요 | 쇼핑해요 | 등산해요 | 야구해요 |
| 외식해요 | 에어로빅해요 | 농구해요 | 노래해요 | 샤워해요 |
| 한국어 숙제해요 | 방 청소해요 | 설거지해요 | 화장해요 | 빨래해요 |

**Exercise 4.**    **-에 or not?**

Fill in the blanks with the time marker -에 only if it is needed.

1) **조셉** 씨는 매일____ 어디에 가요?

2) **조수아** 씨는 주말____ 엄마 집에 가요.

3) **제시카** 씨는 매주____ 한 번 외식을 해요.

4) 다음 주____ 친구하고 배구를 해요.

5) **시드니** 씨는 평일____ 공부 안 해요.

6) 일주일____ 몇 번 아빠하고 전화해요?

7) 얼마나 자주____ 청소해요?

**Exercise 5.**    **Connector practice**    그래서? 그리고? 그렇지만?

Conjoin the following sentences with appropriate connectors!

> 제 이름은 **이은비**에요. _____ 저는 대학교 3 학년이에요. 제 전공은
>
> 수학이에요. _____ 저는 이번 학기에 중국어를 공부해요. _____ 매일 중국어를
>
> 공부해요. 저는 가난한* 학생이에요. _____ 돈이 별로 없어요.     *가난한:
>
> poor

**Exercise 6.**    **How often do you…?**

Ask your partner how often he/she does the following in the specified place. Be sure to use the location particle for activities!

*Example*: 도서관-공부

     A: **은비** 씨, 일주일에 몇 번 도서관에서 공부해요?

     B: 저는 -- 월요일, 수요일, 금요일 -- 일주일에 <u>세 번</u> 도서관에서 공부해요.

                       or

     A: **은비** 씨, 얼마나 자주 도서관에서 공부해요?

1) 체육관 – 운동

2) 백화점 – 쇼핑

3) 식당 – 외식

4)  기숙사 - 청소

5)  교실- 친구하고 전화

6)  운동장 – 축구

7)  노래방 – 노래

8)  엄마집 - 빨래

## Exercise 7.    What classes are you taking?
Find out what courses your classmates are taking this quarter.  Interview at least four classmates.

## Lesson 8      Checkpoint

**대화  1** 　　　　우리는 언제 데이트해요?

몽룡: **춘향** 씨 이번 학기에 무슨 수업을 들어요?

춘향: 이번 학기에 언어학 수업하고 심리학을 들어요. 그리고 아르
　　　바이트도 해요. 그래서 평일에 시간이 없어요.

몽룡: 학교는 일 주일에 몇 번 가요?

춘향: 학교는 월요일, 화요일, 그리고 수요일 세 번 가요. 그렇지만
　　　목요일하고 금요일에는 한국식당에서 아르바이트를 해요.

몽룡: 그럼, 우리는 언제 데이트해요?

춘향: 그렇지만 주말에는 시간이 있어요, **몽룡** 씨.

## 대화  2        한국에 얼마나 자주 전화해요?

수미:  **정미** 씨, **정미** 씨는 하루에 몇 번 샤워해요?

정미:  저는 아침하고 밤, 하루에 두 번 샤워해요.

수미:  **정미** 씨는 한국에 얼마나 자주 전화해요?

정미:  저는 한국에 일주일에 한 번 전화해요.

수미:  **정미** 씨는 한 달[17]에 몇 번 쇼핑을 가요?

정미:  한 달에 두 번쯤 쇼핑을 가요.

수미:  **정미** 씨는 일 주일에 몇 번 외식을 해요?

정미:  저는 거의 외식을 안 해요.

## 읽기  1        백수

나는 직업이 없어요. 그래서 나는 백수에요. 백수는 보통 시간이 많이[18] 있어요. 그렇지만 나는 시간이 없어요. 매일 매일 아르바이트를 해요. 아르바이트는 세 개를 해요. 나는 평일에 두 번 우체국에서 일해요. 그리고 평일에 세 번 도서관에서 일해요. 주말에는 한국식당에서 일해요. 그렇지만 나는 돈이 별로 없어요. 쇼핑하고 외식도 거의 안 해요.

## 읽기  2        타미의 운동

**타미**는 자주 체육관에 가요. 일주일에 두 번 정도 가요. **타미**는 체육관에서 보통 친구들하고 같이 농구를 해요 . 그리고 가끔 배구도 해요. 그렇지만 축구는 전혀 안 해요. 그래서 축구장[19]에는 전혀 안 가요. **타미**는 집에서 매일 농구 연습[20]을 해요. 또, **타미**는 한 달에 한 번 산에 가요. 항상 어머니하고 같이 가요. **타미**의 어머니는 주말에 항상 등산을 해요.

---

[17] month
[18] a lot
[19] football field
[20] practice

163

## Culture Point          *I don't do much*

Regardless of culture and society, there are always people who don't enjoy work. In Korea, education precedes all else in life.  Junior high and middle school students are expected to study from dawn till late at night to prepare for college entrance exam.  Those who do not show interest in studying or who take interest in what is outside the school curricula are called 날라리, someone who is flaky and not serious about their studies. Then there are people who are jobless after college graduation.  They are called 백수, literally *white hands*, as they have no work to dirty their hands with.

## Pronunciation Points

### Silent ㅎ

ㅎ sounds often become silent in casual speech. Practice saying these words.

김동호          친구하고    문학          연필하고    안 해요

The ㅎ sound in the beginning of words, however, must be pronounced.

학생          화학          하나          하고          혼자

# 쉬어갑시다!

# LET'S TAKE A BREAK!

> How many brothers and sisters do you have?

# CHAPTER 2.5  우리 가족

**My family**

## Vocabulary

1. 가족  family

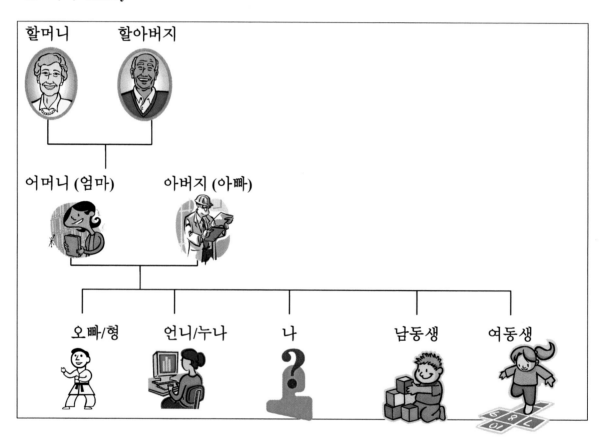

| | |
|---|---|
| 2. 어머니 (엄마) | mother (mom) |
| 3. 아버지 (아빠) | father (dad) |
| 4. 부모님 | parents |
| 5. 딸 | daughter |
| 6. 아들 | son |
| 7. 아이들/애들 | children |
| 8. 아기 [애기] | baby |
| 9. (외/친)할머니 | (maternal/paternal) grandmother |
| 10. (외/친)할아버지 | (maternal/paternal) grandfather |

11. (큰/작은) 오빠      female's older brother
12. (큰/작은) 형      male's older brother
13. (큰/작은) 언니      female's older sister
14. (큰/작은) 누나      male's older sister
15. (남/여-) 동생      (male/female) younger sibling

> Ask your teacher about how 큰 오빠 is different from 작은 오빠!

16. 강아지/개      puppy/dog
17. 고양이      cat

18. 명      (counter for people)
19. 마리      (counter for animals)

20. 그렇게      like so
21. 모두      all together (adv.)

# Supplemental vocabulary: More family terms

22. 형제      siblings; male sibling
23. 남매      male-female siblings
24. 자매      female sibling(s)

> Ask your teacher how to say *the second son* or *the third daughter*!

25. 맏이 [마지] (= 큰 아들/딸)      oldest child
26. 막내 [망내]      youngest child
27. 쌍둥이      twins
28. 외동딸      only daughter
29. 외아들/독자      only son

30. 손녀      granddaughter
31. 손자      grandson; grandchildren
32. 이모(부)      aunt on mother's side (aunt's husband)
33. 삼촌      uncle
34. 고모(부)      aunt on father's side (aunt's husband)
35. 사촌      cousin
36. 조카      niece, nephew

## Grammar Notes

**How many people are there in your family?**
A: 가족이 모두 몇 명이에요? (몇 명 → [면 명]: how many people)
B: 엄마, 아빠, 나, (그렇게) 셋이에요.  (= we are three)

> *It's 3 o'clock* and *We are three* (or *they are three*) are pronounced the same, right?

**How many siblings do you have?**
A: 형제가 몇 명이에요?)                    (How many (siblings) are you?)
B: 넷이에요. or 네 명이에요.  or 네 명<u>이 있어요</u>    (*including yourself!*)
*or* B: 오빠 두 명하고 언니 한 명<u>이 있어요</u>.        (There are…)

## Exercises

**Exercise 1.    Which picture is it?**
Match the picture to the sentence that describes it, and circle the narrator.

1) 우리 가족은 아빠하고 나하고, 그리고 엄마, 모두 세 명이에요.

2) 우리 가족은 모두 네 명이에요.  엄마하고 아빠하고 나. 저는 여동생이 하나 있어요.

3) 우리 가족은 모두 둘이에요.  그냥 아빠하고 저예요.

4) 저는 언니가 한 명있어요.  오빠는 없어요.  동생도 없어요.

a.     b.     c.     d.

**Exercise 2.    How many are there in your family?    가족이 모두 몇이에요?**
**식구가 몇이에요?**
Find out about your friends' families by asking if they have various relatives.

Two things to remember:
 a)  be sure to use the right words for older siblings based on the gender of the person you are asking,
 b)  for grandparents and parents, use the honorific 계세요 in place of  있어요.

**Exercise 3.  What's your sister's name? 동생 이름이 뭐에요?**
Continue finding out about your friends' family members by asking their names and their activities. (언니 있어요? 형이 공부해요?, etc.)

**Exercise 4.  Who's who?**
Study the family tree and fill in the blanks in the sentences below according to the family tree.

*Example:*    김 민수는 최 미진의 <u>할아버지</u>에요.

## 나의 가족

김 민수 ——————— 박 영미
(남자)                          (여자)
          김 지영 ——————— 최 민수
          (여자)                      (남자)

최 수진    최 영진    최 미진    최 은진    최 하진
(여자)     (남자)    (나-여자)   (여자)     (남자)

1) 박 영미는 최 미진의 _____에요.

2) 김 지영은 최 미진의 _____에요.

3) 최 민수는 최 미진의 _____에요.

4) 최 수진은 최 미진의 _____에요.

5) 최 영진은 최 미진의 _____에요.

6) 최 은진은 최 미진의 _____에요.

7) 최 하진은 최 미진의 _____에요.

8) 최 영진은 최 하진의_____에요.

9) 최 수진은 최 하진의_____에요.

10) 김 기영하고 최 민수는 최 수진의 _____에요.

**Exercise 5.     What's your sister's name? 동생 이름이 뭐에요?**
Write at least 12 sentences about your family.  Write about your family members' activities.
(e.g. 형은 대학생이에요.  매일 도서관에서 공부해요).

_____

_____

_____

_____

_____

_____

_____

_____

**Exercise 6.     My Family**
Bring a picture of your family to class and describe each family member to your classmates.
Ask your teacher in advance how to say the occupation of your family members in Korean!

*Example*: 이 사람은 우리 아빠예요.  우리 아빠는 선생님이에요.

## *Culture Point*          Once a child, always a child!

Children are still children until they marry and move out of the house.  Most men and women live with their parents (without paying rent!) even after they graduate from college.  Only when they get married do they leave the house.  Even after marriage, the oldest son in the family (맏아들) is expected to live with the parents in the same house, supporting them economically.

# CHAPTER 3  일요일은 괜찮아요.

**Sunday is O.K.**

## Preliminary Dialogue

| | |
|---|---|
| 미라: **알렌** 씨는 집에서 뭐 해요? | |
| 알렌: 평일에는 공부하고 숙제해요. **미라** 씨는요? | |
| 미라: 나는 친구하고 전화해요. 또, 텔레비전도 봐요[1] . | [1] watch |
| 알렌: 공부는 안 해요? | |
| 미라: 하하하! 나는 날라리[2] 에요! | [2] slacker |

**Dialogue practice**

Practice the preliminary dialogue with a classmate.

# LESSON 9
# 파티에 못 가요.

## Lesson 9 vocabulary  Daily Activity Verbs A

**Consonant-ending verbs (in the order of final consonants)**

| Polite<br>Present tense | Citation Form | Meaning |
|---|---|---|
| 1. 먹어요 | (핏자를) 먹다 | **eat** (pizza) |
| 2. 닦아요 | (이빨을/차를) 닦다 | **wipe, clean** (teeth/a car) |
| 3. 안아요 | (아기를) 안다 | **hold** (a baby) |
| 4. 앉아요 | (의자에) 앉다 | **sit** (on a chair) |
| 5. 닫아요 | (창문을) 닫다 | **close** (the window) |
| 6. 받아요 | (A 를) 받다 | **receive, get** (an A) |
| 7. 살아요 | 살다 | **live** |
| 8. 알아요 | 알다 | **know** |
| 9. 열어요 | (문을) 열다 | **open** (the door) |
| 10. 놀아요 | (친구하고) 놀다 | **play** (with a friend) |
| 11. 만들어요 | (샌드위치를) 만들다 | **make** (a sandwich) |
| 12. 울어요 | 울다 | **cry** |
| 13. 읽어요 | (신문을) 읽다 | **read** (newspapers) |
| 14. 남아요 | 남다 | **remain; be left over** |
| 15. 입어요 | (잠옷을) 입다 | **wear, put on** (pajamas) |
| 16. 웃어요 | 웃다 | **laugh, smile** |
| 17. 씻어요 | (손을) 씻다 | **wash** (hands) |
| 18. 잡아요 | (손을) 잡다;<br>(택시를) 잡다 | **hold, grab** (hands);<br>**catch** (a bus) |
| 19. 찾아요 | (친구를) 찾다;<br>(은행에서 돈을) 찾다 | **look for** (a friend);<br>**withdraw** (money from the bank) |
| 20. 넣어요 | (가방에 책을) 넣다 | **put** (a book **in** the bag) |
| 21. 놓아요 = 놔요 | (펜을 테이블에) 놓다;<br>(손을) 놓다 | **put** (a pen **on** the table); **let go** (of a hand) |

몰라요 means *(I) don't know.*

173

## Vocabulary Exercise 1.  What is the object?

Match each verb at the bottom with the picture of an object that might undergo the action expressed in the verb (be its object).

1)    2)    3)    4)

5)    6)    7)    8)

찾아요  입어요  먹어요  만들어요  열어요  읽어요  씻어요  알아요

## Vocabulary Exercise 2.  Odd one out – picture style

Choose the verb *cannot* take the item in the picture as its *object* (direct or indirect).

1)  닦아요, 먹어요, 앉아요, 씻어요

2) 알아요, 닫아요, 읽어요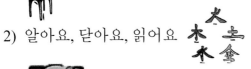

3)  열어요, 닫아요, 찾아요, 입어요, 받아요

4) 입어요, 살아요, 놀아요, 넣어요, 알아요, 앉아요, 놓아요, 찾아요

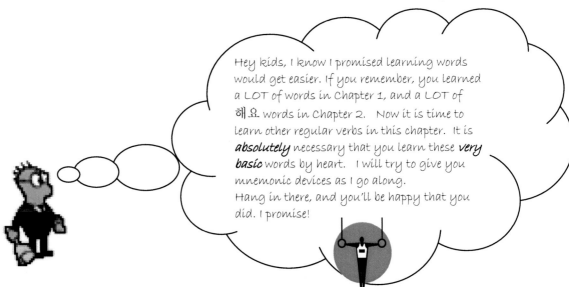

Hey kids, I know I promised learning words would get easier. If you remember, you learned a LOT of words in Chapter 1, and a LOT of 해요 words in Chapter 2.   Now it is time to learn other regular verbs in this chapter.  It is *absolutely* necessary that you learn these *very basic* words by heart.   I will try to give you mnemonic devices as I go along.

Hang in there, and you'll be happy that you did. I promise!

## Lesson 9 dialogue 🐧🐧       미안해요. 파티에 못 가요.

딩동~

제인: 누구세요[1]?

찰스: 안녕하세요, **제인** 씨! 이번 주 토요일에 **수미** 씨
     파티에 가요?

제인: 아, **찰스** 씨! 아니오, 못[2] 가요.

찰스: 왜[3]요?

제인: 토요일에는 항상 집에서 뭐[4] 해요.

찰스: 뭐 해요?

제인: 오후에는 공부하고 집 청소해요.

찰스: 청소하고 나서[5] 못 가요?

제인: 청소하고 나서는 아빠하고 차를[6] 닦아요.

찰스: 아빠하고 차를 닦고 나서 못 가요?

제인: 아빠하고 차를 닦고 나서는 엄마하고 김치를 만들어요.

찰스: 아, 그래요? 배추[7] 김치 만들어요?

제인: 아니오, 이번 주에는 오이로[8] 만들어요.

찰스: 아, 네. 흠...
     에이[9]... 그럼[10] 정말 못 가요?

제인: 네, 못 가요. 미안해요. 근데,[11] 그 꽃[12] 누구 거에요?

찰스: **제인** 씨 거에요...

[1] Who is it? (answering the door)

[2] can't

[3] why

4. something

[5] after doing housecleaning
6. car

7. cabbage

8. with cucumber

9. shucks!
10. if so; then

11. by the way
12. flowers

그런데 and 그러면 are often shortened to 근데, and 그럼 in conversational speech.

## Lesson 9 grammar

### 1. Focus
**Conjugating Consonant-final verbs for the polite present-tense**

| -아 + 요 | after roots (with final) ㅗ, ㅏ |
|---|---|
| -어 + 요 | after all other vowels |

You have seen two verbs conjugated for the polite present tense, 가요 (가다), and 해요 (하다), which is irregular. In this lesson, you learn how to form the polite present tense of some regular verbs and adjectives in order to talk about common activities.

For the present tense, you need to conjugate the verb into the *-어/아 form* first. To show politeness, 요 can be added to the 어 form of the verb.

*Here is how to make the 어 form of the verb:*

Add -아 to the **verb stem** if the last vowel of the stem is 아 or 오. Otherwise add 어. 아 and 오 (and the vowels that contain 아 and 오 like 애, 애, 와, 왜, 외) are considered *light* and *bright* vowels in Korean whereas 어 and 우 (along with 에, 예, 워, 웨, 위) and all other vowels are considered *heavy* and *dark*. This is called 'harmonizing the vowels'. Don't forget to group the vowels of the same kind (or, easier, 아~오)!

**To show politeness, add 요 to the -어/아 conjugated verb.**

For all the verbs above in the **Vocabulary** section we have given the **Citation form**, which is used to list verbs in the dictionary. The citation form is not handy for speaking Korean, because it has no politeness or tense markers. It is a simple form used to refer to the basic verb. When speaking, the verb stem is combined with appropriate politeness, mood and tense suffixes.

The citation form is made up of the verb stem + the suffix 다, so *to determine the verb stem, drop the 다 ending from the citation form*.

|  | **Citation Form** | **Stem** |  | **어 form** | **Politeness marker** |
|---|---|---|---|---|---|
| Stem with 아, 오 | 닫 다 → | 닫 | → | 닫아 | 요 |
| | 놓 다 → | 놓 | → | 놓아 | 요 |
| Others | 먹 다 → | 먹 | → | 먹어 | 요 |
| | 읽 다 → | 읽 | → | 읽어 | 요 |

Once the verb is conjugated, the 어요 (or 아요) ending can express a statement, a question, a proposal, or a command.

• **Statement:** Statements always end in a period.

### *about general facts or habitual actions*
(Usually cued with time adverbs like 보통, 항상 or 매일)

나는 학생이에요.                                     I am a student.

우리는 매일 한국 식당에 가요.                          We go to the Korean restaurant every day.

한국은 북동 아시아에 있어요.                            Korea is in Northeast Asia.

> There is a little more complicated way to emphasize actions in progress. You will learn it in a later chapter!

### *about an action going on now*
(Usually cued with time adverbs like 지금)

A: 지금 뭐 해요?                                    What are you doing now?
B: 지금 친구하고 공부해요.                             I am studying with my friend now.

아빠는 밖에서 차를 닦아요.                              Dad is washing the car outside.

### *about an immediate plan*
(Usually cued with time adverbs like 내일 and 오늘 오후)

미안해요. 내일 파티에 못 가요.                          Sorry -- I can't go to the party tomorrow.

• **Question:** Questions always end in a question mark.

오늘 무슨 요일이에요?                                 What day is it today?

• **Proposal:** -어/아 proposals are rare, but do happen with the expression "(우리) 같이"

A: 우리 같이 체육관에 가요.                             Let's go to the gym together.
B: 네, 좋아요. 10 시에 만나요!                          OK. Let's meet at 10 o'clock.

오늘 같이 점심 먹어요.                                Let's have lunch together.

• **Command**: Commands look suspiciously similar to statements and can be interpreted as commands by context or by an occasional exclamation mark.

창문을 닫아요.                                       Close the window.

손을 씻어요!                                         Wash your hands!

 -어요 commands are quite direct and can be taken as rude. You will learn how to make polite requests in later chapters.

## Quick Review

Here are some more verbs used frequently in daily conversations. The conjugated
−어/아요 form is given for each verb. Can you guess its citation form?

| Polite Present tense | Citation Form | Meaning |
|---|---|---|
| 웃어요 | (엄마가) _____ | laugh |
| 울어요 | (아기가) _____ | cry |
| 씹어요 | (껌을) _____ | chew (gum) |
| 잡아요 | (손을/택시를) _____ | hold (hands); catch (a taxi) |
| 밀어요 | (문을) _____ | push (the door) |
| 맡아요 | (냄새를) _____ | smell (a smell) |
| 믿어요 | _____ | trust, believe |
| 덮어요 | (책을) _____ | close, cover (a book) |
| 안아요 | (아기를) _____ | hold, hug (a baby) |
| 남아요 | (핏자가) _____ | (Pizza) remain, be left over |
| 묻어요 | _____ | bury |
| 업어요 | (아기를) _____ | carry, put (a baby on the back) |

## 2. Other Grammar Notes

### 1. *can't* 못

못 is used just like 안, being placed directly in front of the verb, but 못 means *cannot*.

| | |
|---|---|
| 저는 한국말 잘 못 해요. | I can't speak Korean well. |
| 제 동생은 핏자를 못 먹어요. | My brother cannot eat pizza. |

Like 안, 못 is inserted between [noun] and [해요] for NOUN 해요 verbs.

~~아타샤 씨는 주말에 안 공부해요.~~

아타샤 씨는 주말에 공부(를) 안 해요. Atasha doesn't study on weekends.

~~언니는 못 노래해요.~~

언니는 노래(를) 못 해요. My older sister cannot sing.

> As you have learned by now, what you see in writing is not always what you would say or hear in Korean. 못, especially, can have many different pronunciations depending on what it meets. Practice saying the following sentences aloud over and over and get used to the sound! (If you need to review the pronunciation rules, re-read the Pronunciation Guide in the Preliminary Chapter.)
>
> | | |
> |---|---|
> | 한국어 잘 못 읽어요 | [항구거 잘 모딜거요] or even [몬닐거요] |
> | 친구 집에 못 가요 | [칭구 지베 목까요] |
> | 이거 못 먹어요 | [이거 몸 머거요] |
> | 산책 못 해요 | [산챙 모태요] |

The expressions 못 *can't do (something)* and 잘 못 *can't do (something) very well* or *not good at (something)* are often used contrastively with the expression 잘 해요 (can) *do something well.*

| | |
|---|---|
| 한국어 잘 읽어요? | Do/can you read Korean well? |
| 아니오, 아직 잘 못 읽어요. | No, I can't (do it) very well. |
| | |
| 한국 음식 잘 먹어요? | Do you eat Korean food well? |
| 네, 잘 먹어요! | Yes, I do! |
| 아니오, 잘 못 먹어요. | No, I can't really. |
| 아니오, 잘 안 먹어요. | No, I don't eat it often. |

> *Eat certain food well* might sound weird in English, but it is a very commonly used expression in Korean. It means something like, "Do you eat (it) with ease? Does it sit well with you?" Also don't forget that the adverb 잘 can also mean *frequently*. So the sentence 한국 음식 잘 먹어요? can also mean "Do you eat Korean food frequently?"

179

"잘못하다" written without any space between words is an idiom that means *do it wrong* or *do the wrong thing*. You may hear people say "잘못했어요" (*I am sorry for what I have done*). You may even see 잘못 as a noun:

"제 잘못이에요." *It's my fault.* or "제 잘못이 아니에요." *It is not my fault.*

 When a language is its *object*, 하다 means *to speak*. Can you guess the meaning of the following sentence?                    한국어 잘 해요?

## 2. -고 *and,* & -지만 *but*

The sentence connectors 그리고 and 그렇지만 each have a shorter version that is used as a verb suffix. They are –고, and –지만. They are added to the **stem** of the verb or adjective.

| Citation form | stem | -고 | -지만 |
|---|---|---|---|
| 먹다 | 먹- | 먹고 | 먹지만 |
| 읽다 | 읽- | 읽고 | 읽지만 |
| 가다 | 가- | 가고 | 가지만 |
| 하다 | 하- | 하고 | 하지만 |
| 알다 | 알- | 알고 | 알지만 |

 The verb 이다 *BE* in Korean acts unstably. You saw that it doesn't quite act like an independent word (thus there is no space between it and the noun it attaches to). "이" also often *disappears* before various markers, especially when it comes after a noun that ends in a vowel.

> 오른쪽 사람은 <u>오빠고</u> 왼쪽 사람은 <u>동생이고</u> 가운데 사람은 언니에요.
> The person on the right is my elder brother, the person on the left
> is my younger brother and the person in the middle is my elder sister.

 -하고 can mean three things! *with, and* (for nouns), and *do-and* (하다 verb + 고 connector). In the example sentence below, can you figure out what each -하고 means?
어머니는 친구들**하고** (같이) 얘기**하고** 아버지는 책**하고** 신문을 읽어요.

## 3. -고 나서     *and then*

-고 나서 is a verb connector that is based on the 고 connector. Adding 나서, however, places emphasis on the time *sequence* of the actions; the fact that the first action is completed before the second is undertaken.

> 저는점심을 먹고 나서 도서관에 가요.    After having lunch, I go to the library.
>
> 저는 숙제를 하고 나서 놀아요.            I do my homework and then play.

## 4. -으로     *with, by*

-으로 is a particle that is added to nouns to indicate that the noun is a tool or an instrument. It can be translated as *with* or *by*, or sometimes *in*. Use -으로 when the noun ends in a consonant (other than ㄹ) and -로 when the noun ends in a vowel or ㄹ.

| | |
|---|---|
| 펜으로 싸인해요. | One signs (one's name) with a pen. |
| 학교에 버스로 가요. | I go to school by bus. |
| 'Dog'은 한국어로 개에요. | 'Dog' is 개 in Korean. |

 When the noun ends in ㄹ (and you make 로로) be sure to pronounce a double-ㄹ sound.

| | |
|---|---|
| **조이**는 연필로 숙제를 해요. | Joey does his homework with a pencil. |
| 저는 지하철로 학교에 가요. | I go to school by subway. |

## 5. 뭐     *something*

Question words such as 뭐 are often used to express *indefiniteness*. You already know 뭐 means *what*. 뭐 can mean *something* if the sentence is not a question. In speech, indefinite expressions are followed by a short pause.

| | |
|---|---|
| 언제 ˇ 우리 집에 (한 번) 와요. | Come over to my house (once) some time. |
| 지금 뭐 ˇ 해요? | Are you doing something now? |
| 어디 ˇ 가요? | Are you going somewhere? |

Can you guess the meaning of other question words when they are used as indefinite pronouns?

| | question words | Indefinite pronouns |
|---|---|---|
| 누가, 누구 | who | someone |
| 언제 | when | |
| 어디 | where | |
| 무엇/뭐 | what | |
| 어떻게 | how | somehow |

 The question-indefinite alternation does not work for *why*.

*Quick Review*

You have learned most of the Wh-question words and have probably noticed that they can simply replace what is unknown (what is being asked about); they are not placed at the beginning of the sentence.

> Koreans often give "그냥" as an answer to the 왜 question, meaning *Just because.*

|  | Question word |
|---|---|
| 누가 (← 누구 + 가) 누구 | Who (only as the subject of sentence) Whom |
| 언제 | When |
| 왜 | Why |
| 어디 | Where |
| 무엇/뭐 | What |
| 누구 거 [누구 꺼] | whose |

| 제임스: | 오늘 **누가** 파티에 못 가요? | Who cannot go to the party today? |
|---|---|---|
| 알렌: | 제가 못 가요. | I cannot go to the party. |
| 제임스: | **왜** 못 가요? | Why can't you go to the party? |
| 알렌: | 좀 바빠요. 그런데 제임스 씨는 **누구**하고 파티에 가요? | |
| | I am a little busy. James, who are you going to the party with? | |
| 제임스: | 미라 씨하고 가요. | I am going with Mira. |
| 알렌: | **언제** 파티에 가요? | When are you going to the party? |
| 제임스: | 6 시에 가요. | I am going at 6 o'clock. |
| 제임스: | 파티는 **어디**에서 해요? | Where is the party? |
| 알렌: | 학교 앞 술집(bar)에서 해요. | At the bar in front of the school. |
| 제임스: | 파티에서 **뭐** 해요? | What do you do at parties? |
| 알렌: | 친구들하고 얘기해요. | I talk to my friends. |

You do not need to put the question word at the beginning of the sentence, and more than one question word can be used at the same time (e.g. Who did what when?).

거기에 왜 누구하고 가요?        Why are you going there and with whom?

## Lesson 9 exercises

**Exercise 1.    Dialogue practice**
Practice the dialogue with a classmate.


**Exercise 2.    못해요!**
Ask your partner whether she/he does/can do the following things (using 잘 to indicate 'can' in natural Korean).  The negative answer can use (잘) 못… .

*Example*: 김치를 잘 먹어요?    예! 잘 먹어요.    OR    아니오! 못 먹어요.

1) speak French

2) sing

3) eat anchovy (멸치) pizza

4) read Korean books

5) play baseball

6) read Chinese

7) *make up some more!*


**Exercise 3.    I can do this, but I can't do that**
Make up a sentence explaining what you do and don't do or can and can't do, according to the pictures.  Use -고 and –지만 to make one nice long sentence.  Your partner will respond about his/her abilities.

1) speak …     2) sing

3) eat     4) do sports

or *(나라)음식 (food)*

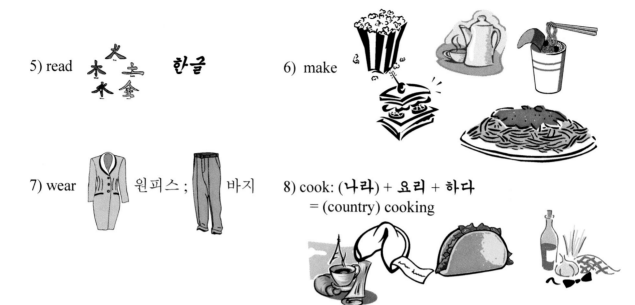

5) read 木人소木金 한글   6) make

7) wear 원피스 ; 바지   8) cook: (나라) + 요리 + 하다
                                         = (country) cooking

**Exercise 4.        언제, 어디서, 누가, 무엇을...**
Guess what the meaning of the following sentences might be. Do any sentences have more than one meaning (that depends on their intonation)?

1) 집에 누가 있어요?

2) 집에 누가 있어요.

3) 우리 언제 한 번 외식해요, 네?   (한 번: once)

4) 내일 어디에서 공부해요?

5) 우리 뭐 좀 먹어요. (좀: a little)

6) 점심에 뭐 먹어요?

**Exercise 5.        뭘로? (with what?)**
What do you use to do the following activities? Ask your partner what he/she uses to do the activities represented at the left. Take turns answering using the items at the right.

1)          포크

2)

Have you talked to your Korean friends yet and noticed that when they speak they actually say "뭘로" rather than "뭐로"? You should, too!

3)          비누: soap

4)          빵 :

*Exercise 6.*       *And then?*
Make up a sentence explaining the order of each person's activities.

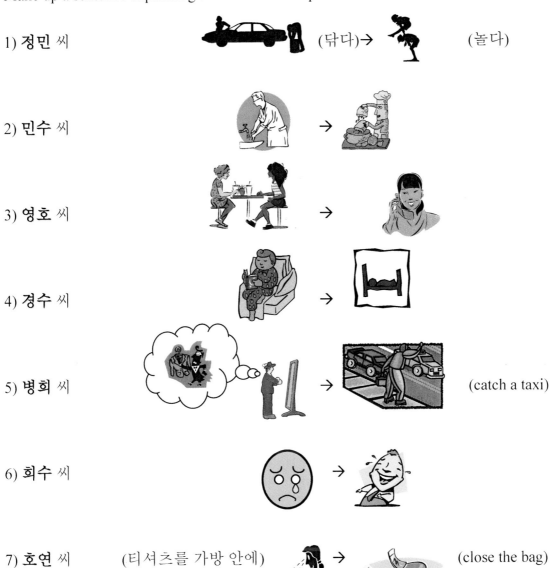

1) 정민 씨                  (닦다)→          (놀다)

2) 민수 씨

3) 영호 씨

4) 경수 씨

5) 병희 씨                                       (catch a taxi)

6) 희수 씨

7) 호연 씨     (티셔츠를 가방 안에) →         (close the bag)

8) *How about you?* What do you do today? On Mondays? On Saturdays?

185

**Exercise 7.          Pieces**
Make a sentence out of the following words.  Be sure to include the necessary particles and connectors and to conjugate the verbs correctly.  Also make sure your sentence makes sense!

1) 엄마 / 사탕 / 못 / 먹다

2) 누가 / 저 방 (room) / 웃다

3) **현수** 씨/ 전혀 / 꽃 / 냄새를 (smell) 맡다 (to smell)

4) 아침 / 옷 (clothes) / 입다 / -고 나서 / 머리 (hair) / 빗다 (to comb) / -고 나서 / 택시 / 잡다

5) 나 / 자주 / 껌 / 씹다 (to chew) / 고 / 신문 / 읽다

6) 왜 / 항상 / **현진** 씨가 / 먹다 / -고 나서 / 음식이 (food) / 남다?

7) 은행 / 돈 / 찾다 / 고 나서 / 지갑 / 넣다

8) **에밀리** 씨/ 다 (all, everything) / 알다 / -고 / 항상 / A / 받다

9) 커피 컵 / 종이 / -(으)로/ 덮다

10) 아버지 / 아기 / 안다

**Exercise 8.          Reading Practice**
Read the following passage and determine the citation form of all the verbs you find.

**나의 하루       My Day**

나는 매일 아침 7 시에 세수를 해요. 그리고 이를 ¹ 닦아요. 7 시 반 쯤에 ² 옷을 ³ 입어요. 그리고 빗으로 ⁴ 머리를 ⁵ 빗어요. 7 시 45 분 쯤에 햄으로 ⁶ 샌드위치를 만들어요. 가방에 햄 샌드위치를 넣고 나서 8 시 쯤에 학교에 가요. 학교에는 버스로 ⁷ 가요. 버스에서 샌드위치를 먹어요.

이번 학기에 나는 한국어 수업을 들어요. 한국어 수업은 8 시 30 분에 시작해요. 한국어 수업 시간에는 내 친구 **타미** 씨하고 첫째 줄에 ⁸ 앉아요. 우리는 큰 소리로 ⁹ 한국어 책을 읽어요. 한국어 선생님은 농담을 잘 해요. 정말 ¹⁰ 재미 있어요 ¹¹. 그래서 저는 **타미** 씨하고 수업 시간에 큰 소리로 웃어요. 그렇지만 우리는 시험 시간에는 못 웃어요.

나는 오후 6 시에 집에서 저녁을 먹고 나서 컴퓨터로 이메일을 써요. 밤 10 시 쯤에 한국어 숙제를 하고 나서 잠옷을 ¹² 입어요. 그리고 이를 닦아요. 나는 매일 10 시 30 분 쯤에 잠이 들어요.

1. teeth
2. about 7:30
3. clothes
4. with a comb
5. hair
6. with ham

7. by bus

8. first row
9. in a loud voice
10. really
11. a lot of fun

12. pajamas

## Lesson 9　　　　Checkpoint

**대화 1**　　　　숫가락[21] 젓가락[22]

철이: **순이** 씨, **순이** 씨는 김치를 어떻게 먹어요?

순이: 저는 젓가락으로 못 먹고 숫가락으로 먹어요.

순이: **철이** 씨, **철이** 씨는 콜라를 어떻게 마셔요[23]?

철이: 저는 그냥 입으로 마셔요. 순이씨는요?

순이: 저는 입으로 못 마시고 항상 빨대[24]로 마셔요.

철이: 2 시에요. 우리 뭐 좀 먹어요.

순이: 네, 우리 점심으로 일본 음식을 먹어요.

**대화 2**　　　　일요일에 뭐해요?

철이: **준이** 씨, **준이** 씨는 일요일에 뭐 해요?

준이: 일요일 아침에 신문을 읽고 나서 차를 닦아요.

철이: 오후에는 뭐 해요?

준이: 오후에는 점심을 먹고 나서 도서관에서 한국어 공부를 해요.

철이: 언제 한 번 같이 한국어 공부해요.

준이: 네, 그럼 이번 주 일요일에 같이 도서관에 가서 공부해요.

철이: 미안해요. 이번 주에는 같이 공부 못 해요.

준이: 왜요? 뭐 해요?

철이: 예, **순이** 씨하고 데이트해요.

---

[21] spoon
[22] chopsticks
[23] to drink
[24] straw

# LESSON 10
# 친구를 만나요.

# Lesson 10 vocabulary  Daily Activity Verbs B

**Vowel-ending verbs (in the order of vowels)**

| Polite Present tense | Citation Form | Meaning |
|---|---|---|
| 1. 끝나요 [끈나요] | (영화가) 끝나다 | (a movie) ends |
| 2. 나가요 | (밖에) 나가다 | go out(side) |
| 3. 들어가요 | (집에) 들어가다 | go (home), enter |
| 4. 떠나요 | (한국을) 떠나다 | leave (Korea) |
| 5. 만나요 | (친구를) 만나다 | meet (a friend) |
| 6. 일어나요 | (침대에서) 일어나다 | get up (get out of bed) |
| 7. 사요 | (책을) 사다 | buy, purchase (a book) |
| 8. 자요 | (늦잠을) 자다 | sleep (late, in) |
| 9. 타요 | (버스를) 타다 | ride, get on (the bus) |
| 10. 깨요 | (잠이) 깨다; (컵을) 깨다 | (one) wakes up; break (a cup) |
| 11. 끝내요 [끈내요] | 끝내요 | end, finish (something) |
| 12. 내요 | (숙제를) 내다 | turn in (homework) |
| 13. 세요 | (숫자를) 세다 | count (numbers) |
| 14. 서요 | 서다 | stand, stop |
| 15. 써요 | (이름을 칠판에) 쓰다 | write (name on board); use |
| 16. 나와요 | (밖에) 나오다 | come out(side) |
| 17. 봐요/보아요 | (TV를, 책을) 보다 | look, watch (TV); read (books) |
| 18. 와요 | (학교에) 오다 | come (to school) |
| 19. 들어와요 | (집에) 들어오다 | come (home), come in |
| 20. 배워요 | (수학을) 배우다 | learn, study (math) |
| 21. 싸워요 | (친구하고) 싸우다 | fight, have an argument |
| 22. 주어요/줘요 | (선물을) 주다 | give (a gift) |
| 23. 가르쳐요/가르치어요 | (한국어를) 가르치다 | teach (Korean) |
| 24. 기다려요 | (친구를) 기다리다 | wait (for a friend) |
| 25. 그려요 | (그림을) 그리다 | draw (pictures) |
| 26. 마셔요 | (주스를) 마시다 | drink (juice) |
| 27. 쳐요/치어요 | (테니스/기타를) 치다 | play (tennis/the guitar) |
| 28. 쉬어요 | (라운지에서) 쉬다 | rest (in the lounge) |
| 29. 좋아해요 | (김치를) 좋아하다 | like (kimchi) |
| 30. 싫어해요 | (숙제를) 싫어하다 | dislike (homework) |

This is a tough vocabulary lesson! It might help to *study the grammar focus* of this lesson first and then come back to these words. We'll help you memorize these words along the way!

## Vocabulary Exercise 1. Odd one out
Circle the verb that does not fit the theme of the others.

1) 열어요, 먹어요, 닫아요

2) 싸워요, 입어요, 빗어요 (comb)

3) 잡아요, 넣어요, 놓아요

4) 들어가요, 나가요, 사요

5) 자요, 일어나요, 깨요

6) 받아요, 줘요, 놓아요, 잡아요, 살아요

## Vocabulary Exercise 2. Matching
Draw a line to match the verbs at the left with verbs at right that are their opposite *or* their thematic 'match' (for example, *eat* and *drink*). Use each verb only once.

| | |
|---|---|
| • 먹어요 | • 배워요 |
| • 앉아요 | • 놓아요 |
| • 가르쳐요 | • 끝내요 |
| • 알아요 | • 닫아요 |
| • 잡아요 | • 받아요 |
| • 열어요 | • 떠나요 |
| • 와요 | • 써요 |
| • 읽어요 | • 몰라요 (not know) |
| • 줘요 | • 쉬어요 |
| • 시작해요 (begin, start) | • 마셔요 |
| • 일해요 | • 일어나요, 서요 |

**Vocabulary Exercise 3.  뭐를?**
Give the verb that might take each pictured item as its object.  Give as many as possible.
Also list the verbs from **Vocabulary 2** that do not take any of these as objects.

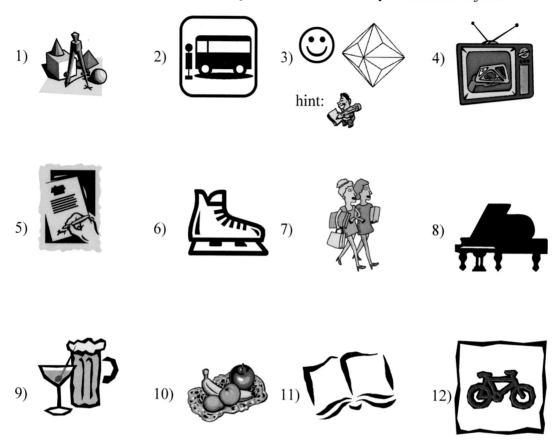

1)

2)

3)   hint:

4)

5)

6)

7)

8)

9)

10)

11)

12)

## Lesson 10 dialogue     친구를 만나요.

따르릉~

제인: 여보세요 [1].

경수: 제인 씨 있어요?

제인: 전데요 [2]. 누구세요?

경수: 제인 씨? 나 경수에요. 여기 수미 씨 파티에 있어요. 파티가 5 시부터[3]에요. 왜 안 와요?

제인: 어머 [4], 경수씨! 너무 너무 [5] 미안해요. 오늘 못 가요.

경수: 파티는 밤 1 시까지에요. 정말로 못 와요?

제인: 네, 오늘 친구들하고 백화점에 가요.

경수: 쇼핑 끝나고 나서 뭐 해요?

제인: 오늘 친한 친구가 한국에 가요. 그래서 그 친구가 떠나기 전에 [6] 다른 친구들하고 같이 만나요.

경수: 몇 시부터 몇 시까지 친구들하고 만나요? 친구들하고 만나기 전에 [7] 잠깐 [8] 못 와요?

제인: 네, 못 가요. 정말 미안해요. 다음에 같이 가요.

경수: 여기에서 나만 [9] 혼자 뭐 해요? 재미 없어요[10]!

[1.] Hello? (answering the phone)

[2.] Speaking. (answering the phone)

[3.] From 5:00

[4.] Oh, my gosh! (used by female speakers)
[5] too (really)

[6.] before the friend leaves
[7.] before meeting the friend
[8.] for a short while

[9.] me only
[10.] it's no fun

# Lesson 10 grammar

## 1. Focus   Conjugating V-verbs for polite present-tense

| -아 + 요 | after verbs with final ㅗ, ㅏ |
|---|---|
| -어 + 요 | after all other vowels |

Based on the vowel harmony mentioned in Focus 1 (this chapter), vowel-ending verbs also use 아요 if the last stem vowel is ㅏ or ㅗ and 어요 after other vowels.

Korean avoids sequences of vowels without consonants separating them. This results in contractions that can seem difficult. It may be easier to memorize the correct 어/아요 forms of V-ending verbs by saying and hearing them than by trying to memorize the rules, but the following rules are provided to give you guidelines about contractions for future reference.  We will learn the conjugated forms with the politeness ending (요) attached.

| Verbs | Citation form | Stem | Conjugation Rule: Verb Stem + | 어/아요 forms |
|---|---|---|---|---|
| Verbs with ㅏ, ㅓ, ㅐ, ㅔ | 가다<br>내다 | 가-<br>내- | Add nothing + 요 | 가요<br>내요 |
| Verbs with ㅗ | 오다<br>보다 | 오-<br>보- | Add ㅏ + 요 | 와요<br>봐요 |
| Verbs with ㅜ | 배우다<br>주다 | 배우-<br>주- | Add ㅓ + 요 | 배워요<br>줘요 |
| Verbs ending in ㅣ | 치다<br>가르치다 | 치-<br>가르치- | Add ㅓ +요<br>(ㅣ + ㅓ becomes ㅕ) | 쳐요<br>가르쳐요 |
| Verbs with complex vowels | 쉬다 | 쉬- | Add 어요 | 쉬어요 |
| Verbs with ㅡ | 쓰다 | 쓰- | ① Drop ㅡ<br>② Is receding vowel 오 or 아?<br>→ add -아요<br>③ Is other vowels?<br>→ add -어요 | 써요 |
| 하다 Verbs | 하다<br>요리하다 | 하-<br>요리하- | Change 하 into 해 | 해요<br>요리해요 |
| Noun + Copula (이다) | 학생이다<br>친구다 | 이- | ① Consonant-ending Noun + 이에요<br>② Vowel ending Noun + 에요 | 학생이에요<br>친구에요 |

consider ㅡ to be a weak vowel.

In the course of studying Korean, you will encounter forms like 이어요 or 이여요 (instead of 이에요), and 하여요 (instead of 해요). These are archaic conjugations that show up mainly in literature or older texts.

## 2. Other Grammar Notes

### 1. -기 전에            *before doing …*

-기 전에 is a phrase that attaches to a verb stem to mean 'before VERB-ing'.
Add -기 전에 to the *stem* of the verb (without 어/아!) whether it ends in a consonant or a vowel.

| | |
|---|---|
| 밖에 나가기 전에 점심 먹어요. | Before going outside, I eat lunch. |
| 점심 먹기 전에 숙제를 해요. | Before eating lunch, I do my homework. |

When a whole sentence with its own subject is used, -기 전에 means 'before (someone) VERBs':

| | |
|---|---|
| 수업이 끝나기 전에 숙제 내요! | Before <u>class ends</u>, turn in your homework! |

### 2. -만        *only, just*

-만 is a noun marker that means *only*.   The marker -만 is added to a noun to indicate "NOUN and no other", or, "only NOUN."

| | |
|---|---|
| 여기는 <u>저만</u> 있어요. | It's only me here./ I am the only one here. |
| <u>저만</u> 한국어 책을 읽어요 | Only I read Korean books.  (*only me*) |
| 저는 한국어 <u>책만</u> 읽어요 | I only read Korean books. (*only Korean books*) |

Like –도 ("also"), -만 takes the place of -가, -는, or –를 but can be used simultaneously with other markers like 에 and 에서.

찰리는 월, 수, 금요일<u>에만</u> 학교에 가요.
Charlie goes to school only on Monday, Wednesday, and Friday.

경아는 도서관<u>에서만</u> 공부해요.        경아 studies only in the library.

### 3. 와요 vs. 가요     *come* vs. *go*

Note the use of the verbs 가요 and 와요 in the dialogue in this lesson.  In places where you might expect "와요" based on English or other languages, 가요 is being used.

찰스: 그러면 파티에 못 와요?          Then you can't come to the party?

제인: 네, 못 가요. 미안해요.          Right, I can't *come*.  Sorry.

In Korean, the selection of the verbs 가요 and 와요 is based on where the speaker is at the time of the utterance.  One can only *come* (오다) to where he/she is when speaking:

I come (here) often.     / Come (here) again.                 use 오다
저는 여기 자주 와요.      / 다시 와요!

⚠ Pay special attention to the use of **가요** in the following situations!

(*answering a call*) Yes, I'm coming (to where *you* are)      use 가다!
네, 가요!

Are you coming to Jen's party tonight (too)?                  use 가다!
오늘 밤 **젠** 씨 파티에 가요?

Wait! I'm coming with you, too.                               use 가다!
잠깐! 나도 같이 가요.

Otherwise use 오다 when the (second or third person) subject is coming toward you (the speaker) and 가다 when the subject is going away from you (the speaker).

It's raining. (Rain is coming (down).)                       use 오다
비가 와요.

I can't sleep.  (Sleep doesn't come to me.)                  use 오다
잠이 안 와요.

When are you coming (here)?                                   use 오다
언제 와요?

### 4. ... 부터...-까지   *from .. until (time)/up to (place)*

The markers -부터 and -까지 often show up together. They designate a point (rather than the space an item takes up) and can be used with time and place expressions. When –까지 is used with a place noun, *up to* is a good translation.  When it is used with a time noun, *to* or *until* makes a natural translation. 부터 means *from*.

뉴욕부터 시카고까지              from N.Y. to Chicago

3시부터 4시까지                  from 3:00 till/to 4:00

196

When -까지 is used with a person, it often means, *up to, including (even)* that member.

현진이까지 와요.                                          Even 현진 will come.

 -부터 can only be used to indicate a starting point in time or space.  It cannot be used to mean (e.g., a gift) *from a person*.

~~엄마부터 선물을 많이 받아요.~~                ~~I get a lot of gifts from my mother.~~
(Instead, use 엄마로부터 선물을 많이 받아요.)

## Lesson 10 exercises

**Exercise 1.          Dialogue practice**
Practice the dialogue with a classmate.

**Exercise 2.          Reading Practice**
Read the following passage and identify the citation forms of all the verbs you find.

나의 주말                  **My Weekend**

나는 토요일에는 아침 늦게까지 [1]  늦잠을 자고, 9 시 반 쯤에 침대에서 일어나요. 계란 후라이를 [2]  먹고  커피를 마시고 11 시 쯤에 집에서 나가요. 혼자 산책해요. 공원까지 걸어 가요. 가끔 우리 개 해피하고 같이 가요. 그러면 공원까지 뛰어 가요.

산책이 끝나고 12 시 쯤에 집에 와요. 그리고 컴퓨터 앞에 앉아요. 오랫동안 [3] 친구들한테 [4] 이메일을 해요. 그리고 나서 [5] 친한 [6] 친구 집에 가요. 친구한테서 [7] 요즘 유행하는 [8] 컴퓨터 게임을 배워요. 나는 게임을 배우고 집에 와요. 그리고 조금 쉬어요. 집에서는 텔레비전을 보고 이메일을 또 [9] 해요. 그러면 한국어 숙제가 생각나요. 그 때부터 한국어 숙제를 해요. 매주 월요일 아침 8 시 30 분까지 한국어 숙제를 내요! 그래서 나는 일요일 밤 늦게까지 잠을 못 자요.

[1] till late
[2] fried eggs

[3] for a long time
[4] to (a person)
[5] and then later
[6] close
[7] from (a person)
[8] popular

[9] again

**Exercise 3.          Make a question**
Conjugate the underlined verbs appropriately.  Then pose the questions to your partner as shown in the example.

*Example*: 어디에서 책을 <u>사다</u>          →        Q: 어디에서 책을 사요?
                                                               A: 학교 앞 서점에서 사요

1) 매일 (everyday) 버스를 <u>타다</u>

2) 내일 (tomorrow) 학교에 <u>안 가다</u>

3) 기타를 잘 <u>치다</u>

4) 학교 안 어디에서 <u>쉬다</u>

5) <u>대학생이다</u>

6) 어디에서 한국어를 <u>배우다</u>

7) 한국어 책을 매일 <u>보다</u>

8) 친구하고 보통 어디에서 <u>만나다</u>

9) 한국어를 잘 <u>쓰다</u>

10) 누가 한국어를 <u>가르치다</u>


**Exercise 4.          -만 or another particle**
Fill in the blanks with the correct particles.

| | | |
|---|---|---|
| 1) 나_____ 연필_____ 있어요. | I have only a pencil. |
| 2) 나_____ 연필_____ 있어요. | Only I have a pencil. |
| 3) 나_____ 내 방_____ 청소해요. | I only clean my room. |
| 4) 나_____ 내 방_____ 청소해요. | Only I clean my room. |
| 5) 나_____ 학교에 _____ 가요. | I only go to school. |
| 6) 나_____ 학교에 _____ 가요. | Only I go to school. |
| 7) 선생님_____ 학생_____ 가르쳐요. | Only the teacher teaches students. |
| 8) 선생님_____ 학생_____ 가르쳐요. | The teacher teaches students only. |
| 9) 우리_____ 물_____ 마셔요. | Only we drink water. |
| 10) 우리_____ 물_____ 마셔요. | We drink water only. |

**Exercise 5.        Only what?**
Rewrite the sentence with 만 according to the meaning given in English.

1) 저는 집에서 공부해요.    → I study only at home.

2) 선생님은 피자를 먹고 학생들은 물을 마셔요.
→ Only the teacher is eating pizza and students are just drinking water.

3) 제시는 금요일에 학교에 와요.
→ Jesse comes to school only on Friday.

4) 수미는 제시하고 놀아요.
→ Sumi plays only with Jesse.


**Exercise 6.        와요 or 가요?**
Fill in the blanks with 가요 or 와요.

멜리: **티나** 씨, 오늘 **제인** 씨 파티에 _____?

티나: 네, _____. 또 누가 **제인**씨 파티에 _____?

멜리: **제임스** 씨하고 **린다**씨가 _____.

티나: 다음 주에는 우리 집에서 파티가 있어요. **멜리** 씨도 ____!

멜리: 네, 그래요.  저는 파티는 다 _____. **티나** 씨 파티에 또 누가 _____?

티나: **토니**하고 **브렌다** 씨가 _____.


Now read the conversation again as if it were a phone conversation.  Do any of the verbs need changing?


**Exercise 7.        From when till when?**
Make a sentence according to the pictures (and time adverbs), that indicates 승희's schedule.  Look carefully to read the start and end tiems from the clocks.

1) 매일

 →

2) Monday-Friday

 →

3) 매일

4) 토요일

5) 일요일

다운타운

*6)* How about your schedule?  Talk to your partner about your schedules.

## Exercise 8.          Let's have lunch!

Find out who in the class you could have lunch with on each day of the week, based on their schedules.  Write down the times during which you have lunch each day (from when to when -- in the TIME box).  Ask what your classmates do at those times on those days.  If the partner also eats lunch then, or can, write his/her name in the YES box.  In the NO box, write the names of people who cannot have lunch with you, and write what that person does at that time. Later you can make up sentences about other's schedules to report to the class.

|      | 월요일 | 화요일 | 수요일 | 목요일 | 금요일 |
|------|--------|--------|--------|--------|--------|
| TIME |        |        |        |        |        |
| YES  |        |        |        |        |        |
| NO   |        |        |        |        |        |

**Exercise 9.**　　　-도, -만, -은/는, -이/가, 하고
Fill in the blanks with an appropriate marker.

1) 뉴욕에는 엠파이어 스테이트 빌딩_____ 있어요. 센트럴 파크___ 있어요.

2) 잭_____ 존_____ 남학생이에요. 벤_____ 남학생이에요. 진_____ 여학생이에요.

3) 리사_____ 자니_____ 오늘 없어요. 그래서 캐씨_____ 아기를 봐요.

4) 저는 사탕_____ 싫어해요. 과자_____ 싫어해요. 콜라_____ 좋아해요.

**Exercise 10.**　　　**Before this and having done that**
**Part A**　　　Based on 승희's schedule in Exercise 7, make up 6 sentences that indicate the order of his activities. Use -기 전에 or -고 나서 in each sentence.

**Part B**　　　*How about you?* What do you do on Mondays? Saturdays? Weekdays? Weeknights? Indicate the order of your activities.

**Exercise 11.**　　　**Pieces**
Make a Korean sentence of the given words, being sure to add all necessary particles and conjugations.

1) weekdays // study // Chinese // library // 3 o'clock - 4 o'clock // and // home // play

2) like // Korean // but // cannot // eat // Korean food (음식)

3) Saturdays // wash // car // and then // go out // restaurant // with // friends // until // 11:00

4) Before // turn in // homework // write // name

5) from now // learn // Hancha (Chinese characters) // and // only Saturdays // watch // TV

6) only I // before // sleep // don't // close // window

7) 선생님: you // *come/go* // Korean class // tomorrow ? – 학생: yes // *go/come*

8) from // before // I // go out // until // I // come back (use 기!) // grandma (할머니) // rests

9) Mom // like // candy // but // dislike // chocolate

## Lesson 10    Checkpoint

대화 1        브람스를 좋아해요?

> 미라:  리라 씨, 브람스를 좋아해요?
>
> 리라:  네, 너무 너무 좋아해요. 저는 매일 브람스만 들어요.
>
> 미라:  내일 5시부터 8시까지 학교에서 브람스 음악회[25]가 있어요.
>
> 리라:  내일만 음악회가 있어요? 내일은 못 가요.
>
> 미라:  왜 못 가요? 무슨 일 있어요?
>
> 리라:  네, 오늘부터 내일까지 심리학 보고서[26]를 써요.
>
> 미라:  음악회는 모레까지에요. 그렇지만 저는 모레 아르바이트를 해요.
>
> 리라:  그럼 제가 내일 음악회 시작하기 전에 보고서를 끝낼게요.[27]
>
> 미라:  고마워요.

대화 2        김치를 좋아해요?

> 미라:  리라 씨, 김치를 좋아해요?
>
> 리라:  네, 너무 너무 좋아해요. 저는 매일 김치만 먹어요.
>
> 미라:  내일 2시부터 5시까지 학교에서 김치 박람회[28]가 있어요.
>
> 리라:  내일만 박람회가 있어요? 내일은 못 가요.
>
> 미라:  왜 못 가요? 무슨 일 있어요?
>
> 리라:  네, 오늘부터 내일까지 심리학 리포트를 써요.
>
> 미라:  박람회는 모레까지에요. 그렇지만 저는 모레 아르바이트를 해요.
>
> 리라:  그럼 제가 내일 박람회 시작하기 전에 보고서를 끝낼게요.
>
> 미라:  고마워요.

---

[25] Classical concert (c.f. for rock music, use 콘서트)
[26] report, paper (also, 보고서)
[27] will finish
[28] exhibition [방남외; 방남회]

## 노래하고 갑시다!

| | |
|---|---|
| 둥근 해가 떴습니다. | The round sun rose. |
| 자리에서 일어나서, | I get up out of bed |
| 제일 먼저 이를 닦자. | First thing, let's brush our teeth. |
| 윗니, 아랫니 닦자. | Upper teeth, lower teeth, let's brush our teeth. |
| 세수 할 때는 깨끗이 | When I wash my face, *cleanly*! |
| 이 쪽, 저 쪽 목 닦고, | Wash my neck this way and that way. |
| 머리 빗고 옷을 입고, | I comb my hair and get dressed, |
| 거울을 봅니다. | look myself in the mirror. |
| 꼭꼭 씹어 밥을 먹고, | Chew-chew, I have a meal, |
| 가방 메고 인사하고, | Put the bag on my back, say good-bye, and |
| 학교에 갑니다. | I am going to school. |
| 씩씩하게 갑니다. | Energized and happy, I'm going to school. |

# LESSON 11
# 일요일이 어때요?

# Lesson 11 vocabulary          *Adjectival verbs*

**(presented in opposite pairs where possible)**

| Polite Present tense | Citation Form | Meaning |
|---|---|---|
| 1. 바빠요 | 바쁘다 | busy |
| 2. 한가해요 | 한가하다 | not busy, have a lot of free time |
| 3. 맞아요 | 맞다 | correct, right |
| 4. 틀려요 | 틀리다 | incorrect, wrong |
| 5. 커요 | 크다 | big |
| 6. 작아요 | 작다 | small |
| 7. 좋아요 | 좋다 | good; be liked |
| 8. 싫어요 | 싫다 | be disliked |
| 9. 나빠요 | 나쁘다 | bad |
| 10. 많아요 | 많다 | abundant, be a lot |
| 11. 적어요 | 적다 | be only a little |
| 12. 같아요 [가태요] | 같다 | be alike, the same |
| 13. 달라요 | 다르다 (irreg) | different |
| 14. 비슷해요 [비스태요] | 비슷하다 | similar |
| 15. 어때요 | 어떻다 (irreg.) | be how |
| 16. 괜찮아요 | 괜찮다 | O.K. |
| 17. 예뻐요 | 예쁘다 | pretty |
| 18. 필요해요 | 필요하다 | be necessary, needed |
| 19. 필요없어요 | 필요없다 | be unnecessary; not needed |
| 20. 재미있어요 | 재미있다 | a lot of fun |
| 21. 재미없어요 | 재미없다 | no fun |
| 22. 편해요 | 편하다 | comfortable |
| 23. 편리해요 | 편리하다 | convenient |
| 24. 불편해요 | 불편하다 | uncomfortable; inconvenient |
| 25. 이상해요 | 이상하다 | weird, strange |
| 26. 신기해요 | 신기하다 | weird, curious, odd |
| 27. 피곤해요 | 피곤하다 | tired |
| 28. 아파요 | 아프다 | sick, hurts |
| 30. 졸려요 | 졸리다 | sleepy |

ㅎ disappears when you say these words fast:
필요해요, 편해요, 편리해요, 불편해요, 이상해요, 피곤해요
Remember to pronounce the ㅎ when you are articulating the words slowly.

ㅎ always drops out of:
좋아요 → [조아요]
싫어요 → [시러요]
괜찮아요 → [괜차나요]
많아요 → [마나요]

Be sure to pronounce only one ㄹ or ㄴ when there is only one, and two when there are two. 달라요 and 달아요 are different!
Also, 많아요 → [마나요] and 만나요 are two different words!

205

## Vocabulary Exercise 1.  What is?
Think of a subject that fits each adjectival verb.

1) _____ 이/가  많아요

2) _____하고 _____ 이/가  달라요(needs two subjects!)

3) _____하고 _____ 이/가  비슷해요 [비스태요]  (needs two subjects!)

4) _____ 이/가  예뻐요

5) _____ 이/가  필요해요

6) _____ 이/가  재미있어요

7) _____ 이/가  편리해요

8) _____ 이/가  이상해요

## Vocabulary Exercise 2.  Opposites
Give the vocabulary word that means the opposite of the word given.

1) 달라요

2) 커요

3) 틀려요

4) 싫어요

5) 많아요

## Vocabulary Exercise 3.  Label the picture
Describe what's in each picture using new vocabulary.

1) 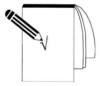   2)    3)    4)

5)    6)    7)    8)

## Lesson 11 dialogue 일요일이 어때요?

경수: **제인** 씨, 재미있는[1] 영화가[2] 있어요. 우리 같이 봐요.

제인: 좋아요. 언제요?

경수: 내일 시간이[3] 있어요?

제인: 아니오, 시험이 있어서[4] 내일은 바빠요.

경수: 그럼 언제가 좋아요?

제인: 토요일이 괜찮아요. 일요일에도 시간이 많아요.
　　　일요일이 어때요?

경수: 좋아요. 일요일도 좋아요.

제인: 근데, 무슨 영화에요?

경수: **재키 찬**의 코메디 액션 영화에요.

제인: 어디에서 해요[5]?

경수: **씨네라마**에서도 하고 **머제스틱**에서도 해요.

제인: 그럼, **씨네라마**에 가요. **씨네라마** 극장은 팝콘도
　　　맛있고 의자도 편해서[6] 내가 좋아해요.

경수: 맞아요[7]. **씨네라마**는 원래[8] 손님들한테[9] 콜라도
　　　공짜로[10] 줘요.

1. fun (modifier)
2. movie
3. time (duration)
4. there is a test so
5. play
6. comfortable so
7. That's right.
8. usually, customarily, originally
9. to (customers)
10. for free

---

You should have already guessed that '해요' is probably the most versatile verb in Korean. You can add 해요 to many, many nouns and turn them into verbs: 농구해요, 배스킷볼해요, 등산해요, 하이킹해요, 조깅해요, 운동해요, 에어로빅해요, etc., etc.

해요 can also be used after a language name to mean 'speak' that language:
한국어 잘 못 해요. *I can't speak Korean well.*
영어를 잘 해요. *(Someone) speaks English well.*

Finally, there are many idiomatic expressions that involve 해요. One of them is 지금 극장에서 그 영화를 해요, which menas *The movie is playing at theaters now.*

## Lesson 11 grammar

### 1. Focus     Conjugating Adj-verbs for polite present tense

> **Adjectives conjugate like verbs do!**

In Korean, you might say there are no adjectives. This does not mean that there is no word for "good," for example, but rather, the word for "good" conjugates as if it were a verb; it requires politeness and tense suffixes when it occurs at the end of a sentence. You can see that this is the case in 바빠요 *busy* and 좋아요 *good* in the lesson dialogue above and in the following examples.

| | |
|---|---|
| 워싱톤 대학교는 아주 커요. | The University of Washington is very big. |
| 우리 언니는 아주 예뻐요. | My elder sister is very pretty. |
| 한국어 수업에는 남학생이 많지만 여학생은 적어요. | |

There are many male students but only a few female students in the Korean class.

You should note, however, that there are differences between adjectives and verbs in Korean grammar – in the way they conjugate for some endings. One difference is that even though some adjectives end in 해요, they are still adjectives: object markers (을/를), 안 (*not*) and spaces are never inserted before the 해요

| | |
|---|---|
| 내 여동생하고 나는 비슷해요. | My younger sister and I are similar. |
| 내 여동생은 나하고 비슷해요. | My younger sister is similar to me. |
| 우리 언니는 나하고 안 비슷해요. | My older sister is not similar to me. |

Also note that, like all other adjectives, the 해요 adjectives 이상해요 (*weird/strange*) and 필요해요 (*needed*) or 비슷해요 (*similar*) take the **subject** marker!

Finally, notice that there may be differences between Enlgish and Korean in what is communicated using adjectives versus verbs. For example, Korean doesn't use a *verb* that means *to need*, but instead has an *adjective* that means *needed*. This means that the thing needed is the *subject* of the adjectival verb in Korean. The negative is also worth noting.

| | |
|---|---|
| ~~펜을 필요해요~~ 펜이 필요해요. | I need a pen. (A pen is needed.) |
| ~~펜이 필요 안 해요/안 필요해요.~~ | I don't need a pen. |
| 펜이 필요**없어요**. | (I have no need for a pen.) |

> Korean speakers will likely refer to this as the 어서 ending.

## 2. Other Grammar Notes

**1. -어서**    *so*

You learned to connect two sentences using the connector -고 *and*. 그래서 also corresponds to a suffix, -서, that can be attached to the 어/아 form of a verb or adjective to indicate the logical precedent for a following action.

모레 시험이 있어요. <u>그래서</u> 오늘하고 내일은 아주 바빠요.

→ 모레 시험이 <u>있어서</u> 오늘하고 내일은 아주 바빠요.
There is a test the day after tomorrow *so* I am very busy today and tomorrow.

그 사람은 한국어 가르쳐요. <u>그래서</u> 한국어 문법을 잘 알아요.

→ 그 사람은 한국어 <u>가르쳐서</u> 한국어 문법을 잘 알아요.
That person teaches Korean so she knows Korean grammar really well.

 Remember to conjugate the verb in the -어 form to add the connector (어)서!

|  | **Citation form** | **어요/아요** | **-서** |
|---|---|---|---|
| Verbs | 먹다 | 먹어요 | 먹어서 |
|  | 가다 | 가요 | 가서 |
|  | 쉬다 | 쉬어요 | 쉬어서 |
|  | 오다 | 와요 | 와서 |
|  | 쓰다 | 써요 | 써서 |
|  | 치다 | 쳐요 | 쳐서 |
| Adjectives | 크다 | 커요 | 커서 |
|  | 작다 | 작아요 | 작아서 |
| Noun + (이)다 | 학생이다 | 학생이에요 | 학생이어서/학생이라서 |
|  | 친구다 | 친구에요. | 친구여서/친구라서 |

⚠️ The verb 이다 has alternate forms for this suffix.

## 2. "으" Irregular verbs and adjectives

Some verbs and adjectives ending in the vowel ─ are called 으-irregulars. The irregular verb "쓰다" was already introduced in lesson 10.  In this section, you will focus on 으-irregular adjectives.

The conjugation of 으 irregular stems depends on the vowel that comes right before "─". When the preceding vowel is ㅏ or ㅗ, ─ is dropped and 아요 is added.  Otherwise, ─ is dropped and 어요 is added – this includes case like 쓰다 where there is no other vowel after ─ is dropped: in those cases also add -어요.

| Adjectives/ Verbs | Citation form | Stem | Conjugation Rule: Verb Stem + | 어/아요 forms |
|---|---|---|---|---|
| the preceding vowel is ㅏ or ㅗ | 나쁘다 바쁘다 배고프다 | 나쁘 바쁘 배고프 | Drop ─, add 아요 | 나빠요 바빠요 배고파요 |
| Others | 예쁘다 크다 | 예쁘 크 | Drop ─, add 어요 | 예뻐요 커요 |

A: 오늘 날씨가 어때요?

B: 아주 나빠요.

A: 여자 친구가 예뻐요.

B: 아니에요.

How's the weather today?

Very bad.

Your girlfriend is pretty.

Not at all.

> Though it might sound odd or rude, according to the traditional Korean culture, it is very appropriate to *deny* any compliments bestown on one's spouse or significant other, let alone oneself.

## 3. 우리 같이 ... 어요/아요          *let's*

As suggested in the lesson 9 grammar focus, the 어요 (or 아요) ending can express a proposal.

A: 내일 몇 시에 만나요?

B: 10 시에 만나요.

What time are we meeting tomorrow?

Let's meet at 10 o'clock.

When 어요/아요 is used in a proposal, "우리 (같이)" is frequently used in the sentence.

우리 같이 영화 봐요.

우리 내일 같이 만나요.

Let's watch the movie together.

Let's meet (together) tomorrow.

210

## 4. 어때요?          *How is it?*

어때요 is an adjective, and it means *to be how*. It can only be used in a question, asking for the other person's opinion.

> Subject Noun + Particle (Optional) + 어때요?
> 한국어는 어때요?                          How is Korean? / What is Korean like?

> A: 한국어 선생님 어때요?                    How is the Korean teacher?
> B: 아주 재미있는 선생님이에요!               He/she is a really fun teacher!

어때요 is an irregular verb and its citation form is 어떻다. You will learn about this type of verb in a later lesson.

## 5. 어디, 거기 + 에, 에서       *where, there* + location particles

The location particle 에 is often omitted after the deictic expressions 여기, 거기, and 저기 as well as after the question word 어디:

> A: 우체국이 어디에 있어요?                   Where is the post office?
> B: 저기에 있어요.                          It's over there.

에 also optionally disappears after these expressions when it is part of the particle 에서:

> A: 어디에서 만나요?                         Where are we meeting?
> B: 거기에서 만나요.                         Let's meet there.

## 6. -한테      *to (a person)* ...

The marker –한테 means *to* and is used when its object (the receiver) is animate (*to a person*, etc.).

> 돈을 항상 엄마한테 줘요.                    I always give my money <u>to my mother</u>.
> 토요일에 프랑스 친구한테 편지를 써요.      On Saturdays I write to my French friend.

English phrases like "gave <u>him</u> the book," "show <u>me</u> the movie" must be translated "gave the book <u>to him</u>," etc. in Korean. Then you can use the marker –한테 for the *indirect object* (*to him*) and 을/를 for the direct object (*book*).

Here are some other cases where you will need to use 한테:

> (친구)한테 전화해요 (<u>하고</u> is also fine)     to call a friend (to talk on the phone with a friend)

(친구) 한테 얘기해요 (하고 is also fine)      to talk to a friend/with a friend

(친구) 한테 물어봐요                to ask a friend

 Re-read the example phrases from vocabulary lessons 9 and 10 to check for unexpected markers that go with each verb.

### 7. 좋아하다/좋다    *to like / to be good*

 You have learned two sets of very similar verbs and adjectives. 좋아해요 and 싫어해요 are both **verbs** that mean *to like* and *to dislike*, respectively. The thing that is liked or disliked is marked with the *object* marker 을/를 when you use these verbs.

저는 한국어 숙제를 좋아해요.      I like Korean homework.

저는 생선을 싫어해요.      I don't like fish.

좋다 and 싫다 are **adjectives** that mean *good* (or *liked*) and *disliked*, respectively. Whatever is good or disliked is marked with the *subject* marker, 이/가.

언제 가요? – 토요일이 좋아요.      When are you going? – Saturday is good.
이 펜이 아주 좋아요.      This pen is really good!

생선이 싫어요.      I don't like fish.

To express one's own dislikes, then, either 싫어요 or 싫어해요 can be used – there is no other English translation. People often use 좋아요 to reflect their likes in addition to its usage as "*good*", however.

저는 한국어 숙제가 좋아요.      I like Korean homework.
                             (Literally: "As for me, Korean homework is good")

Don't let this confuse you; translate such sentences in your mind as something like "As for me, Korean homework is good," and be sure to use the *subject* marker on [Korean homework]. Note that "as for me" in these cases, uses the *topic* marker, 은/는.

 Be aware however, that you cannot speak for others! You cannot use 좋아요 and 싫어요 to express *others'* likes and dislikes; you can only use 좋아해요 and 싫어해요 to talk about what other people like and dislike.

정민이는 바나나가 아주 좋아해요.

정민이는 바나나를 아주 좋아해요.      Chung-min really likes bananas.

정민이는 계란이 싫어해요.

정민이는 계란을 싫어해요.      Chung-min doesn't like eggs.

## Language Point　　　　　시간 있어요?

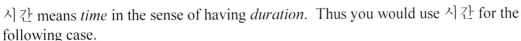

There are many Korean words that correspond to the English word "time". You already know 시 that can only be used in the context

지금 몇 **시**에요?　　　　　*What time is it now?*

시 means *time*, but it usually comes with some other syllable as in 시간:
내일 **시간**이 있어요?　　　*Do you have time tomorrow?*
아니오, 내일은 바빠요.　　*No, I am a little busy tomorrow.*

시간 means *time* in the sense of having *duration*. Thus you would use 시간 for the following case.
몇 **시간** 동안 공부해요?　*For how many hours do you study?*

Finally, don't forget to use 몇 번 in order to express 'how many *times*", which asks for *repetitions* rather than time *duration*:
일주일에 몇 번 체육관에 가요?
*How many times a week do you go to the gym?*

## Lesson 11 exercises

### Exercise 1.　　　Dialogue practice
Practice the dialogue with a classmate.

### Exercise 2.　　　Making conversation
Work with a partner. Ask a question using the words in column A. Your partner will answer the question using the words in column B. Be sure to conjugate the verbs or adjectives correctly.

*Example*:

| A | B |
|---|---|
| 교실에 여학생이 많다 | 적다 |

Q: 교실에 여학생이 많아요?　　　A: 아니오. 적어요.

| A | B |
|---|---|
| 1) 교실에 남학생이 많다 | 적다 |
| 2) 지갑에 돈이 많다 | 많다 |
| 3) 내일 바쁘다 | 바쁘다 |
| 4) 매일 신문을 읽다 | 매일 TV 를 보다 |
| 5) 액션 영화가 좋다 | 액션 영화가 싫다 |
| 6) 한국어 교실이 작다 | 한국어 교실이 크다 |
| 7) 한국어를 가르치다 | 한국어를 배우다 |

**Exercise 3.          Reading Practice**
Read the passage in the box and the following dialogue between Jane and Tina.  Determine the citation form of all the adjectives (adjectival verbs) you find for the passage and the dialogue.

**커피가 어때요?**                    *How about coffee?*

이번 주말에는 파티가 있어요. 그렇지만 나는 아주 바빠서
파티에 못 가요. 왜냐하면 <sup>1</sup>, 친구 **혜미**가 곧 <sup>2</sup> 한국으로
돌아가요 <sup>2</sup>. 그래서 친구한테 작은 <sup>3</sup> 선물을 사 줄 거에요 <sup>4</sup>.
쇼핑은 항상 재미있어요. 그래서 나는 쇼핑을 좋아해요.

<sup>1.</sup> because

<sup>2.</sup> right away
<sup>3.</sup> return, go back

<sup>4.</sup> small
<sup>5.</sup> will buy (for her)

옷이
어때요?

Jane: 선물로 옷이 어때요?  (선물로: as a present)

Tina: **혜미**는 옷이 많아요.

Jane: 그럼, **혜미** 씨는 뭐가 필요해요?

Tina: **혜미**는 항상 피곤해요...

Jane: 그럼 커피가 어때요?

Tina: **혜미**는 커피를 싫어해요.

       참, **혜미**는 농구를 좋아해요.  농구공이 어때요? (참! Oh! 농구공: basketball)

Jane: 네, 그거 좋은 생각이에요. (That's a good idea.)

## Exercise 4.        Make it one sentence
Connect the sentences using –어서/아서.

1) 내일 친구가 와요. 그래서 오늘 청소를 해요.

2) 집이 커요. 그래서 좋아요.

3) 아주 바빠요. 그래서 못 놀아요.

4) 숙제가 많아요. 그래서 시간이 없어요.

5) 학생이에요. 그래서 돈이 없어요.

6) 내일 시험이 있어요. 그래서 공부를 많이 했어요.


## Exercise 5.        Complete the passage.
Complete the passage with the correct adjectives and verbs in the polite present tense. (The meanings of the asterisked words* follow the passage).

안녕하세요? 제 이름은 미미(이다)_____. 저는 한국말을 조금 (읽다) _____. 그래서 저에 대해* 한국말로 (쓰다) _____. 저는 키*가 (작다) _____. 그리고 머리*가 (좋다) _____. 저는 자전거*를 잘 (타다)_____. 기타도 잘 (치다)_____. 저는 영화를 가끔 (보다) _____. 저는 한국 친구가 (많다) _____. 저는 한국 음식을 잘 (먹다) _____. 김치가 (좋다) _____. 하지만 김*은 (싫다) _____. 저는 한국 친구들을 자주 (만나다)_____. 그리고 한국 친구들하고 같이 한국 식당에 점심 먹으러 가끔 (가다)_____. 저는 _____씨에 대해 하나도* 몰라요. _____ 씨는 어떤 사람이에요?

저에 대해: about me/myself
머리가 좋다: smart (head good)
자전거: bicycle
하나도: (none) at all

머리: head
키: height
김: seaweed
어떤 사람: what kind of a person

**Exercise 6.          What is a likely reason?**
Use adjectives and the 어/아서 connector to make up a likely reason behind each phrase and complete the sentences.

1) _____ 파티에 못 가요.

2) _____ *Who wants to be a millionaire?* 를 봐요.

3) _____ 이 옷을 못 입어요. (옷: clothes)

4) _____ 내일 같이 못 만나요.

5) _____ 그 여자/남자한테 매일 전화해요.

6) _____ 이 음식을 안 먹어요. (음식: food)

7) _____ 숙제를 못 해요.

8) _____ 그 사람하고 데이트 안 해요.


**Exercise 7.        Invitations**
Work with a partner.  Invite your partner to do the following activities.  Your parner will either accept or decline your invitation.

*Example*: 내일 테니스 치다
A: 우리, 내일 같이 테니스 쳐요.
B: 좋아요. 같이 쳐요.
B': 미안해요. 내일은 시간이 없어요. 모레 같이 쳐요.

1)  도서관에서 공부하다

2)  영화를 보다

3)  한국어 숙제를 하다

4)  책을 읽다

5)  HUB 에서 핏자를 먹다

6)  일요일에 만나다

7)  여행가다 (travel), 하와이

8)  영화 보다, 액션 영화

9)  도서관에서 공부하다

10) 책을 읽다, 한국어 책

11) 내일 만나다, 12 시

## Exercise 8.        Pieces
Make complete sentences out of the words given. Be sure to add all necessary markers and conjugations.

1) 나 // 한국어 책 // 친구 // 주다

2) 이 버스 // 대학교 // 까지 // 가다          (까지: to the point of)

3) 저 // 학교 도서관 // 세 시 // 공부하다

4) 내 친구 // 우리 집 // 오늘 오후 // 오다

5) 나 // 한국 음식 // 만 // 좋다

6)  우리 엄마 // 일본 음식 // 만 // 좋아하다

7)  이 // 스웨터 // 너무 (too) // 크다 . // 오빠 (older brother) // 주다

## Exercise 9.        Me and my … alter ego.
Your partner (짝) likes everything you dislike and dislikes everything you like.  Make up a sentence telling whether you like or dislike the following items and stating that your 짝 does the opposite.

bananas: 저는 바나나를 좋아하지만 제 짝은 바나나를 싫어해요.

1)  chocolate

2)  opera

3)  Korean (language)

4)  tests

5)  parties

6)  homework

7)  France

8)  books

9)  chips (snacks, crackers)

10)  coffee

**Exercise 10.        Translate the sentences**

1)  I am always right, and you are always wrong!

2)  My older brother is busy on Saturdays too.

3)  How is your Korean teacher? (She/he) is pretty good/O.K.

4)  Have (drink) coffee with me this afternoon.  Meet me there.

5)  Call John tomorrow.

6)  I don't like that show (쇼) so I don't watch it often.

7)  John is busy this weekend so he is not coming to the party. (it's NOT *your* party)

8)  I am tired so I am not going to the party tonight. (it's NOT your party)

9)  Tony has a lot of money.

10) This and that are very different!  No, this and that are exactly the same!

11) Micheal Jackson is a little weird, but I like him.  Do you like him?

12) I need something.

13) Korean is really fun. (really 정말)

## Lesson 11     Checkpoint

대화 1       여보, 나 어때요?

아내: 여보, 나 어때요?

남편: 정말[29] 예뻐요. **김희선**같아요. 그 옷을 사요.

아내: 그렇지만 색깔[30]이 싫어요. 사이즈[31]도 너무 커요.

남편: 아니에요. 색깔도 사이즈도 괜찮아요.

아내: 여보, 이 옷은 어때요?

남편: 그것도 예뻐요. 그런데 새[32] 옷이 꼭 필요해요?

아내: 네, 내일 파티가 있어서 새 옷이 필요해요.

남편: 여보, 나 오늘 피곤해요. 우리 이제 집에 가요.

아내: 당신[33] 정말 재미없어요!

대화 2       우리 어느 도서관에서 공부해요?

철이: 우리 어디서 같이 한국어 공부해요?

준이: 저는 보통 문대[34] 도서관에서 공부해요. **철이** 씨는요?

철이: 저는 전공이 전자공학이라서 공대[35] 도서관에서 공부해요.

준이: 문대 도서관이 책이 많아서 좋아요. 그리고 열람실[36]도 커요.

철이: 그렇지만 남자 화장실이 적어서 불편해요.

준이: 그래요? 공대 도서관은 어때요?      (cont.to next page)

---

[29] really
[30] color
[31] size
[32] new
[33] a second person pronoun. It is often used to refer to one's spouse.
[34] The College of Liberal Arts (short for 문리대)
[35] The College of Engineering
[36] reading room

철이: 우리 도서관은 남자 화장실이 많아요. 그렇지만 열람실이 작아서 나빠요.

준이: 그리고 또 여기는 여학생이 많아서 좋아요. 공대 도서관에 여학생 많이 와요?

철이: 아니오, 공대 도서관에는 여학생이 거의 없어요.

준이: 그럼 우리 어디서 공부해요?

철이: 우리 이제부터 문대 도서관에서만 공부해요. 어때요?

## 읽기 1          나의 토요일

나는 매주 토요일 시내[37] 서점에 가요. 나는 토요일 오전 10 시에 집을 나와요. 10 시 10 분에 버스를 타고 서점에 가요. 서점 안의 커피숖에서 커피를 마셔요. 커피를 마시고 나서 11 시부터 한국에 관한[38] 책을 찾아요. 나는 한국에 관심[39]이 많이[40] 있어요. 그렇지만 학교에는 한국에 관한 책이 거의 없어요. 그래서 시내 서점에 가서 책을 읽어요. 그렇지만 책은 자주 못 사요.

책을 보고 나서 1 시 반 쯤 서점을 나와요. 서점 옆에 샌드위치 집에 가서 점심을 먹어요. 주인[41] 아주머니는 김치로 샌드위치를 만들어요. 나는 김치를 좋아하고 잘 먹어요. 김치 샌드위치는 정말 맛있어요.

점심을 먹고 나서 5 시까지 학교 운동장에 가요. 6 시까지 **타미**와 같이 테니스를 쳐요. 6 시에 우리는 학교 앞 술집에 가요. 나는 저녁을 먹고 술도 마시지만 **타미**는 술만 마셔요. **타미**는 술고래[42]에요.

---

[37] downtown
[38] 한국에 관한 책 means books about Korea.
[39] interest
[40] a lot
[41] owner
[42] 술 means *liquor* or *alcohol* and 고래, *whale*. 술고래 refers to *someone who drinks like a fish.*

## 읽기 2        은비

**은비**는 제 사촌 동생이에요. **은비**는 한 살이에요. 우리 막내 이모의 딸이에요. 월요일부터 수요일까지 우리 집에 와요. 막내 이모는 월요일부터 수요일까지 부산에서 일해요. **은비**는 나를 보고 잘 웃어요. 정말 예뻐요. 그런데 밤에는 잘 울어요. 그래서 나는 밤에 잠을 잘 못 자요. **은비**는 항상 뭘 먹어요. **은비**는 아무거나 잘 먹지만 풍선껌을 제일 좋아해요. **은비**는 풍선껌을 좋아하지만 잘 못 씹어요. 그냥 먹어요. 그래서 저는 **은비**가 보기 전에 빨리 풍선껌을 입 안에 넣고 혼자 씹어요. **은비**는 입 안의 풍선껌을 못 찾아요.

# LESSON 12
# 재미 없었어요.

# Lesson 12 vocabulary    *Adverbs*

1. 정말(로)          **really, truly (진짜(로) is another often used adverb)**
2. 아주             **very  (되게, 굉장히 -slang)**
3. 너무             **too, very** ———

> Adverbs such as 아주 and 너무 are quantifying adverbs that need to modify adjectives or other adverbs. They can't modify verbs!!
> 아주 바빠요. OR 너무 많이 먹어요.
> When they modify verbs directly, they have a special meaning:
> 그 사람 한국에 아주 가요.
> He is leaving for Korea for good.
> 너무 해요!
> You can't do this to me. Too mean!
> 그 아이는 텔레비전을 너무 봐요. 그리고 밥을 너무 먹어요.
> He watches too much TV; he eats too much.
> *This works only with certain verbs*

4. 많이             **a lot**
5. 조금/좀 [쪼금/ 쫌]   **a little bit**
6. 다              **all**
7. 거의 다           **almost**
8. 더              **more**

9. 벌써             **already**
10. 아직            **(not) yet**

11. 열심히          **diligently, (*work*) hard, whole-heartedly**
12. 오랫동안         **for a long time**
13. 잠깐 = 잠시       **for a short while; just a minute**
14. 방금            **just now**
15. 갑자기          **suddenly**

16. -(이)나         **as many as**

> 지난 is not an adverb, but it will come in handy as you express events and activities that occurred in the past, which you will learn in this lesson. Learn these very useful expressions!
>
> 지난 주에          last week
> 지난 주말에         last weekend
> 지난 학기에         last semester/quarter
> 지난 주 수요일에      last Wednesday
> 지난 해에 = 작년에    last year
> 지난 밤 = 어젯밤      last night

17. 그제 = 그저께      **the day before yesterday**
18. 어제 = 어저께      **yesterday**
19. 지난            **past, last**
20. 지난 해에 = 작년에  **last year**

21. 이 주일 전에       **two weeks ago**
22. 한 달 전에        **a month ago**

**23. 거의 다 했어요** means *almost done/almost finished*, and it has to be conjugated in the past/perfective tense.  You can substitute other verbs for 했어요.

**Vocabulary Exercise 1.  How?**
Fill in the blanks with an adverb from the box to complete a natural phrase (that describes the picture).  *Memorize some of these phrases-- they're useful!* ☺ Try to use all the adverbs.

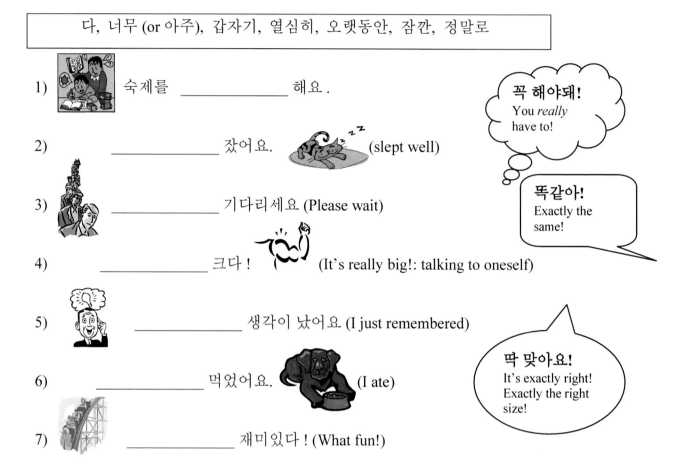

다, 너무 (or 아주), 갑자기, 열심히, 오랫동안, 잠깐, 정말로

1)  숙제를 _____ 해요 .

2)  _____ 잤어요.  (slept well)

3)  _____ 기다리세요 (Please wait)

4)  _____ 크다 !  (It's really big!: talking to oneself)

5)  _____ 생각이 났어요 (I just remembered)

6)  _____ 먹었어요.  (I ate)

7)  _____ 재미있다 ! (What fun!)

꼭 해야돼!
You *really* have to!

똑같아!
Exactly the same!

딱 맞아요!
It's exactly right!
Exactly the right size!

**Vocabulary Exercise 2.  Conversations**
Make up a sentence about your daily life using the following adverbs.  You partner should reply using an adverb – the same or opposite meaning, perhaps.

1)  벌써

2)  방금

3)  조금

4)  거의 다

5)  너무

6)  정말(로)

## Lesson 12 dialogue 제인 씨가 없어서 재미없었어요!

제인: **경수** 씨, 토요일 파티 어땠어요 [1]?

경수: 너무 너무 재미 없어서 [2] 집에 그냥 일찍 갔어요.

제인: 왜 재미가 없었어요?

경수: 사람들은 다 같이 자기 [3] 파트너하고 게임도 하고 춤도
췄어요. 그런데 제인 씨가 안 와서 [4] 나만 혼자 짝 [5] 이
없었어요! 그런데, 토요일에 김치는 잘 만들었어요?

제인: 네. 아주 많이 만들었어요. 김치 필요해요?

경수: 아니오. 방금 한국 마케트에서 샀어요.

제인: 그래요? 그런데 **경수** 씨, 월요일 시험공부 [6] 했어요?

경수: 네. 토요일에 집에 가서 [7] 오랫동안 공부했어요. 밤
12시까지 했고, 일요일에 조금 더 했어요. 숙제도 벌써
거의 다 했어요.

제인: 와 – **경수** 씨, 공부 정말 열심히 했네요 [8]. 나는 세
시간이나 [9] 했지만, 숙제가 많아서 아직 다 못 끝냈어요.

경수: 그럼 빨리 집에 가서 공부 더 해요. 이번 한국어 숙제는
정말 많아요!

[1] How was it?

[2] because it wasn't fun at all

[3] one's

[4] because you weren't there, Jane
[5] partner

[6] study for Monday's test

[7] went home and there...

[8] Wow, you really studied hard.

[9] as many as 3 hours

You are not familiar with some of the verb endings, but they are not glossed on purpose. Based on the meaning of 어땠어요, can you guess what they might mean?

**Comprehension Exercise.**
Based on the passage above answer the following questions.

지난 주일은 어땠어요? (Circle the correct answer or, T or F next to the sentence.)

1) 숙제가 많았지만 시험은 별로 없었어요. (T, F)

2) 한국어, 수학, 그리고 화학 시험을 봤어요. (T, F)

3) 주말에는 극장에 갔지만 돈이 없어서 외식은 안 했어요. (T, F)

4) 다음 주의 숙제는 아직 다 못 했어요. (T, F)

5) 대학 생활은 재미있고 힘이 별로 많이 안 들어요. (T, F)

## Lesson 12 grammar

### 1. Focus                                    Past tense

| -ㅆ어요 | polite past tense |
|---|---|

To form the past tense (or *perfective)* of verbs and adjectives (for completed events), add
ㅆ어 after the 어/아 form of the verbs and adjectives.  To indicate politeness, you can add 요.

| Citation Form | Stem | 어 form | Perfective | Politeness |
|---|---|---|---|---|
| 가다 | 가 | [가 | ㅆ어 | 요] = 갔어요 |
| 작다 | 작 | [작아 | ㅆ어 | 요] = 작았어요 |
| 있다 | 있 | [있어 | ㅆ어 | 요] = 있었어요 |
| 하다 | 하 | [하여/해 | ㅆ어 | 요] = 했어요 |
| 이다 | 이 | [이어/여 | ㅆ어 | 요] = 였어요, 이었어요 |

> Koreans may think of it as adding 았, but that's not exactly true!

> Some consider 갔, for example, altogether the past or perfective stem.

The Korean "past tense" is not quite like the English past tense.  It expresses whether an
activity is *completed* and not necessarily whether it occurred in the past:

| 숙제 다 **했어요**. | I *did* all the homework. *or* I *have done* all the homework. |
|---|---|
| 그 때 거기 **있었어요**. | I *was* there at that time. |
| 지금까지 거기 **있었어요**. | I *was* there until now. |
| 저는 학생**이었어요**. | I *was* a student. |
| 저는 지금까지 학생**이었어요**. | I *have been* a student up until now. |

어제, 지난 (last), 작년 (last year) are adverbs that indicate the past tense.

| 어제 뭐 했어요? | What did you do yesterday? |
|---|---|

작년에 시애틀에 있었어요?       Were you in Seattle last year?

The form 이었어요 is used after a noun that ends in a consonant and 였어요 after a noun that ends in a vowel:

저는 학생**이었어요**.               I *was* a student.

저 사람은 제 친구**였어요**.        That person *was/used to be* my friend (but not any more).

Be *extra* careful *not* to say 이엤어요!!

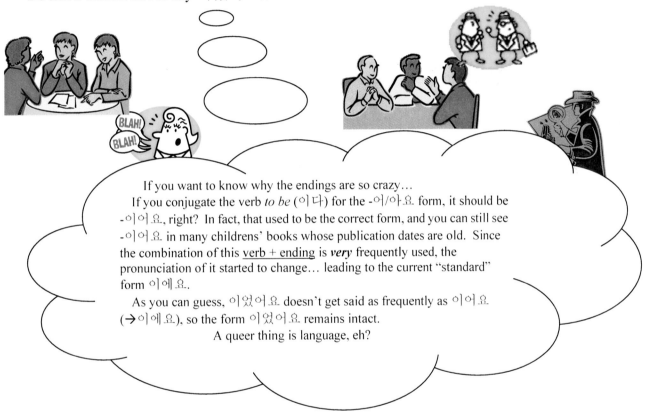

If you want to know why the endings are so crazy…
   If you conjugate the verb *to be* (이다) for the -어/아요 form, it should be -이어요, right? In fact, that used to be the correct form, and you can still see -이어요 in many childrens' books whose publication dates are old. Since the combination of this verb + ending is *very* frequently used, the pronunciation of it started to change… leading to the current "standard" form 이에요.
   As you can guess, 이었어요 doesn't get said as frequently as 이어요 (→이에요), so the form 이었어요 remains intact.
   A queer thing is language, eh?

 Make an effort to pronounce 쌍시옷 (ㅆ) in the past tense *heavily*, as 먹어서요 and 먹었어요 mean two different things. Also remember that the polite past (or perfective) ending *always* ends in -어요, and *never* -아요.

## On the side

Rather than having the past-present-future *tense system* like English, Korean verbs make a distinction between whether an activity is completed (perfect) or on-going (imperfect). To ease your understanding, however, we will call the present imperfect forms "present tense."

## 2. Other Grammar Notes

### 1. -고, -지만, -어서/-아서　　　Connecting past tense phrases with

When a series of completed events are connected with –고 (*and*), only the final predicate is required to have the past tense/perfective marker ㅆ. Any preceding verbs and adjectives may either be conjugated in the past tense, or be left without a tense marker. This difference does not have a big affect on the meaning of the sentence.

토요일에는 극장에 **가고** 외식도 했어요.

***OR*** 토요일에는 극장에 **갔고** 외식도 했어요.
I *went* to the movie and also ate out.

The connector –지만 (*but*) is attached to a verb with the past tense marker if the action is completed. (The sentence-final verb may also have past tense marking.)

~~토요일에 극장에 **가지만** 외식은 안 했어요.~~

토요일에 극장에 **갔지만** 외식은 안 했어요.
I went to the movie on Saturday but did not eat out.

When sentences are connected with the shortened marker –어서/아서, the past tense/perfective marker ㅆ can *only* be used in the sentence-final verbs/adjective.

어제는 시험이 두 개 있었어요. 그래서 바빴어요.

어제는 시험이 두개 **있어서** 바빴어요.
I was busy because I had two tests yesterday.

공부를 많이 했어요. 그래서 시험을 잘 봤어요.

공부를 많이 **해서** 시험을 잘 봤어요.
I did well on the test because I studied hard.

> It will be easier for you if you just remember that **and** and **but** can "take" the past tense but *so* cannot. Remember this mnemonic phrase:
>
> for past tense: 했고, 했지만, 해서

### 2. -은/는 and -이/가　　　Use of the markers (review)

Another use of the topic vs. subject marker to learn is when they appear in the [Topic, subject + predicate] structure. Topic marker 은/는 provides a topic to discuss (*as for…, speaking of…*). It can be attached to the subject, object, place, and time nouns in the sentence:

대학 생활은 힘이 들어요.　　　College life, it's tough.

| | |
|---|---|
| 한국학은 숙제가 많았어요. | (As for) Korea studies, there was a lot of homework. |
| 어제는 아주 바빴어요. | (As for) yesterday, I was very busy. |
| 여기는 항상 바빠요. | (As for) this place, it's always busy. |
| 저는 생선은 안 먹어요. | (As for) fish, I don't eat (it). |

-은/는 often adds the sense of ***contrast*** if more than one noun is listed:

저는 가고 **제시카**는 안 가요.
Me, I am going, and *Jessica* is not going.

저는 맥주는 마시지만 콜라는 못 마셔요.
Me, I drink *beer*, but I cannot drink *coke*.

 Though 이/가 is called the 'subject marker,' it is not *always* used to mark the subject. Other markers like –만 (*only*), -도 (*also*) and even -은/는 mark the subject when there is some additional meaning attached to the subject noun – and this is very often the case!

| | |
|---|---|
| 대학 생활은 힘이 들어요. | *College life* is tough. (*Speaking of* college life, it is tough.) |
| 대학 생활이 힘이 들어요. | *College life* is tough. (Answer to *What's* tough?) |
| 대학 생활만 힘이 들어요. | College life alone is tough. |
| 대학 생활도 힘이 들어요. | College life also is tough. |

## 3. Use of the marker -도

You learned in earlier lessons that the marker -도 is used to *list* additional items.

지우개가 있어요. 그리고 펜**도** 있어요.
There is an eraser. There is a pen, *too*.

You can also use -도 to list additional events. If the verb happens to be one of the compound 하다 verbs, 도 appears where you would expect the object marker 을/를.

토요일에는 극장에 갔고 외식**도** 했어요.
Saturday I went to a movie and (also) ate out.

Sometimes -도 *anticipates* a list and thus *emphasizes* the listed items.

지난 주에는 숙제**도** 많았고 시험**도** 3 개나 있었어요.
Last week I had tons of homework, and I *also* had three (!) exams.

그리고 숙제**도** 벌써 거의 다 했어요
I have *also/even* already almost finished the homework.


## 4. -이나    *as many as ...*

The marker -이나 means *as many as...* in sentences like 손을 세 번이나 씻었어요!
*I washed my hands (as many as) three times!* It marks some surprise as to the (large) number of things/happenings. Use -이나 when the preceding noun ends in a consonant and -나 when it ends in a vowel.

이번 학기에 수업을 다섯 과목**이나** 들어요.   (과목: subject, counter for classes)
She's taking as many as 5 classes this quarter.

**사이몬**은 사탕을 열 개**나** 먹었어요.
Simon ate *ten* candies!

숙제를 세 시간**이나** 했어요.
I did homework for *three* hours!


## Language Point   The shape of adverbs

You have seen many time adverbs with various shapes (어제, 오늘, 가끔, 별로, etc.).  You also have seen adverbs that are *derived* from a noun or an adjective.

정말로 (정말 + 로: truthfully)
큰 소리로 (큰 소리 + 로: loudly)
많이 (많 + 이: a lot)
바쁘게 (바쁘 + 게: busily)
열심히 (열심 + 히: diligently, whole-heartedly)

There are systematic ways to derive adverbs from other parts of speech, but there are also many independent adverbs.  It is important that you learn them as you encounter them.

## Lesson 12 exercises

### Exercise 1.      Reading practice

Read the dialogue aloud once. As you are reading aloud, pay attention to the pronunciation of each word and how it is changed when connected with other words. Then read it one more time silently. This time, force yourself to move your eyes *fast* and recognize word shapes rather than consonant and vowel combinations. (You need to have memorized the vocabulary for this practice. If you are not sure about the meaning of one or two words, read on and try to guess the meanings from the context. If you do not recognize more than 3-4 words, go back to the **Vocabulary** section and study the words first.)

### Exercise 2.      Conjugation practice

Change the verbs and adjectives in the dialogue into the *polite present tense*. Then change all the predicates back to the *past/perfective tense*.

### Exercise 3.      거의 다 ... 했어요 (Almost done!)

What have the following people *almost* finished doing? Make up a sentence to explain.

1) **타일러**, 커피, 마시다

2) **게일**, 신문, 읽다 (신문: newspaper)

3) **요한**, 콜라, 마시다

4) **안젤로**, 핏자, 만들다

**Exercise 4.          and/but/so**
Make each pair of sentences into one using an appropriate connector-suffix.

1)  오늘은 시험이 없어요. 그리고 숙제도 없어요.

2)  어제는 집에서 청소를 했어요. 그리고 빨래도 했어요.

3)  돈이 없어요. 그래서 선물을 못 사요.

4)  지난 학기에 한국어를 배웠어요. 그래서 한국어를 잘 해요.

5)  한국 사람은 저녁에 목욕해요.  그리고 미국 사람은 아침에 샤워해요.

6)  어제 바빴어요. 그래서 친구를 못 만났어요.

7)  돈이 없었어요. 그렇지만 외식을 했어요.

8)  차를 닦았어요. 그래서 예뻐요.

9)  늦게 (late) 일어났어요. 그래서 이빨을 안 닦았어요.


**Exercise 5.          Complete the passage**
Complete the sentence with the correct verb in the polite past/perfective tense or the present tense.

안녕하세요? 제 이름은 미미(이다)_____. 저는 한국말을 조금 (알다)

_____.   지난 주말에 저는 자전거를 (타다)_____. 기타도

(치다)_____. 저는 영화도 (보다) _____. 아주 (바쁘다)

_____.    저는 지난 주말에 또, 한국 친구들도 (만나다)_____.

한국 친구들하고 같이 한국 식당에 (가다)_____. 김치하고 불고기를 (먹다)

_____. 그리고 집에 10 시에 (가다) _____. 재미있는 하루* (이다)

_____.

*하루: one day

**Exercise 6.　　　The difference between you and me**
Using the chart below, try to discover as many differences and similarities as you can between you and your partner. Then write a sentence about them as shown in the example.

*Example*:　　　A 씨는 농구를 잘 하지만 나는 농구를 잘 못 해요. OR
　　　　　　　　A 씨도 농구를 잘 하고 나도 농구를 잘 해요.

|  | 나 | 파트너 |
|---|---|---|
| 차가 있어요? | O | X |
| 피아노를 잘 쳐요? |  |  |
| 도서관에 매일 가요? |  |  |
| 지난 주말에 파티에 갔어요? |  |  |
| 지난 주말에 공부했어요? |  |  |
| Your own question |  |  |

**Exercise 7.　　　-은/는 vs. -이/가 vs. -을/를**
Complete the sentences with the correct markers – 은/는 or -이/가.

1) 저＿＿ 수학＿＿ 안 좋아하지만, 물리(학)＿＿ 좋아해요.

2) 저＿＿ 월요일에 수업＿＿ 세 개 있어요.

3) 저＿＿ 오늘 수업＿＿ 세 개 있고, 토니＿＿ 수업＿＿ 다섯 개 있어요.

4) 돈＿＿ 있어요? -- 아니오, 돈＿＿ 없지만, 크레디트 카드＿＿ 있어요.

5) 화장실＿＿ 어디에요? -- 화장실＿＿ 저기 오른쪽에 있어요. (화장실: restroom)

6) 화장실＿＿ 오른쪽에 부엌＿＿ 왼쪽에 있어요. (부엌: kitchen)

**Exercise 8.　　　-이나**
Make up a sentence about yourself or someone you know using the words below and -이나.
*Example*:　A: 스타워즈 몇 번 봤어요? B: 세 번이나 봤어요.

1) How many hours, Korean homework

2) How many times, call your girl/boyfriend

3) How many times, call your mother per week

4) How many CD's, have (개)

233

5) How many times, eat Korean food

6) How many people, take Korean class

7) (make your own)

**Exercise 9.**       **Reading Practice**

Read the following passage and circle all the adverbs you find. Then make up sentences of your own for each adverb.

### 나의 주말             My weekend

>     지난 주말은 아주 바빴어요. 숙제도 많았고 시험도 3 개[1]나 있었어요. 월요일에는 한국어 시험, 수요일에는 수학 시험, 그리고 목요일에는 화학 시험을 봤어요. 경제학하고 한국학은 숙제가 많았어요. 정말로 바쁜[2] 일주일이었지만, 주말에는 좀 괜찮았어요. 토요일에는 친구들하고 극장에 가고 외식도 했어요. 일요일에는 집에서 쉬었어요. 다음 주에도 숙제가 많지만, 시험은 없어요. 그리고 숙제도 벌써 거의 다 했어요. 대학 생활은 힘이 많이 들지만 재미있어요![2]

[1] general counter for things

[2] busy (modifying form)

[3] 힘이 많이 들다: really tough

---

*Life*          생활

생활 is a noun that means *life*, usually, the daily life one experiences belonging to a particular community. It is mostly used as part of a compound. Can you guess the meaning of the following compounds?

대학 생활, 학교 생활, 미국 생활, 한국 생활, 유학 생활 (유학: study abroad)

## Language Point *Idioms*

It is important to learn as many as associated idioms when you learn a new word.
Can you guess what the following expressions might mean?

조수아는 힘이 좋아요

빌은 오늘 힘이 없어요.

이 일에 벤자민이 힘을 많이 썼어요.

힘: energy, strength          일: day (suffix); one; job, task

## Lesson 12          Checkpoint

대화 1          주희의 유학 생활

경옥:  **주희** 씨, 안녕하세요? 언제 서울에 돌아왔어요?

주희:  어제요. 방학이라서 잠깐 서울에 나왔어요.

경옥:  미국 유학 생활은 어땠어요?

주희:  많이 힘들었지만 재미있었어요.

경옥:  석사[43]는 언제 끝나요?

주희:  사실은[44] 지난 학기에 석사가 벌써 끝났어요.

경옥:  어머, 축하해요.[45] 서울에 언제까지 있어요?

주희:  오랫동안은 못 있어요. 다음 학기가 다음 달에 시작해요.

경옥:  **주희** 씨가 미국가기 전에 우리 언제 한 번 만나요!

주희:  좋아요. 전화해요!

---

[43] Master's program, degree (short for 석사 과정)
[44] actually
[45] congratulations

## 대화 2      철이의 데이트

준이: **철이** 씨, 어제 **순이** 씨랑 데이트해서 피곤해요?

철이: 네, 조금. 그렇지만 기분은 정말 좋아요.

준이: 어디 가서 뭐 했어요?

철이: 영화를 보고 나서 저녁을 먹고 공원을 산책했어요.

준이: 공원에서 산책만 했어요?

철이: 네, 세시간이나 공원을 산책해서 힘들었지만 아주 재미있었어요 .

준이: 거짓말![46]

철이: 사실은 어제 **순이** 씨 손을 잡았어요.

준이: 손만 잡았어요?

철이: 네. 정말로 손만 잡았어요.

## 읽기 1      동현이, 그리고 눈

어제 갑자기 눈[47]이 왔어요. 눈이 우리 집 마당[48]을 거의 다 덮었어요. 어제 미도리는 눈을 처음 봤어요. **동현이**는 아주 오랫동안 눈을 쳐다보았어요.[49] 나는 **동현이**하고 마당으로 나갔어요. **동현이**는 너무 좋아했어요. 우리는 손을 꼭 잡고 눈을 구경했어요.[50] 나는 열심히 눈사람을 만들었어요. 그런데 눈이 적어서 눈사람이 작았어요. 눈사람은 **동현이**같았어요. 저녁에 **동현이**는 피곤해서 일찍 잤어요. 어제 밤에 **동현이**가 안 울어서 잠을 잘 잤어요. 어제는 **동현이**하고 정말 재미있었어요.

---

[46] lie
[47] snow
[48] yard
[49] 쳐다보다 to stare
[50] to see (the sight of something)

236

## 읽기 2          이번 주말

이번 주말은 정말 바빴어요. 전공 숙제도 많았고 한국어 숙제도 많았어요. 그리고 아르바이트도 있었어요. 전공 숙제는 오늘까지여서 일요일에 다 했어요. 한국어 숙제는 너무 많아서 아직 다 못 했어요. 그렇지만 오늘 저녁때 열심히 해서 다 끝내고 내일 낼 거에요.[51] 갑자기 공부를 많이 해서 좀 힘들었어요. 사실 이번 학기에 한국어 수업을 두 개나 들어요. 그래서 매일 한국어 공부를 네 시간이나 해요. 많이 어렵고 힘들지만 저는 한국어가 정말로 좋아요.

---

[51] will submit

# 쉬어갑시다!
# LET'S TAKE A BREAK!

# CHAPTER 3.5    숫자 세기
## Counters

## Grammar Notes

### 1. Counters
Counters are words used to mark the type of noun being counted. They are attached to *the Native Korean number*.

Counting items in Korean takes a particular construction:

> NOUN + NUMBER + COUNTER
>
> **맥주 한 병**        *one bottle of beer*

Interestingly, there are counters for many other kinds of noun, or noun class: some of them are based on shape or other semantic similarity.  See what helps you to memorize each counter's usage:

| Counter | Things counted | Examples | |
|---|---|---|---|
| 개 | items | 사과 한 개 | an apple |
| 사람, 명, 분 | people | 친구 두 사람, 두 명, 두 분 | two friends (honorific) |
| 잔, 컵 | glasses, cups of… | 커피 세 잔, 주스 네 잔/컵 | three cups of coffee four glasses of juice |
| 병 | bottles of… | 맥주 다섯 병 | five bottles of beer |
| 대 | computers, cars | 차 여섯 대 | six cars |
| 상자 | boxes of… | 사과 일곱 상자 | seven boxes of apples |
| 권 | volumes, books | 책 여덟 권 | eight books |
| 장 | sheets (of…) | 종이 아홉 장, CD 열 장 | nine sheets of paper ten CD's |
| 마리 | animals | 개 열한 마리 | eleven dogs |
| 살 | *for* age | 스무 살 | twenty years old |

239

## 2. Native Korean Numbers (Review)

Remember that some native Korean numbers have alternate forms such as 하나 and 한. The shortened forms (e.g. 한) are adjective forms of the full forms (e.g. 하나). They are used when followed by a counter or a noun.

| | | |
|---|---|---|
| one = 하나 | vs. | one person = 한 사람 |
| two = 둘 | vs. | two people = 두 사람 |
| three = 셋 | vs. | three people = 세 사람 |
| four = 넷 | vs. | four people = 네 사람 |
| | ... | |
| twenty = 스물 | vs. | twenty people = 스무 사람 |
| twenty one = 스물 하나 | vs. | twenty one people = 스물 한 사람 |

Can you write the following numbers as native Korean numbers?

| Arabic Numeral | 한글 | Arabic Numeral | 한글 |
|---|---|---|---|
| 1* | 하나, 한 | 20* | |
| 2* | | 21* | |
| 3* | | 30 | |
| 4* | | 40 | 마흔 |
| 5 | | 50 | |
| 6 | | 60 | |
| 7 | | 70 | |
| 8 | | 80 | |
| 9 | | 90 | |
| 10 | 열 | 100 | 백 |
| 11* | | 1000 | |
| 12* | | 10,000 | |
| 13* | | 100,000 | 십만 |
| 14* | | 1,000,000 | |
| 15 | | 10,000,000 | |
| 19 | | 100,000,000 | 일억 |

* Asterisk marks numbers that have alternate forms.

## Exercises

**Exercise 1. Write the proper number and counter for each picture.**

1) 개 _____

2) 사람 _____

3) 책 _____

4) 우유 _____

5) 차 _____

6) 쵸콜렛 _____(box)

7) 사과 _____

8) 차 _____

9) 종이 _____

**Exercise 2. Fill in the blanks with appropriate counters.**

A.  오늘 아침에는 오렌지 주스를 한 (        ) 마시고 배를 두 (        ) 먹었어요.
                                              glass

점심에는 햄버거 한 (        )하고 콜라 한 (        )을 마셨어요. 간식 시간에 친구
                                                        bottle

세 (        )하고 초콜렛 한 (        )를 다 먹었어요. 그리고 서점에서 책을 두
                                          box

(        ) 샀어요. 또 종이도 백 (        ) 샀어요.

B.  내 친구는 집이 아주 커요. 방이 다섯 (        )가 있어요. 가족은 네 (        )이에요.

차도 많아요. 모두 네 (        )나 있어요. 그리고 컴퓨터도 두 (        ) 가 있어요.

내 친구의 동생은 개를 좋아해요. 그래서 개가 세 (        ) 나 있어요. 고양이 (cat)도

두 (        )나 있어요.


## For those who are motivated...

| More counters | | Examples | |
|---|---|---|---|
| 자루 | pencils, pens | 연필 한 자루 | a pencil |
| 봉지 | bags of… | 국수 한 봉지 | a bag of noodle |
| 그루 | trees | 나무 한 그루 | a tree |
| 송이 | flowers, grapes | 장미 한 송이 | a rose |
| 다발 | bunches of (flowers) | 꽃 한 다발 | a bunch of flowers |
| 벌 | clothes | 옷 한 벌 | a piece of clothes |
| 켤레 | pairs of shoes | 신발 한 켤레 | a pair of shoes |
| 채 | houses, buildings | 집 한 채 | a house |
| 조각, 쪽 | pieces, slices of… | 피자 한 조각 | a slice of pizza |
| 그릇, 공기 | bowls of… | 밥 한 그릇 | a bowl of rice |
| 포기 | heads (of cabbage) | 배추 한 포기 | a head of Nappa cabbage |
| 단 | bunches of (vegetables) | 파 한 단 | a bunch of green onion |
| 모 | lumps of (tofu) | 두부 한 모 | a lump of tofu |
| 덩어리/ 덩이 | loaves, lumps of… (bread, cooked rice) | 빵 한 덩어리 | a lump of bread |
| 쌍 | couple, pair (people, animals) | 부부 한 쌍 | a couple (husband and wife) |

# ENGLISH~KOREAN GLOSSARY

(Please see referenced lessons for usage
information and models)

**a little bit** 조금/좀 [쪼금/ 쫌] *Ch3 L12 vocab*
**a lot** 많이 *Ch3 L12 vocab*
**a month ago** 한 달 전에 *Ch3 L12 vocab*
**A.M. (around 7 A.M. ~ 11 A.M.)** 오전 *Ch1.5 B vocab*
**about, approximately** -쯤 *Ch 2 L8 vocab*
**abundant, be a lot** 많아요 많고 [만코] 많아서 많다 [만타] *Ch3 L11 vocab*
**across** 건너편, 맞은 편 *Ch1 L4 vocab*
**after** -고 나서 *Ch3 L9 other*
**again, what else (adverb)** 또 *Ch1 L3 vocab*
**age, *counter*** 살 *Ch3.5 vocab*
**air-conditioner** 에어콘 *Ch 2 L5 point*
**all** 다 *Ch3 L12 vocab*
**all together (adv.)** 모두 *Ch2.5 vocab*
**almost** 거의 *Ch 2 L7 vocab*
**almost all** 거의 다 *Ch3 L12 vocab*
**already** 벌써 *Ch3 L12 vocab*
**also (noun particle)** -도 *Ch1 L3 vocab*
**always** 항상 *Ch 2 L7 vocab*
**American (person)** 미국 사람 *Prelim. I vocab*
**and** -고 verb connector *Ch3 L9 other*
**and** 그리고 conjunction *Ch 2 L8 other*
**and** -하고 noun marker *Ch1 L3 vocab*
**and then** -고 나서 *Ch3 L9 other*
**animal, *counter for*** 마리 *Ch3.5 vocab*
**apartment** 아파트 *Ch2 L5 vocab*
**April** 사월 *Prelim. H vocab*
**around** 주위 *Ch1 L4 vocab*
**art** 미학 *Ch 2 L8 point*
**Art/painting** 미술 *Ch 2 L8 supp*
**as many as** -(이)나 *Ch3 L12 vocab*
**at (time)** 에 *Ch 2 L7 other*
**August** 팔월 *Prelim. H vocab*
**aunt on father's side** 고모; 고모부 *Ch2.5 vocab*
**aunt on mother's side** 이모; 이모부 *Ch2.5 vocab*
**baby** 아기 [애기] *Ch2.5 vocab*
**baby-sits** 아기를 봐요 아기를 보고 아기를 봐서 아기를 보다 *Ch2.5 point*
**back; behind** 뒤 *Ch1 L4 vocab*
**bad** 나빠요 나쁘고 나빠서 나쁘다 *Ch3 L11 vocab*
**bag** 가방 *Ch1 L2 vocab*
**bag, *counter for*** 봉지 *Ch3.5 vocab*
**ball field** 운동장 *Ch2 L5 vocab*

**bank** 은행 *Ch2 L5 vocab*
**barely** 별로 *Ch 2 L7 vocab*
**baseball -- plays baseball** 야구해요 야구하고 야구해서 야구하다 *Ch 2 L6 vocab*
**basketball -- plays basketball** 농구해요 농구하고 농구해서 농구하다 *Ch 2 L6 vocab*
**bathe** 목욕해요 목욕하고 [모교카고] 목욕해서[모교캐서] 목욕하다 [모교카다] *Ch 2 L6 vocab* [모교캐요]
**be how** 어때요 (irregular) 어떻고 [어떠코] 어때서 어떻다 *Ch3 L11 vocab*
**be only a little** 적어요 적고 적어서 적다 *Ch3 L11 vocab*
**before doing ...** -기 전에 *Ch3 L10 other*
**behind; back** 뒤 *Ch1 L4 vocab*
**below** 아래 *Ch1 L4 vocab*
**beside; next to** 옆 *Ch1 L4 vocab*
**between** 사이 *Ch1 L4 vocab*
**bicycle** 자전거 *Ch1 L3 vocab*
**big** 커요 크고 커서 크다 *Ch3 L11 vocab*
**Biology** 생물학 *Ch 2 L8 supp*
**birthday** 생일 *Prelim. H vocab*
**book** 책 *Ch1 L2 vocab*
**bookstore** 서점 *Ch2 L5 vocab*
**bottle** 병 *Ch3.5 vocab*
**bowls *counter*** 그릇, 공기 *Ch3.5 vocab*
**box, *counter*** 상자 *Ch3.5 vocab*
**breakfast** 아침(밥) *bonus*
**breaks (e.g., a cup)** 깨요 깨고 깨서 깨다 *Ch3 L10 vocab*
**British (person)** 영국 사람 *Prelim. I vocab*
**brother -- female's older brother** 오빠 *Ch2.5 vocab*
**brother -- female's older brother who is older than another older brother** 큰 오빠 *Ch2.5 vocab*
**brother -- female's older brother who is younger than another brother** 작은 오빠 *Ch2.5 vocab*
**brother -- male's older brother** 형 *Ch2.5 vocab*
**brother -- male's older brother who is older than another older brother** 큰형 *Ch2.5 vocab*
**brother -- male's older brother who is younger than another brother** 작은 형 *Ch2.5 vocab*
**brother -- younger brother** 남동생 *Ch2.5 vocab*
**brothers -- male siblings** 형제 *Ch2.5 vocab*
**building** 건물, 빌딩 *Ch1 L4 vocab*

**bunches of (flowers) counter** 다발  *Ch3.5 vocab*
**bunches of (vegetables)** *counter* 단  *Ch3.5 vocab*
**bus** 버스  *Ch1 L3 vocab*
**Business and Administration** 경영학  *Ch 2 L8 supp*
**busy** 바빠요 바쁘고 바빠서 바쁘다 *Ch3 L11 vocab*
**but** -지만 verb connector  *Ch3 L9 other*
**but** 그렇지만 conjunction  *Ch 2 L8 other* [그러치만]
**buys, purchases** 사요 사고 사서 사다 *Ch3 L10 vocab*
**by oneself** 혼자  *Ch2 L5 vocab*
**cafeteria; diner** 식당  *Ch2 L5 vocab*
**camera** 카메라  *Ch1 L2 vocab*
**can't** 못  *Ch3 L9 other*
**Canada** 캐나다  *Prelim. I vocab*
**Canadian (person)** 캐나다 사람  *Prelim. I vocab*
**candy** 사탕  *Ch1 L3 vocab*
**car** 차  *bonus*
**cat** 고양이  *Ch2.5 vocab*
**catches a bus** 잡아요 잡고 잡아서 잡다 *Ch3 L9 vocab*
**CD (compact disk)** 시디  *Ch1 L3 vocab* [씨디]
**cellular phone** 핸드폰  *Ch1 L3 vocab*
**chair** 의자  *Ch1 L1 vocab*
**chalkboard** 칠판  *Ch1 L1 vocab*
**change of focus** -은/는  *Ch2 L5 other*
**Chemistry** 화학  *Ch 2 L8 supp*
**chewing gum** 껌  *Ch1 L3 vocab*
**children** 아이들/애들  *Ch2.5 vocab*
**China** 중국  *Prelim. I vocab*
**Chinese (language)** 중국어  *Prelim. I vocab*
**Chinese (person)** 중국 사람  *Prelim. I vocab*
**chocolate** 초컬릿, 초컬렛, 초콜렛, 초콜릿  *Ch2 L4 vocab*
**class (course)** 수업  *Ch 2 L8 vocab*
**classroom** 교실  *Ch1 L1 vocab*
**cleans (house, rooms)** 청소해요 청소하고 청소해서 청소하다 *Ch 2 L6 vocab*
**climbs mountains** 등산해요 등산하고 등산해서 등산하다 *Ch 2 L6 vocab*
**clock, watch** 시계  *Ch1 L1 vocab* [시게]
**closes** 닫아요 닫고 [닥꼬, 닫꼬] 닫아서 닫다 *Ch3 L9 vocab*
**clothes,** *counter for* 벌  *Ch3.5 vocab*
**coffee shop** 커피숍  *Ch2 L5 vocab*
**college student** 대학생  *Ch 2 L8 vocab*
**comes** 와요 오고 와서 오다 *Ch3 L10 vocab*
**comes home, comes in** 들어와요 들어오고 들어와서 들어오다 *Ch3 L10 vocab*

**comes out(side)** 나와요 나오고 나와서 나오다 *Ch3 L10 vocab*
**comfortable** 편해요 편하고 편해서 편하다 *Ch3 L11 vocab*
**computer** 컴퓨터  *Ch1 L1 vocab*
**computer lab** 컴퓨터 랩  *Ch2 L5 vocab*
**Computer Science** 컴퓨터 공학  *Ch 2 L8 supp*
**computers, cars,** *counter* 대  *Ch3.5 vocab*
**consonant** 자음  *Prelim. D vocab*
**consonant at end of writtem syllable** 받침  *Prelim. D vocab*
**convenient** 편리해요 편리하고 [펼리아고] 편리해서 [펼리애서] 편리하다 *Ch3 L11 vocab* [펼리애요]
**cookies, crackers, chips** 과자  *Ch1 L3 vocab*
**cooks** 요리해요 요리하고 요리해서 요리하다 *Ch 2 L6 vocab*
**copier** 복사기  *Ch1 L1 supp*
**correct, right** 맞아요 맞고 [막꼬, 맏꼬] 맞아서 맞다 *Ch3 L11 vocab*
**counter for animals** 마리  *Ch2.5 vocab*
*counter for* **sacks pencils, pens** 자루  *Ch3.5 vocab*
**country** 나라  *Prelim. I vocab*
**counts** 세요 세고 세서, 세어서 [서서, 시어서] 세다 [세다, 시다] *Ch3 L10 vocab* [서요], [세요]
**couple, pair,** *counter for* **people, animals** 쌍  *Ch3.5 vocab*
**cousin** 사촌  *Ch2.5 vocab*
**crackers, cookies, chips** 과자  *Ch1 L3 vocab*
**credit card** 신용카드, 크레딧 카드, 크레디트 카드 *Ch1 L3 vocab*
**cries** 울어요 울고 울어서 울다 *Ch3 L9 vocab*
**cup** 컵  *Ch3.5 vocab*
**dad** 아빠  *Ch2.5 vocab*
**daughter** 딸  *Ch2.5 vocab*
**dawn, early morning (around 3, 4 A.M. ~ 6 A.M.)** 새벽  *Ch1.5 B vocab*
**day before yesterday** 그제, 그제께  *Ch3 L12 vocab*
**day time (around 11:30 A.M. ~ 2:30 P.M.)** 점심  *Ch1.5 B vocab*
**day(s) of the week** 요일  *Ch 2 L8 vocab*
**December** 십 이월  *Prelim. H vocab*
**department store** 백화점  *Ch2 L5 vocab* [배콰점]
**desk** 책상  *Ch1 L1 vocab* [책쌍]
**different** 달라요 다르고 달라서 다르다 *Ch3 L11 vocab*

**diligently, (*work*) hard, whole-heartedly** 열심히 *Ch3 L12 vocab*

**dinner** 저녁(밥) *bonus*

**diner; cafeteria** 식당 *Ch2 L5 vocab*

**dishes (does)** 설거지해요 설거지하고 설거지해서 설거지하다 *Ch 2 L6 vocab*

**disliked** 싫어요 싫고 [실코] 싫어서 싫다 [실타] *Ch3 L11 vocab*

**dislikes** 싫어해요 싫어하고 싫어해서 싫어하다 *Ch3 L10 vocab*

**does** 해요 하고 해서 하다 *Ch 2 L6 vocab*

**dog** 개 *Ch2.5 vocab*

**door** 문 *Ch1 L1 vocab*

**dormitory** 기숙사 *Ch2 L5 vocab*

**draws** 그려요 그리고 그려서 그리다 *Ch3 L10 vocab*

**drinks** 마셔요 마시고 마셔서, 마시어서 마시다 *Ch3 L10 vocab*

**drug store** 약국 *Ch2 L5 vocab*

**during vacation** 방학 때(에) *Ch 2 L7 vocab*

**eat** 먹어요 먹고 먹어서 먹다 *Ch3 L9 vocab*

**eats out** 외식해요 외식하고 외식해서 외식하다 *Ch 2 L6 vocab*

**Economics** 경제학 *Ch 2 L8 supp*

**eight (native Korean vocab.)** 여덟 *Prelim. G vocab*

**eight (Sino-Korean vocab.)** 팔 *Prelim. G vocab*

**eighth** 여덟째 *Prelim. G vocab*

**eighty (native Korean vocab.)** 여든 *Prelim. G vocab*

**Electrical Engineering** 전자 공학 *Ch 2 L8 supp*

**email (address)** 이메일 *Ch1 L2 vocab*

**ends** 끝내요 (intransitive) 끝나고 끝나서 끝나다 *Ch3 L10 vocab* [끈나요]

**ends** 끝내요 (transitive) 끝내고 끝내서 끝내다 *Ch3 L10 vocab* [끈내요]

**English (language)** 영어 *Prelim. I vocab*

**eraser** 지우개 *Ch1 L2 vocab*

**evening (around 5, 6 P.M. ~ 8 P.M.)** 저녁 *Ch1.5 B vocab*

**every week, each week** 매주 *Ch 2 L8 vocab*

**everyday, each day** 매일 *Ch 2 L7 vocab*

**excuse me** 실례합니다 실례하고 실례해서 실례하다 *Prelim. F vocab*

**exercise (sports)** 운동해요 운동하고 운동해서 운동하다 *Ch 2 L6 vocab*

**exists; has** 있어요 있고 있어서 있다 *Ch1 L1 vocab* [이써요]

**family** 가족 *Ch2.5 vocab*

**father** 아버지 *Ch2.5 vocab*

**February** 이월 *Prelim. H vocab*

**fifth** 다섯째 *Prelim. G vocab*

**fifty (native Korean vocab.)** 쉰 *Prelim. G vocab*

**fights, has an argument** 싸워요 싸우고 싸워서 싸우다 *Ch3 L10 vocab*

**find; look for; withdraw (money)** 찾아요 찾고 찾아서 찾다 *Ch3 L9 vocab*

**finishes** 끝내요 (transitive) 끝내고 끝내서 끝내다 *Ch3 L10 vocab* [끈내요]

**first** 첫째 *Prelim. G vocab*

**first (day of month)** 일일 *Prelim. H vocab*

**first time** 첫번째 *Prelim. G vocab*

**five (native Korean vocab.)** 다섯 *Prelim. G vocab*

**five (Sino-Korean vocab.)** 오 *Prelim. G vocab*

**flaky person not serious about their studies** 날라리 *Ch 2 L8 point*

**flowers, grapes, *counter for*** 송이 *Ch3.5 vocab*

**for a long time** 오랫동안 *Ch3 L12 vocab*

**for a short while; just a minute** 잠깐 *Ch3 L12 vocab*

**forty (native Korean vocab.)** 마흔 *Prelim. G vocab*

**forty (Sino-Korean vocab.)** 사 십 *Prelim. G vocab*

**four (native Korean vocab.)** 넷, 네 *Prelim. G vocab*

**four (Sino-Korean vocab.)** 사 *Prelim. G vocab*

**fourth** 넷째 *Prelim. G vocab*

**France** 프랜스, 불란서, 프랑스, 프랑스 *Prelim. I point*

**free time, to have (adj.)** 한가해요 한가하고 한가해서 한가하다 *Ch3 L11 vocab*

**French (language)** 프랑스어, 불어 *Prelim. I vocab*

**French (person)** 프랑스 사람 *Prelim. I vocab*

**Friday** 금요일 *Ch1.5 A vocab*

**friend** 친구 *Ch1 L2 vocab* [칭구

**from (time)** -부터 *Ch3 L10 other*

**front** 앞 *Ch1 L4 vocab*

**fun** 재미있어요 재미있고 재미있어서 재미있다 *Ch3 L11 vocab*

**German (language)** 독일어 *Prelim. I vocab*

**German (person)** 독일 사람 *Prelim. I vocab*

**Germany** 독일 *Prelim. I vocab*

**gets up, gets out of bed** 일어나요 일어나고 일어나서 일어나다 *Ch3 L10 vocab*

**give** 줘요, 주어요 주고 줘서, 주어서 주다 *Ch3 L10 vocab*

**glasses, *counter for*** 잔 *Ch3.5 vocab*

**goes** 가요 가고 가서 가다 *Ch2 L5 focus*

**goes home, enters** 들어가요 들어가고 들어가서 들어가다 *Ch3 L10 vocab*

**goes out(side)** 나가요 나가고 나가서 나가다 *Ch3 L10 vocab*

**good; liked** 좋아요 좋고 [조코] 좋아서 좋다 [조타] *Ch3 L11 vocab*

**grabs, holds (hands)** 잡아요 잡고 잡아서 잡다 *Ch3 L9 vocab*

**graduate school** 대학원 *Ch2 L5 vocab*

**graduate student** 대학원생 *Ch 2 L8 vocab*

**grandchild** 손자 *Ch2.5 vocab*

**granddaughter** 손녀 *Ch2.5 vocab*

**grandfather** 할아버지 *Ch2.5 vocab*

**grandfather -- maternal grandfather** 외할아버지 *Ch2.5 vocab*

**grandfather -- paternal grandfather** 친할아버지 *Ch2.5 vocab*

**grandmother** 할머니 *Ch2.5 vocab*

**grandmother -- maternal grandmother** 외할머니 *Ch2.5 vocab*

**grandmother -- paternal grandmother** 친할머니 *Ch2.5 vocab*

**grandson** 손자 *Ch2.5 vocab*

**grocery store** 슈퍼(마켓) *Ch2 L5 vocab*

**ground, field** 장 *Ch 2 L5 point*

**guitar** 기타 *Ch1 L3 vocab*

**gym** 체육관 *Ch2 L5 vocab*

**hall** -관 *Ch 2 L5 point*

**Han'gul; the Korean alphabet** *Prelim. D vocab*

**hard as in *work hard*** 열심히 *Ch3 L12 vocab*

**has** 있어요 있고 있어서 있다 *Ch1 L3 focus*

**heads (of cabbage), *counter for*** 포기 *Ch3.5 vocab*

**here** 여기 *Prelim. C vocab*

**here; right here** 요기 *Ch1 L4 point*

**highlighter** 마커 *Ch1 L1 supp*

**History** 역사학 *Ch 2 L8 supp*

**holds (hands); grab** 잡아요 잡고 잡아서 잡다 *Ch3 L9 vocab*

**holds (hugs, cradles)** 안아요 안고 [앙꼬, 안꼬] 안아서 안다 *Ch3 L9 vocab*

**homework** 숙제 *Prelim. C vocab*

**homework (does)** 숙제해요 숙제하고 숙제해서 숙제하다 *Ch1 L1 vocab* [숙쩨]

**hospital** 병원 *Ch2 L5 vocab*

**hour** 시 *Ch1.5 B vocab*

**house, home** 집 *Ch2 L5 vocab*

**houses, buildings, *counter for*** 채 *Ch3.5 vocab*

**how** 얼마나 *Ch 2 L8 vocab*

**How is it?** 어때요? *Ch3 L11 other*

**how many** 몇 *Ch1.5 B vocab*

**how many times** 몇 번 *Ch 2 L8 other* [뻔]

**how often** 얼마나 자주 *Ch 2 L8 other*

**hugs, holds (baby)** 안아요 안고 [앙꼬, 안꼬] 안아서 안다 *Ch3 L9 vocab*

**hundred** 백 *Prelim. G vocab*

**hundred million** 억 *Prelim. G vocab*

**hundred thousand** 십 만 *Prelim. G vocab*

**hurts; sick** 아파요 아프고 아파서 아프다 *Ch3 L11 vocab*

**I (familiar form)** 나 *Ch 2 L7 vocab*

**I will be obliged to you. (greeting)** 잘 부탁합니다, 잘 부탁해요 잘 부탁하고 잘 부탁해서 잘 부탁하다 *Prelim. I point*

**I, me (humble)** 저 *Ch2 L5 vocab*

**ice cream** 아이스크림 *Ch1 L3 vocab*

**in, at, on** -에 *Ch1 L1 vocab*

**incorrect, wrong** 틀려요 틀리고 틀려서 틀리다 *Ch3 L11 vocab*

**inside** 안 *Ch1 L4 vocab*

**institution** -원 *Ch 2 L5 point*

**introduction** 소개 *Prelim. C vocab*

**introduction of oneself** 자기 소개 *Prelim. C vocab*

**Italian (language)** 이탈리아어 *Prelim. I vocab*

**Italian (person)** 이탈리아 사람 *Prelim. I vocab*

**Italy** 이탈리아, 이태리 *Prelim. I vocab*

**items *counter*** 개 *Ch3.5 vocab*

**January** 일월 *Prelim. H vocab*

**Japan** 일본 *Prelim. I vocab*

**Japanese (language)** 일본어 *Prelim. I vocab*

**Japanese (person)** 일본 사람 *Prelim. I vocab*

**jogging** 죠깅 *Ch 2 L6 focus*

**jogs** 조깅해요 조깅하고 조깅해서 조깅하다 *Ch 2 L6 vocab*

**juice** 주스 or 쥬스 *Ch1 L3 vocab*

**July** 칠월 *Prelim. H vocab*

**June** 유월 *Prelim. H vocab*

**junior, someone socially 'below'** 아랫사람 *Ch1 L4 vocab*

**just a minute; for a short while** 잠깐 *Ch3 L12 vocab*

**just now** 방금 *Ch3 L12 vocab*

**karaoke room** 노래방 *Ch2 L5 vocab*

**key** 열쇠 *Ch1 L3 vocab* [열쒸, 열쎄]

246

**King Sejong, inventor of Han'gul (Korean alphabet)**   *Prelim. D vocab*
**knife**   칼   *Ch1 L1 supp*
**knows**   알아요 알고 알아서 알다   *Ch3 L9 vocab*
**Korea**   한국   *Prelim. I vocab*
**Korea Studies**   한국학   *Ch 2 L8 supp*
**Korea, South Korea**   대한민국   *Prelim. I point*
**Korean (language)**   한국어   *Prelim. I vocab*
**Korean (person)**   한국 사람   *Prelim. I vocab*
**Koreans living in Japan**   재일동포   *Prelim. I point*
**Koreans living in US**   재미동포   *Prelim. I point*
**lacks**   없어요 없고 없어서 없다   *Ch1 L1 vocab* [업써요]
**last**   마지막   *Prelim. G vocab*
**last (Wednesday)**   지난 주 (수요일에)   *Ch3 L12 vocab*
**last night**   지난 밤, 어젯밤   *Ch3 L12 vocab*
**last semester/quarter**   지난 학기에   *Ch3 L12 vocab*
**last week**   지난 주에   *Ch3 L12 vocab*
**last weekend**   지난 주말에   *Ch3 L12 vocab*
**last year**   지난 해에, 작년에   *Ch3 L12 vocab*
**last, past**   지난   *Ch3 L12 vocab*
**laughs, smiles**   웃어요 웃고 [욱꼬, 욷꼬] 웃어서 웃다   *Ch3 L9 vocab*
**laundry (does)**   빨래해요 빨래하고 빨래해서 빨래하다   *Ch 2 L6 vocab*
**learns, studies**   배워요 배우고 배워서 배우다   *Ch3 L10 vocab*
**leaves**   떠나요 떠나고 떠나서 떠나다   *Ch3 L10 vocab*
**left side**   왼쪽   *Ch1 L4 vocab*
**letter opener**   레터 오프너   *Ch1 L3 vocab*
**library**   도서관   *Ch2 L5 vocab*
**like so**   그렇게   *Ch2.5 vocab* [그러케]
**liked; good**   좋아요 좋고 [조코] 좋아서 좋다 [조타]   *Ch3 L11 vocab*
**likes**   좋아해요 좋아하고 좋아해서 좋아하다   *Ch3 L10 vocab*
**Linguistics**   언어학   *Ch 2 L8 supp*
**literally white hands. people who are jobless after college graduation**   백수   *Ch 2 L8 point*
**Literature**   문학   *Ch 2 L8 supp*
**literature studies**   문학   *Ch 2 L8 point*
**live**   살아요 살고 살아서 살다   *Ch3 L9 vocab*
**loaves, lumps, counter**   덩어리   *Ch3.5 vocab*
*Location particle for activities*   에서   *Ch 2 L6 other*
**look for ; find; withdraw (money)**   찾아요 찾고 찾아서 찾다   *Ch3 L9 vocab*

**loudly**   큰 소리로   *Prelim. C vocab*
**loves**   사랑해요 사랑하고 사랑해서 사랑하다   *Ch 2 L6 vocab*
**lumps** *counter*   모   *Ch3.5 vocab*
**lunch**   점심(밥)   *bonus*
**magazine**   잡지   *Ch1 L3 vocab* [잡찌]
**major**   전공   *Ch 2 L8 vocab* [전공, 정공]
**makes**   만들어요 만들고 만들어서 만들다   *Ch3 L9 vocab*
**make-up (puts on)**   화장해요 화장하고 화장해서 화장하다   *Ch 2 L6 vocab*
**male student**   남학생   *Ch1 L1 vocab*
**March**   삼월   *Prelim. H vocab*
**Math**   수학   *Ch 2 L8 supp*
**May**   오월   *Prelim. H vocab*
**Mechanical Engineering**   기계 공학   *Ch 2 L8 supp*
**meets**   만나요 만나고 만나서 만나다   *Ch3 L10 vocab*
**Mexico**   멕시코   *Prelim. I point*
**middle**   가운데   *Ch1 L4 vocab*
**million**   백 만   *Prelim. G vocab*
**minute**   분   *Ch1.5 B vocab*
**mom**   엄마   *Ch2.5 vocab*
**moment; just a moment; for a short while**   잠시   *Ch3 L12 vocab*
**Monday**   월요일   *Ch1.5 A vocab*
**Monday through Friday**   월-화-수-목-금   *Ch1.5 A vocab*
**money**   돈   *Ch1 L3 vocab*
**more**   더   *Ch3 L12 vocab*
**more, one more time**   한 번 더   *Prelim. C vocab*
**morning (around 7 A.M. ~ 11 A.M.)**   아침   *Ch1.5 B vocab*
**mother**   어머니   *Ch2.5 vocab*
**motorcycle ("auto-bike")**   오토바이   *Ch1 L3 vocab*
**motorcycle.**   오토바이   *Ch 2 L5 point*
**movie theater**   극장, 영화관   *Ch2 L5 vocab*
**Mr., Ms.**   씨   *Ch1 L2 vocab*
**Music**   음악   *Ch 2 L8 supp*
**my (familiar form)**   내   *Ch 2 L7 other*
**my (humble), I (humble)**   제   *Ch 2 L7 other*
**name**   이름   *Ch1 L2 vocab*
**needed, necessary**   필요해요 필요하고 필요해서 필요하다   *Ch3 L11 vocab*
**newspaper**   신문   *Ch1 L3 vocab*
**next month**   다음 달에   *Ch 2 L7 vocab*
**next week**   다음 주에   *Ch 2 L7 vocab*

next weekend  다음 주말에  *Ch 2 L7 vocab*
next year  내년에  *Ch 2 L7 vocab*
Nice to meet you  만나서 반가워요 만나서 반갑고 만나서 반가워서 만나서 반갑다 *Prelim. I point*
Nice to meet you  만나서 반갑습니다 만나서 반갑고 만나서 반가워서 만나서 반갑다 *Prelim. I point*
night (around 10, 11 P.M. ~ 2, 3 A.M.) 밤  *Ch1.5 B vocab*
nine (native Korean vocab.)  아홉  *Prelim. G vocab*
nine (Sino-Korean vocab.)  구  *Prelim. G vocab*
ninety (native Korean vocab.)  아흔  *Prelim. G vocab*
ninth  아홉째 열째  *Prelim. G vocab*
no  아니오  *Prelim. C vocab*
no fun  재미없어요 재미없고 재미없어서 재미없다 *Ch3 L11 vocab*
North Korea  북한  *Prelim. I point*
North Korea (old term)  북조선  *Prelim. I point*
not  안  *Ch 2 L7 focus*
not busy, have a lot of free time  한가해요 한가하고 한가해서 한가하다 *Ch3 L11 vocab*
not really, not very, barely  별로  *Ch 2 L7 vocab*
notebook (blank book that you will fill in!) 공책 *Ch1 L2 vocab*
November  십 일월  *Prelim. H vocab*
now  지금  *Prelim. H vocab*
number  숫자  *Prelim. G vocab*
O.K.  괜찮아요 괜찮고 괜찮아서 괜찮다 *Prelim. F vocab* [괜차나요, 갠차나요]
*Object marker*  을/를  *Ch 2 L6 other*
October  시월  *Prelim. H vocab*
office  사무실  *Ch1 L1 vocab*
office, official or government department  -국 *Ch 2 L5 point*
often, very often  자주  *Ch 2 L7 vocab*
often, well  잘  *Ch 3 L8 vocab*
oldest child  맏이  *Ch 2 L6 point* [마지]
oldest son  맏아들, 큰 아들  *Ch2.5 vocab*
on leave (by students)  휴학  *Ch 2 L8 point*
on weekdays  평일에  *Ch 2 L7 vocab*
on weekend(s)  주말에  *Ch 2 L7 vocab*
one (*native Korean vocab.*)  하나, 한  *Prelim. G vocab*
one (Sino-Korean vocab.)  일  *Prelim. G vocab*
only daughter  외동딸  *Ch2.5 vocab*
only son  외아들/독자  *Ch2.5 vocab*
only, just  -만  *Ch3 L10 other*
opens  열어요 열고 열어서 열다 *Ch3 L9 vocab*

our (humble)  저희  *Ch 2 L7 other*
outside  밖  *Ch1 L4 vocab*
over there  저기  *Ch1 L3 vocab*
over there; right over there  조기  *Ch1 L4 point*
P.M. (around 1 P.M. ~ 5)  오후  *Ch1.5 B vocab*
pairs of shoes, *counter for*  켤레  *Ch3.5 vocab*
paper  종이  *Ch1 L2 vocab*
parents  부모님  *Ch2.5 vocab*
park  공원  *Ch2 L5 vocab*
parking lot  주차장  *Ch2 L5 vocab*
partner  짝  *Prelim. C vocab*
part-time work (does)  아르바이트해요 아르바이트하고 아르바이트해서 아르바이트하다 *Ch 2 L6 vocab*
*past tense*  -ㅆ어요  *Ch3 L12 focus*
past, last  지난  *Ch3 L12 vocab*
pen  펜  *Ch1 L2 vocab*
pencil  연필  *Ch1 L2 vocab*
pencil case, holder  필통  *Ch1 L1 supp*
people *counter*  명  *Ch2.5 vocab*
people, (honorific) *counter for*  분  *Ch3.5 vocab*
per  -에  *Ch 2 L8 other*
per day  하루에  *Ch 2 L8 vocab*
per week  일 주일에  *Ch 2 L8 vocab* [일쭈이레]
person  사람  *Prelim. I vocab*
person (honorific)  분  *Ch1 L2 vocab*
phone number  전화번호  *Ch1 L2 vocab* [저나버노]
phones  전화해요 전화하고 전화해서 전화하다 *Ch 2 L6 vocab*
Physics  물리학  *Ch 2 L8 supp*
pieces, slices, *counter for*  조각, 쪽  *Ch3.5 vocab*
play soccer  축구해요 축구하고 축구해서 축구하다 *Ch 2 L6 vocab*
plays  놀아요 놀고 놀아서 놀다 *Ch3 L9 vocab*
plays (tennis/ guitar)  쳐요 치고 쳐서 치다 *Ch3 L10 vocab*
plural marker  들  *Ch2.5 review*
Political Science  정치학  *Ch 2 L8 supp*
portable CD player  워크맨  *Ch1 L3 vocab*
possessive (NOUN's)  -의  *Ch1 L4 vocab*
post office  우체국  *Ch2 L5 vocab*
pretty  예뻐요 예쁘고 예뻐서 예쁘다 *Ch3 L11 vocab*
printer  프린터  *Ch1 L1 vocab*

**problem** 문제 *Prelim. F vocab*

**Psychology** 심리학 *Ch 2 L8 supp* [심니악]

**puppy** 강아지 *Ch2.5 vocab*

**puts (something) in** 넣어요 넣고 [너코] 넣어서 [너~서] 넣다 [너타] *Ch3 L9 vocab* [너~요]

**puts, lets go of** 놓아요 놓고 [노코] 놓아서 [놔서] 놓다 [노타] *Ch3 L9 vocab* [놔요]

**quarter/semester** 학기 *Ch 2 L8 vocab*

**question** 질문 *Prelim. C vocab*

**quickly** 빨리 *Prelim. C vocab*

**quiet** 조용히 하세요 조용히하고 조용히해서 조용히하다 *Prelim. F vocab*

**reads** 읽어요 읽고 읽어서 읽다 *Ch3 L9 vocab*

**really, truly** 정말(로) *Ch3 L12 vocab*

**Really. That is so. / Let's do.** 그래요 *Prelim. F vocab*

**Really? Is that so?** 그래요? *Prelim. F vocab*

**receives, gets** 받아요 받고 받아서 받다 *Ch3 L9 vocab*

**regular days** 평소에 *Ch 2 L7 vocab*

**remains; is leftover** 남아요 남고 [남꼬] 남아서 남다 [남따] *Ch3 L9 vocab*

**repeat (after me), repeats** 따라 하세요 따라하고 따라해서 따라하다 *Prelim. C vocab*

**restroom** 화장실 *Prelim. F vocab*

**rests, rest (takes a)** 쉬어요 쉬고 쉬어서 쉬다 *Ch3 L10 vocab*

**rides, gets on** 타요 타고 타서 타다 *Ch3 L10 vocab*

**right side** 오른쪽 *Ch1 L4 vocab*

**room** 실 *Ch 2 L5 point*

**room** 방 *Ch2 L5 vocab*

**ruler** 자 *Ch1 L1 supp*

**Russia** 러시아 *Prelim. I vocab*

**Russian (language)** 러시아어 *Prelim. I vocab*

**Russian (person)** 러시아사람 *Prelim. I vocab*

**same, alike** 같아요 같고 [각꼬, 갇꼬] 같아서 [가타서] 같다 *Ch3 L11 vocab* [가태요]

**sandwich** 샌드위치 *Ch1 L3 vocab* [쌘드위치]

**Saturday** 토요일 *Ch1.5 A vocab*

**say: How do you say ____ in Korean?** ____ 한국말로 뭐에요? *Prelim. F vocab*

**school** 학교 *Ch2 L5 vocab*

**school vacation** 방학 *Ch 2 L8 point*

**school year** 학년 *Ch 2 L8 point*

**scissors** 가위 *Ch1 L1 supp*

**second** 둘째 *Prelim. G vocab*

**sees, *idiomatically* reads (newspaper, book)** 봐요 보고 봐서, 보아서 보다 *Ch2.5 point*

**self-study** 독학 *Ch 2 L8 point*

**semester/quarter/** 학기 *Ch 2 L8 vocab*

**senior; someone socially 'above'** 윗사람 *Ch1 L4 vocab*

**September** 구월 *Prelim. H vocab*

**seven (native Korean vocab.)** 일곱 *Prelim. G vocab*

**seven (Sino-Korean vocab.)** 칠 *Prelim. G vocab*

**seventh** 일곱째 *Prelim. G vocab*

**seventy (native Korean vocab.)** 일흔 *Prelim. G vocab*

**sheets, *counter for*** 장 *Ch3.5 vocab*

**shops; goes shopping** 쇼핑해요 쇼핑하고 쇼핑해서 쇼핑하다 *Ch 2 L6 vocab*

**shower** 목욕해요 목욕하고 [모교카고] 목욕해서[모교캐서] 목욕하다 [모교카다] *Ch 2 L6 vocab* [모교캐요]

**shower (takes a)** 샤워해요 샤워하고 샤워해서 샤워하다 *Ch 2 L6 vocab*

**sibling -- female sibling** 자매 *Ch2.5 vocab*

**sibling -- male sibling** 형제 *Ch2.5 vocab*

**sick, hurts** 아파요 아프고 아파서 아프다 *Ch3 L11 vocab*

**side (poetic)** 곁 *Ch1 L4 vocab*

**similar** 비슷해요 비슷하고 [비스타고] 비슷해서 [비스태서] 비슷하다 *Ch3 L11 vocab* [비스태요]

**sings** 노래해요 노래하고 노래해서 노래하다 *Ch 2 L6 vocab*

**sister -- female's older sister who is older than another older sister** 큰 언니 *Ch2.5 vocab*

**sister -- female's older sister who is younger than another sister** 언니 *Ch2.5 vocab*

**sister -- female's older sister who is younger than another sister** 작은 언니 *Ch2.5 vocab*

**sister -- male's older sister** 누나 *Ch2.5 vocab*

**sister -- male's older sister who is older than another older sister** 큰 누나 *Ch2.5 vocab*

**sister -- male's older sister who is younger than another sister** 작은 누나 *Ch2.5 vocab*

**sister -- younger sister** 여동생 *Ch2.5 vocab*

**sisters -- female siblings** 자매 *Ch2.5 vocab*

**sits** 앉아요 앉고 [앙꼬, 안꼬] 앉아서 앉다 *Ch3 L9 vocab*

**six (native Korean vocab.)** 여섯 *Prelim. G vocab*

**six (Sino-Korean vocab.)** 육 *Prelim. G vocab*

**sixth** 여섯째 *Prelim. G vocab*

**sixty (native Korean vocab.)** 예순 *Prelim. G vocab*

**sleeps** 자서 자고 자서 자다 *Ch3 L10 vocab*
**slowly** 천천히 *Prelim. C vocab*
**small** 작아요 작고 작아서 작다 *Ch3 L11 vocab*
**smiles, laughs** 웃어요 웃고 [욱꼬, 온꼬] 웃어서 웃다 *Ch3 L9 vocab*
**so** 그래서 *Ch 2 L8 other*
**so** -어서 *Ch3 L11 other*
**Sociology** 사회학 *Ch 2 L8 supp*
**somehow** 어떻게 *Ch3 L9 other* [어떠케]
**someone** 누가, 누구 *Ch3 L9 other*
**something** 뭐 *Ch3 L9 other*
**sometime** 언제 *Ch3 L9 other*
**sometimes, rarely** 가끔 *Ch 2 L7 vocab*
**somewhere** 어디 *Ch3 L9 other*
**son** 아들 *Ch2.5 vocab*
**sorry -- I am sorry** 미안합니다 미안하고 미안해서 미안하다 *Prelim. F vocab*
**South Korea** 남한 *Prelim. I point*
**South Korea (old term)** 남조선 *Prelim. I point*
**Spain** 스페인 *Prelim. I vocab*
**Spanish (language)** 서반아어, 스페인어 *Prelim. I point*
**Spanish (person); Spaniard** 스페인사람 *Prelim. I vocab*
**sports complex; gym** 체육관 *Ch2 L5 vocab*
**stands, stops** 서요 서고 서서 서다 *Ch3 L10 vocab*
**store** 점 *Ch 2 L5 point*
**student** 학생 *Ch1 L1 vocab* [학쌩]
**student center** 학생회관 *Ch2 L5 vocab*
**student ID card** 학생증 *Ch1 L3 vocab* [학쌩쯩]
**student ID number** 학번 *Ch 2 L8 point*
**student, female** 여학생 *Ch1 L1 vocab*
**student, male** 남학생 *Ch1 L1 vocab*
**studies** 공부해요 공부하고 공부해서 공부하다 *Ch 2 L6 vocab*
**study** 공부 *Ch 2 L6 focus*
**subject marker (after a noun ending in a consonant)** -이 *Ch1 L1 vocab*
**subject marker (after a noun ending in a vowel)** -가 *Ch1 L1 vocab*
**suddenly** 갑자기 *Ch3 L12 vocab*
**Sunday** 일요일 *Ch1.5 A vocab*
**swims** 수영해요 수영하고 수영해서 수영하다 *Ch 2 L6 vocab*
**T.V.** 텔레비전, 테레비 *Ch1 L1 vocab*
**table** 탁자 *Ch1 L1 vocab* [탁짜]
**takes (a class); hears, listens** 들어요 (irregular) 듣고 들어서 듣다 *Ch 2 L8 vocab*
**talks** 얘기해요 얘기하고 얘기해서 얘기하다 *Ch 2 L6 vocab*

**talks** 이야기해요 이야기하고 이야기해서 이야기하다 *Ch 2 L6 vocab*
**taxi** 택시 *Ch1 L3 vocab*
**teacher** 선생님 *Prelim. C vocab*
**teaches** 가르쳐요 가르치고 가르쳐서 가르치다 *Ch3 L10 vocab*
**telephone** 전화 *Ch1 L1 vocab* [저놔, 저나]
**ten (Sino-Korean vocab.)** 십 *Prelim. G vocab*
**ten million** 천 만 *Prelim. G vocab*
**ten thousand** 만 *Prelim. G vocab*
**tenth** 열째 *Prelim. G vocab*
**test** 시험 *Ch1 L1 vocab* [시험, 시엄]
**thanks (Thank you!)** 감사합니다 감사하고 감사해서 감사하다 *Prelim. F vocab*
**that (adj.)** 그 *Ch1 L2 vocab*
**that little/exact thing** 고거 *Ch1 L4 point*
**that little/exact thing over there** 조거 *Ch1 L4 point*
**that over there (adj.)** 저 *Ch1 L2 vocab*
**that thing over there (noun)** 저거 *Ch1 L2 vocab*
**that thing over there as opposed to the others (for something that has been introduced in previous utterances or for contrast)** 저건 *Ch1 L2 vocab*
**that thing over there as subject/focus** 저게 *Ch1 L2 vocab*
**that/it** 그거 *Ch1 L2 vocab*
**that/it as opposed to the others (for something that has been introduced in previous utterances or for contrast)** 그건 *Ch1 L2 vocab*
**that/it as subject/focus** 그게 *Ch1 L2 vocab*
**the day after tomorrow** 모레 *Ch 2 L7 vocab*
**there** 거기 *Ch1 L3 vocab*
**there is no** 없어요 없고 없어서 없다 *Ch1 L1 vocab* [업써요]
**there is; exists; has** 있어요 있고 있어서 있다 *Ch1 L1 vocab* [이써요]
**there; right there** 고기 *Ch1 L4 point*
**thing** 것 *Ch1 L2 vocab*
**thing (cf. written form 것)** 거 *Ch1 L2 vocab*
**third** 셋째 *Prelim. G vocab*
**thirty (native Korean vocab.)** 서른 *Prelim. G vocab*
**thirty (Sino-Korean vocab.)** 삼 십 *Prelim. G vocab*
**this (adj.)** 이 *Ch1 L2 vocab*
**this (noun)** 이거 *Ch1 L2 vocab*

**this as opposed to the others (for something that has been introduced in previous utterances or for contrast)** 이건   *Ch1 L2 vocab*
**this as subject/focus** 이게   *Ch1 L2 vocab*
**this little/exact thing** 요거   *Ch1 L4 point*
**this month** 이번 달에   *Ch 2 L7 vocab*
**this morning** 오늘 아침   *Ch1.5 B vocab*
**this week** 이번 주에   *Ch 2 L7 vocab*
**this weekend** 이번 주말에   *Ch 2 L7 vocab*
**this year** 금년, 올해   *Ch 2 L7 vocab*
**thousand** 천   *Prelim. G vocab*
**three (native Korean vocab.)** 셋, 세   *Prelim. G vocab*
**three (Sino-Korean vocab.)** 삼   *Prelim. G vocab*
**Thursday** 목요일   *Ch1.5 A vocab*
**time** 시간   *Ch 2 L7 vocab*
**tired** 피곤해요 피곤하고 피곤해서 피곤하다 *Ch3 L11 vocab*
**to (a person)** -한테   *Ch3 L11 other*
**to (a place)** -에   *Ch2 L5 other*
**today** 오늘   *Prelim. H vocab*
**together** 같이   *Ch 2 L6 vocab* [가치]
**tomorrow** 내일   *Ch1 L1 vocab*
**tonight** 오늘 밤   *Ch1.5 B vocab*
**top; above (n.)** 위   *Ch1 L4 vocab*
**topic marker** -은/는   *Ch1 L2 vocab*
**transfer (schools)** 전학   *Ch 2 L8 point*
**trees** *counter* 그루   *Ch3.5 vocab* [구루]
**truly** 정말(로), 진짜(로)   *Ch3 L12 vocab*
**Tuesday** 화요일   *Ch1.5 A vocab*
**turns in (work); put out** 내요 내고 내서 내다 *Ch3 L10 vocab*
**twenty (native Korean vocab.)** 스물, 스무   *Prelim. G vocab*
**twenty (Sino-Korean vocab.)** 이 십   *Prelim. G vocab*
**twins** 쌍둥이   *Ch2.5 vocab*
**two (native Korean vocab.)** 둘, 두   *Prelim. G vocab*
**two (Sino-Korean vocab.)** 이   *Prelim. G vocab*
**two weeks ago** 이 주일 전에   *Ch3 L12 vocab*
**uncle** 삼촌   *Ch2.5 vocab*
**uncomfortable; inconvenient** 불편해요 불편하고 불편해서 불편하다 *Ch3 L11 vocab*
**underneath** 밑   *Ch1 L4 vocab*
**United Kingdom** 영국   *Prelim. I vocab*
**United States of America** 미국   *Prelim. I vocab*
**university, college** 대학교   *Ch2 L5 vocab*
**unnecessary; not needed** 필요없어요 필요없고 필요없어서 필요없다 *Ch3 L11 vocab*

**until (time); up to (place)** -까지   *Ch3 L10 other*
**usually, on regular days** 보통   *Ch 2 L7 vocab*
**VCR** 비디오   *Ch1 L1 vocab*
**very** 아주   *Ch3 L12 vocab*
**very (slang)** 핑장히, 되게   *Ch3 L12 vocab* [핑장이, 갱장이]
**very; too** 너무   *Ch3 L12 vocab*
**Vietnam** 월남, 베트남   *Prelim. I vocab*
**Vietnamese (language)** 베트남어   *Prelim. I vocab*
**Vietnamese (person)** 베트남 사람   *Prelim. I vocab*
**volleyball -- plays volleyball** 배구해요 배구하고 배구해서 배구하다 *Ch 2 L6 vocab*
**volumes, books** *counter* 권   *Ch3.5 vocab*
**vowel** 모음   *Prelim. D vocab*
**waits** 기다려요 기다리고 기다려서 기다리다 *Ch3 L10 vocab*
**wakes up** 깨요 깨고 깨서 깨다 *Ch3 L10 vocab*
**walk (takes a)** 산책해요 산책하고 [산채카고] 산책해서 [산채캐서] 산책하다 *Ch 2 L6 vocab* [산채캐요]
**wall** 벽   *Ch1 L1 vocab*
**wallet** 지갑   *Ch1 L3 vocab*
**wash** 씻어요 씻고 씻어서 씻다 *Ch3 L9 vocab*
**wash face** 세수해요 세수하고 세수해서 세수하다 *Ch 2 L6 vocab*
**watches (TV, movie)** 봐요 보고 봐서, 보아서 보다 *Ch2.5 point*
**we, our (familiar form)** 우리   *Ch 2 L7 vocab*
**we, our (familiar form)** 우리;저   *Ch 2 L7 other*
**wears, puts on (clothes)** 입어요 입고 입어서 입다 *Ch3 L9 vocab*
**Wednesday** 수요일   *Ch1.5 A vocab*
**weird, strange** 이상해요 이상하고 이상해서 이상하다 *Ch3 L11 vocab*
**what (무엇)** 뭐   *Ch1 L1 vocab*
**what (adj.)** 무슨   *Ch 2 L8 vocab*
**what (noun)** 무엇, 뭐   *Ch3 L9 other*
**what date** 며칠   *Prelim. H vocab*
**what day(s) of the week** 무슨 요일   *Ch1.5 A vocab* [무슨뇨일]
**what month** 몇월   *Prelim. H vocab* [며뤌]
**when** 언제   *Ch3 L9 other*
**when there is a test** 시험 때(에)   *Ch 2 L7 vocab*
**where** 어디   *Ch3 L9 other*
**which** 어느   *Prelim. I vocab*
**white-out** 화이트   *Ch1 L1 supp*

251

**who** 누구  *Ch1 L2 vocab*
**who (as subject)** 누가  *Ch2 L5 other*
**who/whom** 누구  *Ch2 L5 other*
**whom** 누구  *Ch3 L9 other*
**whose** 누구 거  *Ch3 L9 other* [누구 꺼]
**why** 왜  *Ch3 L9 other*
**window** 창문  *Ch1 L1 vocab*
**wipes, cleans** 닦아요 닦고 닦아서 닦다 *Ch3 L9 vocab*
**with** -하고  *Ch2 L5 vocab*
**with/by** -으로  *Ch3 L9 other*
**withdraw (money from the bank); look for; find** 찾아요 찾고 찾아서 찾다 *Ch3 L9 vocab*
**within** 속  *Ch1 L4 vocab*

## KOREAN-ENGLISH GLOSSARY

(all verbs listed in –어요/아요 form, with additional conjugation forms)

–(이)나   as many as *Ch3 L12 vocab*
_____ 한국말로 뭐에요?  say: How do you say _____ in Korean? *Prelim. F vocab*
-가   subject marker (after a noun ending in a vowel) *Ch1 L1 vocab*
가끔   sometimes, rarely *Ch 2 L7 vocab*
가르쳐요 가르치고 가르쳐서 가르치다 teaches *Ch3 L10 vocab*
가방   bag *Ch1 L2 vocab*
가요 가고 가서 가다 goes *Ch2 L5 focus*
가운데   middle *Ch1 L4 vocab*
가위   scissors *Ch1 L1 supp*
가족   family *Ch2.5 vocab*
감사합니다 감사하고 감사해서 감사하다 thanks (Thank you!) *Prelim. F vocab*
갑자기   suddenly *Ch3 L12 vocab*
강아지   puppy *Ch2.5 vocab*
같아요 같고 [각꼬, 간꼬] 같아서 [가타서] 같다 same, alike *Ch3 L11 vocab* [가태요]
같이   together *Ch 2 L6 vocab* [가치]
개   dog *Ch2.5 vocab*
개   items *counter Ch3.5 vocab*
거   thing (cf. written form 것) *Ch1 L2 vocab*
거기   there *Ch1 L3 vocab*
거의   almost *Ch 2 L7 vocab*
거의 다   almost all *Ch3 L12 vocab*
건너편   across *Ch1 L4 vocab*
건물   building *Ch1 L4 vocab*
것   thing *Ch1 L2 vocab*
경영학   Business and Administration *Ch 2 L8 supp*

**Women Studies** 여성학  *Ch 2 L8 supp*
**works** 일해요 일하고 일해서 일하다 *Ch 2 L6 vocab*
**write; use** 써요 쓰고 써서 쓰다 *Ch3 L10 vocab*
**written syllable** 글자  *Prelim. D vocab* [글짜]
**year (in school)** 학년  *Ch 2 L8 vocab* [항년]
**yes** 네, 예  *Ch1 L1 vocab*
**yesterday** 어제 = 어저께  *Ch3 L12 vocab*
**yet; not yet** 아직  *Ch3 L12 vocab*
**you all (respect)** 여러분  *Ch 2 L8 vocab*
**younger sibling** 동생  *Ch2.5 vocab*
**youngest child** 막내  *Ch2.5 vocab* [망내]

경제학   Economics *Ch 2 L8 supp*
곁   side (poetic) *Ch1 L4 vocab*
-고   and *Ch3 L9 other*
–고 나서   and then *Ch3 L9 other*
고거   that little/exact thing *Ch1 L4 point*
고기   there; right there *Ch1 L4 point*
고모   aunt on father's side *Ch2.5 vocab*
고모부   aunt on father's side *Ch2.5 vocab*
고양이   cat *Ch2.5 vocab*
공부   study *Ch 2 L6 focus*
공부해요 공부하고 공부해서 공부하다 studies *Ch 2 L6 vocab*
공원   park *Ch2 L5 vocab*
공책   notebook (blank book that you will fill in!) *Ch1 L2 vocab*
과자   cookies, crackers, chips *Ch1 L3 vocab*
-관   a large hall *Ch 2 L5 point*
괜찮아요 괜찮고 괜찮아서 괜찮다 O.K. *Prelim. F vocab* [괜차나요, 갠차나요]
굉장히   very (slang) *Ch3 L12 vocab* [굉장이, 갱장이]
교실   classroom *Ch1 L1 vocab*
구   nine (Sino-Korean vocab.) *Prelim. G vocab*
구월   September *Prelim. H vocab*
-국   office, official or government department *Ch 2 L5 point*
권   volumes, books *counter Ch3.5 vocab*
그   that (adj.) *Ch1 L2 vocab*
그거   that/it *Ch1 L2 vocab*
그건   that/it, as opposed to the others (for something that has been introduced in previous utterances or for contrast) *Ch1 L2 vocab*
그게   that/it as subject/focus *Ch1 L2 vocab*
그래서   so *Ch 2 L8 other*
그래요   Really. That is so. / Let's do. *Prelim. F vocab*

그래요? Really? Is that so? *Prelim. F vocab*

그렇게 like so *Ch2.5 vocab* [그러케]

그렇지만 but *Ch 2 L8 other* [그러치만]

그려요 그리고 그려서 그리다 draws *Ch3 L10 vocab*

그루 trees *counter Ch3.5 vocab* [구루]

그릇, 공기 bowls *counter Ch3.5 vocab*

그리고 and *Ch 2 L8 other*

그제 day before yesterday *Ch3 L12 vocab*

그제께 day before yesterday *Ch4 L13 vocab*

극장 movie theater *Ch2 L5 vocab*

글자 written syllable *Prelim. D vocab* [글짜]

금년에 this year *Ch 2 L7 vocab*

금요일 Friday *Ch1.5 A vocab*

-기 전에 before doing … *Ch3 L10 other*

기계 공학 Mechanical Engineering *Ch 2 L8 supp*

기다려요 기다리고 기다려서 기다리다 waits *Ch3 L10 vocab*

기숙사 dormitory *Ch2 L5 vocab*

기타 guitar *Ch1 L3 vocab*

-까지 until (time); up to (place) *Ch3 L10 other*

깨요 깨고 깨서 깨다 breaks (e.g., a cup) *Ch3 L10 vocab*

깨요 깨고 깨서 깨다 wakes up *Ch3 L10 vocab*

껌 chewing gum *Ch1 L3 vocab*

끝내요 끝나고 끝나서 끝나다 ends (intransitive) *Ch3 L10 vocab* [끈나요]

끝내요 끝내고 끝내서 끝내다 ends, finishes (something) *Ch3 L10 vocab* [끈내요]

나 I (familiar form) *Ch 2 L7 vocab*

나가요 나가고 나가서 나가다 goes out(side) *Ch3 L10 vocab*

나라 country *Prelim. I vocab*

나빠요 나쁘고 나빠서 나쁘다 bad *Ch3 L11 vocab*

나와요 나오고 나와서 나오다 comes out(side) *Ch3 L10 vocab*

날라리 someone who is flaky and not serious about their studies *Ch 2 L8 point*

남동생 male younger sibling *Ch2.5 vocab*

남아요 남고 [남꼬] 남아서 남다 [남따] remains; is leftover *Ch3 L9 vocab*

남조선 South Korea (old term) *Prelim. I point*

남학생 male student *Ch1 L1 vocab*

남한 South Korea *Prelim. I point*

내 my (familiar form) *Ch 2 L7 other*

내년에 next year *Ch 2 L7 vocab*

내요 내고 내서 내다 turns in (work); put out *Ch3 L10 vocab*

내일 tomorrow *Ch1 L1 vocab*

너무 very; too *Ch3 L12 vocab*

넣어요 넣고 [너코] 넣어서 [너~서] 넣다 [너타] puts (something) in *Ch3 L9 vocab* [너~요]

네 four (native Korean vocab.) *Prelim. G vocab*

네 yes *Ch1 L2 vocab*

넷 four (native Korean vocab.) *Prelim. G vocab*

넷째 fourth *Prelim. G vocab*

노래방 karaoke room *Ch2 L5 vocab*

노래해요 노래하고 노래해서 노래하다 sings *Ch 2 L6 vocab*

놀아요 놀고 놀아서 놀다 plays *Ch3 L9 vocab*

농구해요 농구하고 농구해서 농구하다 plays basketball *Ch 2 L6 vocab*

놓아요 놓고 [노코] 놓아서 [놔서] 놓다 [노타] puts, lets go of *Ch3 L9 vocab* [놔요]

누가 who (as subject) *Ch2 L5 other*

누가, 누구 someone *Ch3 L9 other*

누구 who *Ch1 L2 vocab*

누구 거 whose *Ch3 L9 other* [누구 꺼]

누나 male's older sister *Ch2.5 vocab*

다 all *Ch3 L12 vocab*

다발 bunches of (flowers) counter *Ch3.5 vocab*

다섯 five (native Korean vocab.) *Prelim. G vocab*

다섯째 fifth *Prelim. G vocab*

다음 달에 next month *Ch 2 L7 vocab*

다음 주말에 next weekend *Ch 2 L7 vocab*

다음 주에 next week *Ch 2 L7 vocab*

닦아요 닦고 닦아서 닦다 wipes, cleans *Ch3 L9 vocab*

단 bunches of (vegetables) *counter Ch3.5 vocab*

닫아요 닫고 [닥꼬, 닫꼬] 닫아서 닫다 closes *Ch3 L9 vocab*

달라요 다르고 달라서 다르다 different *Ch3 L11 vocab*

대 computers, cars, *counter Ch3.5 vocab*

대학교 university, college *Ch2 L5 vocab*

대학생 college student *Ch 2 L8 vocab*

대학원 graduate school *Ch2 L5 vocab*

대학원생 graduate student *Ch 2 L8 vocab*

대한민국 Korea, South Korea *Prelim. I point*

더 more *Ch3 L12 vocab*

덩어리 loaves, lumps, *counter Ch3.5 vocab*

덩어리 loaves, lumps, *counter Ch3.6 vocab*

-도 also (noun particle) *Ch1 L3 vocab*

도서관 library *Ch2 L5 vocab*

독일 Germany *Prelim. I vocab*

253

독일 사람   German (person) *Prelim. I vocab*
독일어   German (language) *Prelim. I vocab*
독자   only son *Ch2.5 vocab*
독학   self-study *Ch 2 L8 point*
돈   money *Ch1 L3 vocab*
동생   younger sibling *Ch2.5 vocab*
되게   very (slang) *Ch3 L12 vocab*
두   two (native Korean vocab.) *Prelim. G vocab*
둘   two (native Korean vocab.) *Prelim. G vocab*
둘째   second *Prelim. G vocab*
뒤   back; behind *Ch1 L4 vocab*
들   plural marker *Ch2.5 review*
들어가요 들어가고 들어가서 들어가다 goes home, enters *Ch3 L10 vocab*
들어와요 들어오고 들어와서 들어오다 comes home, comes in *Ch3 L10 vocab*
들어요 **(irregular)** 듣고 들어서 듣다 takes (a class); hears, listens *Ch 2 L8 vocab*
등산해요 등산하고 등산해서 등산하다 climbs mountains *Ch 2 L6 vocab*
따라 하세요 따라하고 따라해서 따라하다 repeat (after me), repeats *Prelim. C vocab*
딸   daughter *Ch2.5 vocab*
떠나요 떠나고 떠나서 떠나다 leaves *Ch3 L10 vocab*
또   again, what else (adverb) *Ch1 L3 vocab*
러시아   Russia *Prelim. I vocab*
러시아사람   Russian (person) *Prelim. I vocab*
러시아어   Russian (language) *Prelim. I vocab*
레터 오프너   letter opener *Ch1 L3 vocab*
마리   counter for animals *Ch2.5 vocab*
마셔요 마시고 마셔서, 마시어서 마시다 drinks *Ch3 L10 vocab*
마지막   last *Prelim. G vocab*
마커   highlighter *Ch1 L1 supp*
마흔   forty (native Korean vocab.) *Prelim. G vocab*
막내   youngest child *Ch2.5 vocab* [망내]
만   ten thousand *Prelim. G vocab*
-만   only, just *Ch3 L10 other*
만나서 반가워요 만나서 반갑고 만나서 반가워서 만나서 반갑다 Nice to meet you *Prelim. I point*
**만나서 반갑습니다** 만나서 반갑고 만나서 반가워서 만나서 반갑다 Nice to meet you *Prelim. I point*
만나요 만나고 만나서 만나다 meets *Ch3 L10 vocab*
만들어요 만들고 만들어서 만들다 makes *Ch3 L9 vocab*
많아요 많고 [만코] 많아서 많다 [만타] abundant, be a lot *Ch3 L11 vocab*
많이   a lot *Ch3 L12 vocab*
맏아들   oldest son *Ch2.5 vocab*
맏이   oldest child *Ch 2 L6 point* [마지]

맞아요 맞고 [맏꼬, 맏꼬] 맞아서 맞다 correct, right *Ch3 L11 vocab*
맞은 편   across *Ch1 L4 vocab*
매일   everyday, each day *Ch 2 L7 vocab*
매주   every week, each week *Ch 2 L8 vocab*
먹어요 먹고 먹어서 먹다 eat *Ch3 L9 vocab*
멕시코   Mexico *Prelim. I point*
며칠   what date *Prelim. H vocab*
명   people *counter Ch2.5 vocab*
몇   how many *Ch1.5 B vocab*
몇 번   how many times *Ch 2 L8 other* [뻔]
몇월   what month *Prelim. H vocab* [며뒬]
모   lumps *counter Ch3.5 vocab*
모두   all together (adv.) *Ch2.5 vocab*
모레   the day after tomorrow *Ch 2 L7 vocab*
모음   vowel *Prelim. D vocab*
목요일   Thursday *Ch1.5 A vocab*
**목욕해요** 목욕하고 [모교카고]
목욕해서[모교캐서] 목욕하다 [모교카다] bathes, take a shower *Ch 2 L6 vocab* [모교캐요]
못   can't *Ch3 L9 other*
무슨   what (adj.) *Ch 2 L8 vocab*
무슨 요일   what day(s) of the week *Ch1.5 A vocab* [무슨뇨일]
무엇   what (written) *Ch3 L9 other*
문   door *Ch1 L1 vocab*
문제   problem *Prelim. F vocab*
문학   Literature *Ch 2 L8 supp*
문학   literature studies *Ch 2 L8 point*
물리학   Physics *Ch 2 L8 supp*
뭐   something *Ch3 L9 other*
뭐   what (무엇) *Ch1 L1 vocab*
미국   United States of America *Prelim. I vocab*
미국 사람   American (person) *Prelim. I vocab*
미술   Art/painting *Ch 2 L8 supp*
미안합니다 미안하고 미안해서 미안하다 I am sorry, sorry *Prelim. F vocab*
미학   art *Ch 2 L8 point*
밑   underneath *Ch1 L4 vocab*
바빠요 바쁘고 바빠서 바쁘다 busy *Ch3 L11 vocab*
밖   outside *Ch1 L4 vocab*
받아요 받고 받아서 받다 receives, gets *Ch3 L9 vocab*
받침   consonant at end of writtem syllable *Prelim. D vocab*
밤   night (around 10, 11 P.M. ~ 2, 3 A.M.) *Ch1.5 B vocab*
방   room *Ch2 L5 vocab*
방금   just now *Ch3 L12 vocab*

방학    school vacation *Ch 2 L8 point*

방학 때(에)    during vacation *Ch 2 L7 vocab*

배구해요 배구하고 배구해서 배구하다 plays volleyball *Ch 2 L6 vocab*

배워요 배우고 배워서 배우다 learns, studies *Ch3 L10 vocab*

백    hundred *Prelim. G vocab*

백 만    million *Prelim. G vocab*

백수    literally white hands. people who are jobless after college graduation *Ch 2 L8 point*

백화점    department store *Ch2 L5 vocab* [배과점]

버스    bus *Ch1 L3 vocab*

벌    clothes, *counter for Ch3.5 vocab*

벌써    already *Ch3 L12 vocab*

베트남    Vietnam *Prelim. I vocab*

베트남 사람    Vietnamese (person) *Prelim. I vocab*

베트남어    Vietnamese (language) *Prelim. I vocab*

벽    wall *Ch1 L1 vocab*

별로    not really, not very, barely *Ch 2 L7 vocab*

병    bottle *Ch3.5 vocab*

병원    hospital *Ch2 L5 vocab*

보통    usually, on regular days *Ch 2 L7 vocab*

복사기    copier *Ch1 L1 supp*

봉지    bag, *counter for Ch3.5 vocab*

봐요 보고 봐서, 보아서 보다 sees, watches, *idiomatically* reads (newspaper, book) *Ch2.5 point*

부모님    parents *Ch2.5 vocab*

-부터    from (time) *Ch3 L10 other*

북조선    North Korea (old term) *Prelim. I point*

북한    North Korea *Prelim. I point*

분    minute *Ch1.5 B vocab*

분    people, (honorific) *counter for Ch3.5 vocab*

불란서    France *Prelim. I point*

불어    French *Prelim. I point*

불편해요 불편하고 불편해서 불편하다 uncomfortable; inconvenient *Ch3 L11 vocab*

비디오    VCR *Ch1 L1 vocab*

비슷해요 비슷하고 [비스타고] 비슷해서 [비스태서] 비슷하다 similar *Ch3 L11 vocab* [비스태요]

빌딩    building *Ch1 L4 vocab* [삘딩], [빌딩]

빨래해요 빨래하고 빨래해서 빨래하다 laundry (does) *Ch 2 L6 vocab*

빨리    quickly *Prelim. C vocab*

사    four (Sino-Korean vocab.) *Prelim. G vocab*

사 십    forty (Sino-Korean vocab.) *Prelim. G vocab*

사람    person *Prelim. I vocab*

사랑해요 사랑하고 사랑해서 사랑하다 loves *Ch 2 L6 vocab*

사무실    office *Ch1 L1 vocab*

사요 사고 사서 사다 buys, purchases *Ch3 L10 vocab*

사월    April *Prelim. H vocab*

사이    between *Ch1 L4 vocab*

사촌    cousin *Ch2.5 vocab*

사탕    candy *Ch1 L3 vocab*

사회학    Sociology *Ch 2 L8 supp*

산책해요 산책하고 [산채카고] 산책해서 [산채캐서] 산책하다 walk (takes a) *Ch 2 L6 vocab* [산채캐요]

살    age, *counter Ch3.5 vocab*

살아요 살고 살아서 살다 live *Ch3 L9 vocab*

삼    three (Sino-Korean vocab.) *Prelim. G vocab*

삼 십    thirty (Sino-Korean vocab.) *Prelim. G vocab*

삼월    March *Prelim. H vocab*

삼촌    uncle *Ch2.5 vocab*

상자    box, *counter Ch3.5 vocab*

새벽    dawn, early morning (around 3, 4 A.M. ~ 6 A.M.) *Ch1.5 B vocab*

샌드위치    sandwich *Ch1 L3 vocab* [쌘드위치]

생물학    Biology *Ch 2 L8 supp*

생일    birthday *Prelim. H vocab*

샤워해요 샤워하고 샤워해서 샤워하다 shower (takes a) *Ch 2 L6 vocab*

서른    thirty (native Korean vocab.) *Prelim. G vocab*

서반아어    Spanish (language) *Prelim. I point*

서요 서고 서서 서다 stands, stops *Ch3 L10 vocab*

서점    bookstore *Ch2 L5 vocab*

선생님    teacher *Prelim. C vocab*

설거지해요 설거지하고 설거지해서 설거지하다 dishes (does) *Ch 2 L6 vocab*

세    three (native Korean vocab.) *Prelim. G vocab*

세수해요 세수하고 세수해서 세수하다 wash face *Ch 2 L6 vocab*

세요 세고 세서, 세어서 [셔서, 시어서] 세다 [세다, 시다] counts *Ch3 L10 vocab* [서요], [세요]

세종    King Sejong, inventor of Han'gul (Korean alphabet) *Prelim. D vocab*

셋    three (native Korean vocab.) *Prelim. G vocab*

셋째    third *Prelim. G vocab*

소개    introduction *Prelim. C vocab*

속    within *Ch1 L4 vocab*

손녀    granddaughter *Ch2.5 vocab*

손자    grandson; grandchildren *Ch2.5 vocab*

송이    flowers, grapes, *counter for Ch3.5 vocab*

쇼핑해요 쇼핑하고 쇼핑해서 쇼핑하다 shops; goes shopping *Ch 2 L6 vocab*

수업　class (course) *Ch 2 L8 vocab*

수영해요 수영하고 수영해서 수영하다 swims *Ch 2 L6 vocab*

수요일　Wednesday *Ch1.5 A vocab*

수학　Math *Ch 2 L8 supp*

숙제　homework *Prelim. C vocab*

숙제해요 숙제하고 숙제해서 숙제하다 homework (does) *Ch1 L1 vocab* [숙쩨]

숫자　number *Prelim. G vocab*

쉬어요 쉬고 쉬어서 쉬다 rests, rest (takes a) *Ch3 L10 vocab*

쉰　fifty (native Korean vocab.) *Prelim. G vocab*

슈퍼(마켓)　grocery store *Ch2 L5 vocab*

스무　twenty (native Korean vocab.) (adj.) *Prelim. G vocab*

스물　twenty (native Korean vocab.) *Prelim. G vocab*

스페인　Spain *Prelim. I vocab*

스페인사람　Spanish (person); Spaniard *Prelim. I vocab*

스페인어　Spanish (language) *Prelim. I vocab*

시　hour *Ch1.5 B vocab*

시간　time *Ch 2 L7 vocab*

시계　clock, watch *Ch1 L1 vocab* [시게]

시디　CD (compact disk) *Ch1 L3 vocab* [씨디]

시월　October *Prelim. H vocab*

시험　test *Ch1 L1 vocab* [시험, 시엄]

시험 때(에)　when there is a test *Ch 2 L7 vocab*

식당　diner; cafeteria *Ch2 L5 vocab*

식당　cafeteria; diner *Ch2 L5 vocab*

신문　newspaper *Ch1 L3 vocab*

신용카드　credit card *Ch1 L3 vocab*

실　a single room *Ch 2 L5 point*

실례합니다 실례하고 실례해서 실례하다 excuse me *Prelim. F vocab*

싫어요 싫고 [실코] 싫어서 싫다 [실타] disliked *Ch3 L11 vocab*

싫어해요 싫어하고 싫어해서 싫어하다 dislikes *Ch3 L10 vocab*

심리학　Psychology *Ch 2 L8 supp* [심니악]

십　ten (Sino-Korean vocab.) *Prelim. G vocab*

십 만　hundred thousand *Prelim. G vocab*

십 이월　December *Prelim. H vocab*

십 일월　November *Prelim. H vocab*

-ㅆ어요　past tense *Ch3 L12 focus*

싸워요 싸우고 싸워서 싸우다 fights, has an argument *Ch3 L10 vocab*

쌍　couple, pair, *counter for* people, animals *Ch3.5 vocab*

쌍둥이　twins *Ch2.5 vocab*

써요 쓰고 써서 쓰다 write; use *Ch3 L10 vocab*

씨　Mr., Ms. *Ch1 L2 vocab*

씻어요 씻고 씻어서 씻다 wash *Ch3 L9 vocab*

아기 [애기]　baby *Ch2.5 vocab*

아기를 봐요 아기를 보고 아기를 봐서 아기를 보다 baby-sits *Ch2.5 point*

아니오　no *Prelim. C vocab*

아들　son *Ch2.5 vocab*

아래　below *Ch1 L4 vocab*

아랫사람　junior, someone socially 'below' *Ch1 L4 vocab*

아르바이트해요 아르바이트하고 아르바이트해서 아르바이트하다 part-time work (does) *Ch 2 L6 vocab*

아버지　father *Ch2.5 vocab*

아빠　father (dad) *Ch2.5 vocab*

아이들/애들　children *Ch2.5 vocab*

아이스크림　ice cream *Ch1 L3 vocab*

아주　very *Ch3 L12 vocab*

아직　yet; not yet *Ch3 L12 vocab*

아침　morning (around 7 A.M. ~ 11 A.M.) *Ch1.5 B vocab*

아파요 아프고 아파서 아프다 sick, hurts *Ch3 L11 vocab*

아파트　apartment *Ch2 L5 vocab*

아홉　nine (native Korean vocab.) *Prelim. G vocab*

아홉째 열째　ninth *Prelim. G vocab*

아흔　ninety (native Korean vocab.) *Prelim. G vocab*

안　not *Ch 2 L7 focus*

안　inside *Ch1 L4 vocab*

안아요 안고 [앙꼬, 안꼬] 안아서 안다 hugs, holds (baby) *Ch3 L9 vocab*

안아요 안고 [앙꼬, 안꼬] 안아서 안다 holds (hugs, cradles) *Ch3 L9 vocab*

앉아요 앉고 [앙꼬, 안꼬] 앉아서 앉다 sits *Ch3 L9 vocab*

알아요 알고 알아서 알다 knows *Ch3 L9 vocab*

앞　front *Ch1 L4 vocab*

야구해요 야구하고 야구해서 야구하다 plays baseball *Ch 2 L6 vocab*

약국　drug store *Ch2 L5 vocab*

얘기해요 얘기하고 얘기해서 얘기하다 talks *Ch 2 L6 vocab*

어느　which *Prelim. I vocab*

어디　somewhere *Ch3 L9 other*

어디　where *Ch1 L4 vocab*

어때요 (irregular) 어떻고 [어떠코] 어때서 어떻다 be how *Ch3 L11 vocab*

어때요? How is it? *Ch3 L11 other*

어떻게 somehow *Ch3 L9 other* [어떠케]

어머니 mother *Ch1 L2 vocab*

-어서 so *Ch3 L11 other*

어제 = 어저께 yesterday *Ch3 L12 vocab*

어젯밤 last night *Ch3 L12 vocab*

억 hundred million *Prelim. G vocab*

언니 female's older sister who is younger than another sister *Ch2.5 vocab*

언어학 Linguistics *Ch 2 L8 supp*

언제 sometime *Ch3 L9 other*

언제 when *Ch3 L9 other*

얼마나 how *Ch 2 L8 vocab*

얼마나 자주 how often *Ch 2 L8 other*

엄마 mom *Ch2.5 vocab*

없어요 없고 없어서 없다 there is no; is lacking *Ch1 L1 vocab* [업써요]

-에 at (time) *Ch 2 L7 other*

-에 to (a place) *Ch2 L5 other*

-에 per *Ch 2 L8 other*

-에 in, at, on *Ch1 L1 vocab*

에서 *Location particle for activities Ch 2 L6 other*

에어콘 air-conditioner *Ch 2 L5 point*

여기 here *Prelim. C vocab*

여덟 eight (native Korean vocab.) *Prelim. G vocab*

여덟째 eighth *Prelim. G vocab*

여동생 female younger sibling *Ch2.5 vocab*

여든 eighty (native Korean vocab.) *Prelim. G vocab*

여러분 you all (respect) *Ch 2 L8 vocab*

여섯 six (native Korean vocab.) *Prelim. G vocab*

여섯째 sixth *Prelim. G vocab*

여성학 Women Studies *Ch 2 L8 supp*

여학생 female student *Ch1 L1 vocab*

역사학 History *Ch 2 L8 supp*

연필 pencil *Ch1 L2 vocab*

열쇠 key *Ch1 L3 vocab* [열쐬, 열쎄]

열심히 diligently, (*work*) hard, whole-heartedly *Ch3 L12 vocab*

열심히 hard as in *work hard Ch3 L12 vocab*

열어요 열고 열어서 열다 opens *Ch3 L9 vocab*

열째 tenth *Prelim. G vocab*

영국 United Kingdom *Prelim. I vocab*

영국 사람 British (person) *Prelim. I vocab*

영어 English (language) *Prelim. I vocab*

영화관 movie theater *Ch2 L5 vocab*

옆 beside; next to *Ch1 L4 vocab*

예 yes *Ch1 L1 vocab*

예뻐요 예쁘고 예뻐서 예쁘다 pretty *Ch3 L11 vocab*

예순 sixty (native Korean vocab.) *Prelim. G vocab*

오 five (Sino-Korean vocab.) *Prelim. G vocab*

오늘 today *Prelim. H vocab*

오늘 밤 tonight *Ch1.5 B vocab*

오늘 아침 this morning *Ch1.5 B vocab*

오랫동안 for a long time *Ch3 L12 vocab*

오른쪽 right side *Ch1 L4 vocab*

오빠 female's older brother *Ch2.5 vocab*

오월 May *Prelim. H vocab*

오전 A.M. (around 7 A.M. ~ 11 A.M.) *Ch1.5 B vocab*

오토바이 motorcycle ("auto-bike") *Ch1 L3 vocab*

오후 P.M. (around 1 A.M. ~ 5) *Ch1.5 B vocab*

올해에 this year *Ch 3 L8 vocab*

와요 오고 와서 오다 comes *Ch3 L10 vocab*

왜 why *Ch3 L9 other*

외동딸 only daughter *Ch2.5 vocab*

외식해요 외식하고 외식해서 외식하다 eats out *Ch 2 L6 vocab*

외아들/독자 only son *Ch2.5 vocab*

외할머니 maternal grandmother *Ch2.5 vocab*

외할아버지 maternal grandfather *Ch2.5 vocab*

왼쪽 left side *Ch1 L4 vocab*

요거 this little/exact thing *Ch1 L4 point*

요기 here; right here *Ch1 L4 point*

요리해요 요리하고 요리해서 요리하다 cooks *Ch 2 L6 vocab*

요일 day(s) of the week *Ch 2 L8 vocab*

우리 we, our (familiar form) *Ch 2 L7 vocab*

우체국 post office *Ch2 L5 vocab*

운동장 ball field *Ch2 L5 vocab*

운동해요 운동하고 운동해서 운동하다 exercise (sports) *Ch 2 L6 vocab*

울어요 울고 울어서 울다 cries *Ch3 L9 vocab*

웃어요 웃고 [욱꼬, 욷꼬] 웃어서 웃다 laughs, smiles *Ch3 L9 vocab*

웃어요 웃고 [욱꼬, 욷꼬] 웃어서 웃다 smiles, laughs *Ch3 L9 vocab*

워크맨 portable CD player *Ch1 L3 vocab*

원 an institution *Ch 2 L5 point*

월남 Vietnam *Prelim. I point*

월요일 Monday *Ch1.5 A vocab*

월-화-수-목-금 Monday through Friday *Ch1.5 A vocab*

위 top; above (n.) *Ch1 L4 vocab*

윗사람 senior; someone socially 'above' *Ch1 L4 vocab*

유월 June *Prelim. H vocab*

육　　six (Sino-Korean vocab.) *Prelim. G vocab*

–으로　　with/by *Ch3 L9 other*

-은/는　　*change of focus Ch2 L5 other*

-은/는　　topic marker *Ch1 L2 vocab*

은행　　bank *Ch2 L5 vocab*

을/를　　*Object marker Ch 2 L6 other*

음악　　Music *Ch 2 L8 supp*

–의　　possessive (NOUN's) *Ch1 L4 vocab*

의자　　chair *Ch1 L1 vocab*

이　　two (Sino-Korean vocab.) *Prelim. G vocab*

이　　this (adj.) *Ch1 L2 vocab*

-이　　subject marker (after a noun ending in a consonant) *Ch1 L1 vocab*

이 십　　twenty (Sino-Korean vocab.) *Prelim. G vocab*

이 주일 전에　　two weeks ago *Ch3 L12 vocab*

이거　　this (noun) *Ch1 L2 vocab*

이건　　this as opposed to the others (for something that has been introduced in previous utterances or for contrast) *Ch1 L2 vocab*

이게　　this as subject/focus *Ch1 L2 vocab*

-이나　　as many as　*Ch3 L12 other*

이름　　name *Ch1 L2 vocab*

이메일　　email (address) *Ch1 L2 vocab*

이모　　aunt on mother's side *Ch2.5 vocab*

이모부　　aunt on mother's side *Ch2.5 vocab*

이번 달에　　this month *Ch 2 L7 vocab*

이번 주말에　　this weekend *Ch 2 L7 vocab*

이번 주에　　this week *Ch 2 L7 vocab*

이상해요 이상하고 이상해서 이상하다 weird, strange *Ch3 L11 vocab*

이야기해요 이야기하고 이야기해서 이야기하다 talks *Ch 2 L6 vocab*

이월　　February *Prelim. H vocab*

이탈리아　　Italy *Prelim. I vocab*

이탈리아 사람　　Italian (person) *Prelim. I vocab*

이탈리아어　　Italian (language) *Prelim. I vocab*

이태리　　Italy *Prelim. I point*

일　　one (Sino-Korean vocab.) *Prelim. G vocab*

일 주일에　　per week　*Ch 2 L8 vocab* [일쭈이레]

일곱　　seven (native Korean vocab.) *Prelim. G vocab*

일곱째　　seventh *Prelim. G vocab*

일본　　Japan *Prelim. I vocab*

일본 사람　　Japanese (person) *Prelim. I vocab*

일본어　　Japanese (language) *Prelim. I vocab*

일어나요 일어나고 일어나서 일어나다 gets up, gets out of bed *Ch3 L10 vocab*

일요일　　Sunday *Ch1.5 A vocab*

일월　　January *Prelim. H vocab*

일일　　first (day of month) *Prelim. H vocab*

일해요 일하고 일해서 일하다 works *Ch 2 L6 vocab*

일흔　　seventy (native Korean vocab.) *Prelim. G vocab*

읽어요 읽고 읽어서 읽다 reads *Ch3 L9 vocab*

입어요 입고 입어서 입다 wears, puts on (clothes) *Ch3 L9 vocab*

있어요 있고 있어서 있다 there is; exists; has *Ch1 L1 vocab* [이써요]

자　　ruler *Ch1 L1 supp*

자기 소개　　introduction of oneself *Prelim. C vocab*

자루　　*counter for* sacks pencils, pens *Ch3.5 vocab*

자매　　female sibling *Ch2.5 vocab*

자서 자고 자서 자다 sleeps *Ch3 L10 vocab*

자음　　consonant *Prelim. D vocab*

자전거　　bicycle *Ch1 L3 vocab*

자주　　often, very often *Ch 2 L7 vocab*

작년에　　last year *Ch3 L12 vocab*

작아요 작고 작아서 작다 small *Ch3 L11 vocab*

작은 누나　　male's older sister who is younger than another sister *Ch2.5 vocab*

작은 언니　　female's older sister who is younger than another sister *Ch2.5 vocab*

작은 오빠　　female's older brother who is younger than another brother *Ch2.5 vocab*

작은 형　　male's older brother who is younger than another brother *Ch2.5 vocab*

잔　　glasses, *counter for Ch3.5 vocab*

잘　　often, very often *Ch 3 L8 vocab*

잘 부탁합니다 잘 부탁하고 잘 부탁해서 잘 부탁하다 I will be obliged to you. (greeting) *Prelim. I point*

잘 부탁해요 잘 부탁하고 잘 부탁해서 잘 부탁하다 I will be obliged to you. (greeting) *Prelim. I point*

잠깐　　just a minute; for a short while *Ch3 L12 vocab*

잠시　　moment; just a moment; for a short while *Ch3 L12 vocab*

잡아요 잡고 잡아서 잡다 grabs, holds (hands); catches (a bus) *Ch3 L9 vocab*

잡지　　magazine *Ch1 L3 vocab* [잡찌]

장　　ground, field *Ch 2 L5 point*

장　　sheets, *counter for Ch3.5 vocab*

재미동포　　Koreans living in US *Prelim. I point*

재미없어요 재미없고 재미없어서 재미없다 no fun *Ch3 L11 vocab*

재미있어요 재미있고 재미있어서 재미있다 fun *Ch3 L11 vocab*

재일동포    Koreans living in Japan *Prelim. I point*

저    I, me (humble) *Ch2 L5 vocab*

저    that over there (adj.) *Ch1 L2 vocab*

저거    that thing over there (noun) *Ch1 L2 vocab*

저건    that thing over there as opposed to the others (for something that has been introduced in previous utterances or for contrast) *Ch1 L2 vocab*

저게    that thing over there as subject/focus *Ch1 L2 vocab*

저기    over there  *Ch1 L3 vocab*

저녁    evening (around 5, 6 P.M. ~ 8 P.M.) *Ch1.5 B vocab*

저희    our (humble) *Ch 2 L7 other*

적어요 적고 적어서 적다 be only a little *Ch3 L11 vocab*

전공    major  *Ch 2 L8 vocab* [전공, 정공]

전자 공학    Electrical Engineering *Ch 2 L8 supp*

전학    *Ch 2 L8 point*

전화    telephone *Ch 2 L6 focus*

전화    telephone *Ch1 L1 vocab* [저놔, 저나]

전화번호    phone number *Ch1 L2 vocab* [저나버노]

전화해요 전화하고 전화해서 전화하다 phones *Ch 2 L6 vocab*

점    a store *Ch 2 L5 point*

점심    day time (around 11:30 A.M. ~ 2:30 P.M.) *Ch1.5 B vocab*

정말(로)    really, truly *Ch3 L12 vocab*

정말(로)    truly  *Ch3 L12 vocab*

정치학    Political Science *Ch 2 L8 supp*

제    my (humble), I (humble) *Ch 2 L7 other*

조각, 쪽    pieces, slices, *counter for Ch3.5  vocab*

조거    that little/exact thing over there *Ch1 L4 point*

조금/좀 [쪼금/ 쫌]    a little bit *Ch3 L12 vocab*

조기    over there; right over there *Ch1 L4 point*

조용히 하세요 조용히하고 조용히해서 조용히하다 quiet. *Prelim. F vocab*

종이    paper *Ch1 L2 vocab*

좋아요 좋고 [조코] 좋아서 좋다 [조타] good; liked *Ch3 L11 vocab*

좋아해요 좋아하고 좋아해서 좋아하다 likes *Ch3 L10 vocab*

죠깅    jogging *Ch 2 L6 focus*

죠깅해요 조깅하고 조깅해서 조깅하다 jogs *Ch 2 L6 vocab*

주말에    on weekend(s) *Ch 2 L7 vocab*

주스 or 쥬스    juice *Ch1 L3 vocab*

주위    around *Ch1 L4 vocab*

주차장    parking lot *Ch2 L5 vocab*

중국    China *Prelim. I vocab*

중국 사람    Chinese (person) *Prelim. I vocab*

중국어    Chinese (language) *Prelim. I vocab*

줘요, 주어요 주고 줘서, 주어서 주다 give *Ch3 L10 vocab*

지갑    wallet *Ch1 L3 vocab*

지금    now *Prelim. H vocab*

지난    last, past *Ch3 L12 vocab*

지난 밤    last night *Ch3 L12 vocab*

지난 주 (수요일에)    last (Wednesday) *Ch3 L12 vocab*

지난 주말에    last weekend *Ch3 L12 vocab*

지난 주에    last week *Ch3 L12 vocab*

지난 학기에    last semester/quarter *Ch3 L12 vocab*

지난 해에    last year *Ch3 L12 vocab*

지난 해에 = 작년에    last year *Ch3 L12 vocab*

-지만    but *Ch3  L9 other*

지우개    eraser *Ch1 L2 vocab*

진짜(로)    truly *Ch3 L12 vocab*

질문    question *Prelim. C vocab*

집    house, home *Ch2 L5 vocab*

짝    partner *Prelim. C vocab*

-쯤    about, approximately *Ch 2 L8 vocab*

창문    window *Ch1 L1 vocab*

찾아요 찾고 찾아서 찾다 look for ; find; withdraw (money) *Ch3  L9 vocab*

채    houses, buildings, *counter for Ch3.5  vocab*

책    book *Ch1 L2 vocab*

책상    desk *Ch1 L1 vocab* [책쌍]

천    thousand *Prelim. G vocab*

천 만    ten million *Prelim. G vocab*

천천히    slowly *Prelim. C vocab*

첫번째    first time *Prelim. G vocab*

첫째    first *Prelim. G vocab*

청소해요 청소하고 청소해서 청소하다 cleans (house, rooms) *Ch 2 L6 vocab*

체육관    sports complex; gym *Ch2 L5 vocab*

쳐요 치고 쳐서 치다 play (tennis/ guitar) *Ch3 L10 vocab*

초컬릿, 초킬렛,    chocolate *Ch2 L4 vocab*

초콜릿, 초콜렛    chocolate *Ch1 L3 vocab*

축구해요 축구하고 축구해서 축구하다 play soccer *Ch 2 L6 vocab*

친구    friend *Ch1 L2 vocab* [칭구

친할머니    paternal grandmother *Ch2.5  vocab*

친할아버지    paternal grandfather *Ch2.5  vocab*

칠    seven (Sino-Korean vocab.) *Prelim. G vocab*

칠월    July *Prelim. H vocab*

칠판    chalkboard *Ch1 L1 vocab*

카메라    camera *Ch1 L2 vocab*

칼 knife *Ch1 L1 supp*

캐나다 Canada *Prelim. I vocab*

캐나다 사람 Canadian (person) *Prelim. I vocab*

커요 크고 커서 크다 big *Ch3 L11 vocab*

커피숍 coffee shop *Ch2 L5 vocab*

컴퓨터 computer *Ch1 L1 vocab*

컴퓨터 공학 Computer Science *Ch 2 L8 supp*

컴퓨터 랩 computer lab *Ch2 L5 vocab*

컵 cup *Ch3.5 vocab*

켤레 pairs of shoes, *counter for Ch3.5 vocab*

크레디트 카드 credit card *Ch1 L3 vocab*

크레딧 카드 credit card *Ch1 L3 vocab*

큰 누나 male's older sister who is older than another older sister *Ch2.5 vocab*

큰 소리로 loudly *Prelim. C vocab*

큰 아들 oldest son *Ch2.5 vocab*

큰 언니 female's older sister who is older than another older sister *Ch2.5 vocab*

큰 오빠 female's older brother who is older than another older brother *Ch2.5 vocab*

큰형 male's older brother who is older than another older brother *Ch2.5 vocab*

타요 타고 타서 타다 rides, gets on *Ch3 L10 vocab*

탁자 table *Ch1 L1 vocab* [탁짜]

택시 taxi *Ch1 L3 vocab*

테레비 T.V. *Ch1 L1 vocab*

텔레비전 T.V. *Ch1 L1 vocab*

토요일 Saturday *Ch1.5 A vocab*

틀려요 틀리고 틀려서 틀리다 incorrect, wrong *Ch3 L11 vocab*

팔 eight (Sino-Korean vocab.) *Prelim. G vocab*

팔월 August *Prelim. H vocab*

펜 pen *Ch1 L2 vocab*

편리해요 편리하고 [펼리아고] 편리해서 [펼리애서] 편리하다 convenient *Ch3 L11 vocab* [펼리애요]

편해요 편하고 편해서 편하다 comfortable *Ch3 L11 vocab*

평소에 usually, on regular days *Ch 2 L7 vocab*

평일에 on week days *Ch 2 L7 vocab*

포기 heads (of cabbage), *counter for Ch3.5 vocab*

프랑스 France *Prelim. I vocab*

프랑스 사람 French (person) *Prelim. I vocab*

프랑스어 French (language) *Prelim. I vocab*

프렌스 France *Prelim. I point*

프린터 printer *Ch1 L1 vocab*

피곤해요 피곤하고 피곤해서 피곤하다 tired *Ch3 L11 vocab*

필요없어요 필요없고 필요없어서 필요없다 unnecessary; not needed *Ch3 L11 vocab*

필요해요 필요하고 필요해서 필요하다 needed, necessary *Ch3 L11 vocab*

필통 pencil case, holder *Ch1 L1 supp*

-하고 with *Ch2 L5 vocab*

-하고 and (noun particle) *Ch1 L3 vocab*

하나 one (*native Korean vocab.*) *Prelim. G vocab*

하루에 per day *Ch 2 L8 vocab*

학교 school *Ch2 L5 vocab*

학기 quarter/semester *Ch 2 L8 vocab*

학년 year (in school) *Ch 2 L8 vocab* [항년]

학번 *Ch 2 L8 point*

학생 student *Ch1 L1 vocab* [학쌩]

학생증 student ID card *Ch1 L3 vocab* [학쌩쫑]

학생회관 student center *Ch2 L5 vocab*

한 one (native Korean vocab.) *Prelim. G vocab*

한 달 전에 a month ago *Ch3 L12 vocab*

한 번 더 more, one more time *Prelim. C vocab*

한가해요 한가하고 한가해서 한가하다 not busy, have a lot of free time *Ch3 L11 vocab*

한가해요 한가하고 한가해서 한가하다 free time, to have (adj.) *Ch3 L11 vocab*

한국 Korea *Prelim. I vocab*

한국 사람 Korean (person) *Prelim. I vocab*

한국어 Korean (language) *Prelim. I vocab*

한국학 Korea Studies *Ch 2 L8 supp*

한글 Han'gul; the Korean alphabet *Prelim. D vocab*

-한테 to (a person) *Ch3 L11 other*

할머니 grandmother *Ch2.5 vocab*

할아버지 grandfather *Ch2.5 vocab*

항상 always *Ch 2 L7 vocab*

해요 하고 해서 하다 does *Ch 2 L6 vocab*

핸드폰 cellular phone *Ch1 L3 vocab*

형 male's older brother *Ch2.5 vocab*

형제 siblings; male sibling *Ch2.5 vocab*

혼자 by oneself *Ch2 L5 vocab*

화요일 Tuesday *Ch1.5 A vocab*

화이트 white-out *Ch1 L1 supp*

화장실 restroom *Prelim. F vocab*

화장해요 화장하고 화장해서 화장하다 make-up (puts on) *Ch 2 L6 vocab*

화학 Chemistry *Ch 2 L8 supp*

휴학 on leave (by students) *Ch 2 L8 point*

# Overview of Grammar

## Preliminary Chapter (예비장)

Sections:
- A. 인사 Greetings
- B. 문화 Culture
- C. 교실에서는 In the Classroom
- D. 한글 Hangul
- E. 발음 길잡이 Pronunciation Guide
- F. 유용 표현 Useful Expressions
- G. 숫자 Numbers
- H. 날짜 Days and Months
- I. 국적 묻기 Nationalities

## Lessons by Chapter

| Chapter | Lesson / Section | Focus | Other |
|---|---|---|---|
| 제 1 장 Chapter 1 — 그게 뭐예요? What is it? | **Classroom Nouns** — 제 1 과 Lesson 1 내일은 시험이 있어요? | • A 이/가 있어요 There is A <br> • A 이/가 없어요 There is no A | • 뭐, 무엇 what <br> • -에 in, on, at |
| | **Other Basic Nouns** — 제 2 과 Lesson 2 그게 뭐예요? | • A 은/는 B(이)에요 A is B <br> • A 은/는 B 이/가 아니에요 A is not B | • -이, -그, -저 this, that, that over there <br> • 거, 것 thing <br> • 제, 저의, …씨 my (humble) <br> • compounds <br> • 네/아니요 yes/no |
| | **More Nouns and Markers** — 제 3 과 Lesson 3 사랑도 있어요? | • A 은/는 B 이/가 있어요 A has B <br> • A 은/는 B 이/가 없어요 A doesn't have B | • -도 also <br> • A 하고 B A and B <br> • 여기, 거기, 저기 here, there, way over there |
| | **Location Nouns** — 제 4 과 Lesson 4 선생님의 사무실 | • _(의) 앞에 이/가 있어요 <br> location words & construction | • -의 's <br> • 어디 where <br> • -은/는 contrast <br> • contracted pronouns |
| 제 1.5 장 Chapter 1.5 | 요일 Days of the week / 시간 Telling time | | |
| 제 2 장 Chapter 2 — 뭐 해요? What are you doing? | **Place Nouns** — 제 5 과 Lesson 5 어디 가요? | • "가요" The Verb "Go" | • -에 to <br> • -요 politeness <br> • -은/는 change of focus <br> • -하고 with <br> • 누구/누가 who, whom |
| | **해요-Verbs** — 제 6 과 Lesson 6 지금 뭐 해요? | • "해요" 동사 The Verb "Do" | • -을/를 Object Marker <br> • 같이 together <br> • -에서 at (location of an activity) |
| | **Time Adverbs** — 제 7 과 Lesson 7 평일에 별로 공부 안 해요. | • 안 not | • 나, 네, 우리, 저, 제, 저희 1st person PN <br> • Use of markers, frequency adv, position of time adverbs <br> • -에 in, on at (time) |
| | **Connectors and Time Words** — 제 8 과 Lesson 8 동호의 하루 | • -에도, -에서도, -에는, -에서는 stacking of markers | • 그리고, 그래서, 그렇지만 and, so, but <br> • -에 per <br> • 몇 how many <br> • 얼마나 자주, 몇 번 how often |
| 제 2.5 장 Chapter 2.5 | 가족 Family | | |
| 제 3 장 Chapter 3 — 일요일은 괜찮아요. Sunday is O.K. | **Daily Activity Verbs A** — 제 9 과 Lesson 9 미안해요, 파티에 못 가요. | • 자음으로 끝나는 동사 현재형 Consonant-ending Verbs (*Present Tense*) | • 못 <br> • -고 and -지만 but <br> • -고 나서 and then <br> • -(으)로 with, by <br> • 뭐 something |
| | **Daily Activity Verbs B** — 제 10 과 Lesson 10 친구를 만나요. | • 모음으로 끝나는 동사 현재형 Vowel-ending Verbs (*Present Tense*) | • -기 전에 before doing <br> • -만 only, just <br> • 와요 vs. 가요 come vs. go <br> • -부터…-까지 from until,…up to |
| | **Adjectival Verbs** — 제 11 과 Lesson 11 일요일이 어때요? | • 형용사 현재형 Adjectives (*Present Tense*) | • -어서 so… <br> • -(으) irregular predicates <br> • 우리 같이…어요. Let's <br> • 어때요? How is it <br> • -어디, 거기+에, 에서 <br> • -한테 to a person <br> • 좋아하다, 좋다 to like, to be good |
| | **Adverbs** — 제 12 과 Lesson 12 제인 씨가 없어서 재미없었어요! | • 과거형 *Past Tense* | • -있고, -있지만 vs. -어서/어서 <br> • -은/는 vs. -이/가 (Review) <br> • -도 (usage) <br> • -(이)나 as many as |
| 제 3.5 장 Chapter 3.5 | Counters | | |